The Best AMERICAN SPORTS WRITING 1995

GUEST EDITORS OF
THE BEST AMERICAN SPORTS WRITING

1991 • DAVID HALBERSTAM
1992 • THOMAS McGUANE
1993 • FRANK DEFORD
1994 • TOM BOSWELL
1995 • DAN JENKINS

The Best AMERICAN SPORTS WRITING 1995

EDITED AND WITH
AN INTRODUCTION BY
Dan Jenkins

Glenn Stout, SERIES EDITOR

HOUGHTON MIFFLIN COMPANY
BOSTON · NEW YORK 1995

ISSN: 1056-8034
ISBN: 0-395-70070-1
ISBN: 0-395-70069-8 (pbk.)

Printed in the United States of America

QUM 10 9 8 7 6 5 4 3 2 1

Contents

Foreword

ONE OF THE SIDE benefits of serving as series editor of this annual collection is that I get to talk with, and occasionally meet, many of the writers whose work appears in this book. Over the five-year life of *The Best American Sports Writing*, that list includes more than one hundred writers of all descriptions, including some of the most notable names in journalism today.

The most memorable, and, I think, perhaps the most important, sports writer I've ever met never appeared in this book or any other similar collection. I doubt if any of the writers whose work has appeared here has ever even heard of the man, and I'd be surprised if more than a handful of readers find his name familiar. Yet I think Doc Kountze, without hardly anyone knowing so, may well have been one of the more significant and important sports writers this nation has ever produced. He certainly was to me. Lessons I learned from him probably have been more important in the evolution of this series than anything I have gathered from any other single writer I have met. When I choose from among the thousands of stories I read each year for those seventy or eighty I pass along to the guest editor, I am reminded that there are reasons to write that have little to do with bylines, headlines, or bottom lines, that words have power and do matter, and that while sport may not be a microcosm of anything, it is certainly a significant part of something larger. Each year, for better or worse, I think this book provides evidence of that.

Doc Kountze never wanted to be the subject of any story. The whole idea was antithetical to who he was. He resisted my own efforts to write about him, and on several occasions he outright refused my pleas for him to tell me about himself. From where Doc sat, every other story was larger and more important than he was. He refused to acknowledge his own central role in some of these larger stories, although they were always immediately apparent to me. Kountze was not trying to appear humble or self-effacing. He *was* humble and self-effacing.

I can write about Doc Kountze now without feeling that I am violating either his friendship or his trust. He passed away on September 27, 1994, at age 84. Consider this a eulogy.

I met Doc a decade ago, just a few weeks after I completed and, to my everlasting surprise, published the first sports story I ever wrote, a historical feature for *Boston Magazine* about the suicide of Red Sox manager Chick Stahl in 1907. After my initial success, I was shocked when editor Ken Hartnett turned to me and asked, "Well, what do you want to write about next?"

Every writer longs to hear these words, but I didn't know that yet. I was so shocked someone actually wanted to publish something I had written that I hadn't even thought of writing another story. Yet the question, and the opportunity, was hanging there in the air, and I had to answer it.

In a panic, I responded with a topic I knew nothing about.

"Black baseball in Boston," I blurted out.

"O.K." the editor said.

I have since learned, as John Keats did, that while it is not a bad idea at all to write about something without knowing where it is going, it is usually helpful to know what you don't know before telling someone you'll write about it. But it was too late for that.

Over the next few weeks my research sent me deep into the microfilmed recesses of Boston's black press — the *Chronicle* and the *Guardian,* virtually the only sources of any information about black baseball in Boston. While the city never really had a team in the Negro Leagues, the local community still supported a wide variety of semipro and barnstorming teams. As I scanned through the papers, season by season, I noticed that virtually every sports story, and every baseball story, carried the byline "Mabray 'Doc' Kountze." Almost by accident, I looked for the name in the phone book. He was still alive.

I made the call and met an amazing man. For more than forty

years, Doc's self-designated beat in the sports world was whatever and whoever the *Boston Globe, Boston Herald,* or *Boston Post* didn't write about. Names they designated to agate type and faces they rarely favored with a photograph were Doc's sole subjects. He was a curator of the invisible, a collector in awkward silences.

Over the next several years I spoke with Doc every few months and listened to him talk about athletes I'd never heard of. Doc's heroes weren't named Ted Williams, Eddie Shore, Bob Cousy, or Harry Agganis, but Will Jackman, Sam Langford, and Louise Stokes — athletes of equal merit whose accomplishments were hardly recognized and whose memories were preserved in precious few places apart from where Doc had placed them. Cannonball Jackman was considered the equal of Satchel Paige in New England and the Canadian Maritimes, a barnstorming iron man who, after hurting his arm, pitched into his sixties by developing a submarine knuckleball. The boxer Sam Langford was known as the Boston Tar Baby, and was probably the best pound-for-pound fighter ever. He was certainly the best fighter who was totally blind in one eye and partially blind in the other, who sometimes hit referees by mistake and made a living late in life by approaching white sports writers and telling them his story of woe. They'd write a column about poor old Sam and raise a few thousand dollars on his behalf. The writer would win an award and Langford would live comfortably for a few years. Then Langford would do the same thing over again in another town with another writer and no one would be the wiser.

Louise Stokes was the first African-American female to make the United States Olympic team, but you won't find her name in any record book. She was withdrawn from competition in the 1932 games in Los Angeles out of deference to Babe Didrickson. Four years later, in Berlin, she was pulled to appease the Nazis. Jesse Owens was not expendable, but a black woman, Louise Stokes, was.

For several years my writing career flourished as Doc pointed me toward these stories. He didn't mind telling me about them, was pleased that I was interested, and was delighted in the finished product. I learned a valuable lesson: Most of the good stories haven't been told yet.

But Doc did more for me than feed me stories. He fed my confidence. He took me seriously and gave me time. Where my entreaties to editors were often ignored, Doc always answered. I sent Doc

copies of all my early stories. A week or two later I'd find an enve-
lope in the mail addressed to "Glenn Stout, sports writer."

Inside would be a page or two of nearly transparent paper, filled
margin-to-margin with incredibly small type from an old manual
typewriter — as if paper and words were so precious that neither
could be wasted — wonderful letters filled with praise, criticism,
advice, tips for stories, commentaries on the present, and bits of
scripture, the accumulated wisdom of someone who spent his entire life writing about sports because he thought it was important,
had meaning, and could somehow someday make a difference.
Wonderful things for a young writer to hear.

But Doc rarely told me about himself. In our letters and conversations, only the dimmest outlines of his own biography slowly
slipped out. One of ten children, he was often sick, but loved sports.
Although small, he played whenever he could. Knowing the chances
of his own progress, and that of many others, were halted by the
reality of his race, Doc parlayed his talent as a cartoonist into a
career in journalism, coinciding with a personal commitment to a
larger cause. All this he referred to only indirectly, as side trips in
stories that always ended with someone else. He referred to sports
as his "survival kit." Where once he had been angry, or bitter, he
found that sports was the cure. In his work, he focused not on
himself or his own experiences, but on others, toward larger issues.
In all his writings I never found a hint of bitterness, never any
cynicism or desperation. He knew more about what he was doing
than any writer I have ever met.

I met Doc in person only once. He was a small man, almost
delicate, but not at all infirm. The rooms where he lived were
dominated by words. I remember a table piled high with books and
papers, stacks of magazines and newspapers everywhere, a writing
desk, which I think was actually an old door, upon which rested the
ancient typewriter, articles and photographs taped to the walls. A
writer's room, most definitely.

The more I spoke with Doc the more I became convinced that he
was the real story, for he was the link to so much else. But he
resisted personal questions and consistently deflected my inquiries
elsewhere. It took several years, more phone calls and letters, before Doc finally gave me the story I was looking for.

Baseball was the sport Doc really loved. The mysterious illness when he was young prevented him from playing much, but he never abandoned the game. He committed himself to the cause of the black ballplayer. When Doc was in his early twenties, on his own initiative he forced meetings with Bob Quinn, owner of the Red Sox, and Judge Fuchs, owner of the Boston Braves, and discussed the integration of major league baseball. Later, he became the first African-American admitted to the press box in both Braves Field and Fenway Park.

That was Doc's cause, his single commitment. But how could he, a nearly invisible young writer for the black press, affect such a great change?

In the early 1930s, Doc contacted the sports editors of the major black papers around the country — the *Pittsburgh Courier,* the *New York Age,* the *St. Louis Argus* and others — and formed an organization he named the National Negro Newspaper All-American Association of Sports Editors. Its single goal was to make the white press aware of the black athlete. The NNNAA named their own All-Americans and elected their own all-star teams. Doc was convinced that once people knew, once the veneer of silence about the black athlete was broken in the white press, the major league color line would be similarly breached.

Doc was no great stylist, for style was a luxury rarely afforded in the black press, but for much of the next decade, he wrote with this one goal in mind.

The strategy worked. Years before Branch Rickey of the Brooklyn Dodgers knew who Jackie Robinson was, Doc and his counterparts had selected Robinson as their choice to break the color line. Robinson was familiar to readers of the black press while he was still a student at UCLA. Through the efforts of the NNNAA, Robinson, with his unique set of qualifications, was made familiar to white America. When Branch Rickey went looking for a player to break the color line, his selection of Robinson was no accident. It was what Doc had in mind all along.

The seminal role of Kountze and the other members of the NNNAA in the eventual breakdown of the color line has never been adequately acknowledged. A version that anoints Rickey and Robinson as singular heroes is both more palatable and more easily told. When Doc finally filled me in on the NNNAA, he characteristically wrote, "I participate only to give honors to those before me." He didn't care that the role of the NNNAA was never recognized. They succeeded, and that was what was important. "I never sought the limelight," he wrote in another letter, "beyond focusing my crusades on what I considered a worthy Cause . . . and made no profit from my writings. . . . With me, a worthy Cause is above Cash."

Doc believed what he wrote and lived his beliefs, a worthy goal for anyone, til the very end. Several years ago, I wrote a biography of Ted Williams. I dedicated the book to Doc, and sent him a copy. In the book, I reprinted the speech Williams gave when he was inducted into the Baseball Hall of Fame in 1966. Rather remarkably, in his speech Williams campaigned for the inclusion of players from the Negro Leagues in the Hall. This was not a popular position in 1966, yet only five years later Williams's suggestion became reality.

Several weeks after sending a copy of the book to Doc, I received a letter from him. He was upset and embarrassed. He had always privately believed that Williams had something to do with keeping the Red Sox so white for so long. While he never wrote such a story, or even whispered a mention of that belief to me, Doc had himself believed it. And after reading Williams's speech, he realized his mistake.

Doc was mortified and deeply ashamed. He called me and sheepishly asked for Williams's address. He had to apologize. His embarrassment over his own private misconception required forgiveness.

I was able to provide an address, and get word to Williams that one simple letter meant an awful lot to a certain old sports writer. Doc wrote Williams and apologized profusely for an indiscretion neither Ted nor anyone else knew anything about. Williams wrote back and Doc was delighted. In his last letter to me, Doc Kountze told me about Ted's letter and how pleased he was to learn that Williams, after all these years, was really on the same side he was, and that he should have known so all along, because the cause was just and it was inevitable that everyone would eventually join. He promised to never make that error again, and cautioned me not to make the same mistake. Then Doc ended the letter with the same admonition he always did.

"Keep Faith," he wrote.

As I put this book together each year, I often think of Doc

Kountze. In my mind, sports writing, at its very best, is best represented by this man. As this series continues to grow, I hope the writers represented herein, and the readers for whom this book exists, adhere to their own standards with the same magnanimous spirit and commitment represented by Doc Kountze. He belongs here, and deserves good company.

If you usually stop reading here, I caution you to keep going. *The Best American Sports Writing* has another address change.

Each year, I personally survey each and every issue of some three hundred sports and general interest magazines in search for stories that I believe may merit inclusion in this series. I also read every issue of nearly fifty Sunday supplement magazines from daily newspapers around the country and the Sunday sports section of a like number of newspapers. I do everything I can to make sure that interested parties know that I welcome submissions. Each year I send letters to more than three hundred magazines and more than three hundred sports editors of daily and weekly newspapers and encourage them to submit stories for consideration, or, even better, to provide me with a complimentary subscription. I need the input of others. But writers should be forewarned that they should not depend on any editor to submit a story for them. I suspect many such letters get thrown away or posted on a bulletin board, then to be covered by a posting for a 1976 Chevy Impala station wagon or gobbled up by a writer who sends me his stuff and no one else's. Neither should writers assume that the publication they write for is so important that I "naturally" read everything they write. I try, but my eye isn't "naturally" perfect. Initiative counts here. From my end, I don't care who you are or who you write for; I pick the stories that I enjoy reading over and over.

Each year, I submit the best seventy-five stories or so to the guest editor, who makes the final selection. This year's guest editor, Dan Jenkins, exercised his own prerogative and supplemented my choices with a number of his own. To be considered for inclusion in next year's volume, each nonfiction story must have been published in 1995 in the United States or Canada and must be column length or longer. Reprints or excerpts from published books are not eligible. I must receive all stories by February 1, 1996. This is a real deadline. After that date I let the mail pile up for a few months while I do the dirty work of putting this book out.

All submissions must include the author's name, date of publication, and publication name and address. Photocopies, tearsheets, or complete publications are fine. Submissions cannot be returned, and I do not feel it is appropriate for me to comment on or critique individual submissions. Publications that want to ensure their contributions are considered should provide me with a complimentary subscription.

Submissions or subscriptions should be sent to this precise address:

Glenn Stout
Series Editor
The Best American Sports Writing
P.O. Box 381
Uxbridge, MA 01569

Copies of recent editions of *The Best American Sports Writing* may be ordered through most bookstores. Earlier volumes may be available through out-of-print book dealers. The staff of the Boston Public Library, as usual, provided much-needed help with this project, and I'd also like to thank Marnie Patterson for her role in the success of this series. Siobhan allowed me to live amidst piles of paper for another year, and the dog didn't eat a single submission, although she did run around the house with a few. My greatest thanks are to those who write so well about sports. They make my task a pleasure. Keep faith.

GLENN STOUT

Introduction

SORRY, BUT NOWHERE in here will you be reading that thoughtful piece about the desperate plight of the golden-cheeked warbler.

That's not all.

In none of these pages will you find an essay by the sensitive novelist who turns to sports for a moment and sees a nation's entire struggle for human rights etched into the brow of a New York Knick.

Nor will you find that story by the somber, social-conscious columnist who reflects on sports long enough to fear for the country because he senses that far too many young people are going to football games now instead of reading Karl Marx, building communes, and practicing yogurt — er, yoga.

I'm also afraid you won't find that sporting feature by the brooding playwright who takes a jog around a poet's pond and later finds a microcosm of American life among the insects gnawing on his ankles.

I know you will regret these omissions because "serious literature" is what you have come to expect from most anthologies of good sports writing. All is not lost, however.

To ease the pain, I have generously elected to devote a large amount of this space to recommending a reading list of the year's most literary sports books. I speak of books that touched on the world of sport with a depth and insight no mere sports writer could possibly comprehend.

You missed these books no doubt because they were all snapped up so quickly by the intellectual community, which has recently moved, I hear, from a boarding house in Cambridge, Massachusetts, to a loft in lower Manhattan. The intellectual community is said to have made this move in order to start up a vital publication called *The New York Review of Each Other.*

But about those highly literary sports books.

One of the most uplifting books of the year was *Gloves,* a boxing novel by Jocelyn Stealth. Best known for *Ballpoint,* her 970-page saga of a bookkeeper for a Chrysler-Plymouth dealership in Topeka, Kansas, Ms. Stealth turned to sports and invented a memorable character named Big Bob Lard. Big Bob is a flabby, 45-year-old former heavyweight champion who reclaims his title by knocking out an exceptionally large piece of Samsonite luggage in the eighth round in Atlantic City. Having always harbored an artistic nature, Big Bob then turns to painting and becomes even more famous for his oils of airport conveyor belts.

The novel leaves you wondering if Big Bob will ever have to defend his heavyweight title again, inasmuch as all of the other legitimate contenders seem to be doing hard time in prison.

Rick Faucet was up to his usual high standards in the novel *Ice.* In the first 40,000 words, he describes ice in most of its basic forms, including many of the shapes and sizes that are issued from dispensers on refrigerators. He answers several key questions about ice, such as where it comes from and why.

The novel turns futuristic toward the end when the narrator, Leif, squatting among penguins on a frozen lake in Ottawa, imagines the National Hockey League playing games in such wildly bizarre places as Los Angeles, Miami, Dallas, Tampa, San Jose, and Anaheim. The book leaves the reader with the haunting suspicion that ice hockey may not be played at all in Canada by the year 2010, which of course would leave that nation with nothing to do with all of its ice but stare at it. Most critics found this sci-fi ending in *Ice* not only troublesome but, in fact, a bit too scary.

Dave McWords is primarily known for his deep-thinking political books, such as the lavishly praised *What I Grasped and You Didn't About 1957 and Part of 1958,* but his loyal fans were rewarded when he focused his attention on sports during the past year. The result was *Why Me?,* a sympathetic look at how the Chicago White Sox slugger Zack Thrasher, who makes only $8 million a year, coped with the baseball strike while overseeing the construction of his new home, a 19,000-square-foot mansion in Rodendo del Taco el Pinto, California.

In the first 968 pages, McWords discusses the political ramifications, both domestically and globally, of an intentional walk Thrasher received from a New York Yankee reliever at 4:17 P.M. on August 22, 1989. Throughout the second half of the book, or the last 873 pages, we get a sense of what Thrasher has gone through to keep from touching the $36 million tied up in mutual funds and blue chips. Among other things, we find him forced to use non-union labor on the construction of his new home, to hire replacement people to take his place in picket lines so he can make sure the marble foyer is put down correctly, and finally, to raise his autograph fee to $600 for adults and $400 for children under twelve.

All in all, *Why Me?* presents a touching portrait of an American sports hero and his family caught in a web of dire financial stress.

Miles Trusk gave us another bittersweet fantasy in his novel, *Strikers and Sweepers*. The plot revolves around a group of long-haired hippies who form the nucleus of a United States soccer team in the World Cup tournament. Things go well for the American athletes and their marijuana plants throughout most of the book. In fact, they almost score a goal in a game against Liechtenstein. But in the final chapter, as the fun-loving Yanks are embroiled in a tight contest in the Cotton Bowl against a squad of talented Nigerians, the players on both sides are mistaken for holdover radicals from the 1960s and are beaten to death with nightsticks by members of the Dallas police department.

Certain reviewers said Trusk's shocking conclusion bordered on cynicism, while others felt it was too whimsical.

The daring writer Sumner Clifford can always be counted on to come up with something innovative, and he did so again in his novel, *Michael Jordan Michael Jordan*. To begin with, all fifty-nine chapters start and finish with the same four words, "Michael Jordan Michael Jordan." Odd, of course, but it soon makes sense, for the major character in the story is named Michael Jordan Michael Jordan. He is an immortal basketball player for the Chicago Bulls who becomes the most famous athlete in America. Unfortunately, his fame reaches such gigantic proportions that it eventually causes a raging public backlash against him. In living rooms around the country, people start to throw sneakers at their TV screens when one of Michael Jordan Michael Jordan's commercials appears.

There is a particularly moving scene, set in Los Angeles, when Michael Jordan Michael Jordan is in the city for a game against the Lakers. As he innocently strolls down the street, 450 people suddenly begin vomiting at the very sight of him. The author leads us to believe that this incident is the final blow that causes Michael Jordan Michael Jordan to retire from the game at the peak of his career and disappear for several months.

. Most readers welcome the novel's cheery ending in which Michael Jordan Michael Jordan joins a minor league baseball team in Birmingham, Alabama, and finds true happiness when he goes 0-for-248 at the plate.

Duane W. Scull did not disappoint his followers again with his lyrical musings in *Green Side Up,* a compelling work of nonfiction that centers around Harvard University reverting the field in its football stadium from artificial turf back to natural grass. In the early part of the book, Scull traces the natural grass from its humble beginning as seeds to its unbridled success in full growth.

We learn that the new turf is a mixture of hybrid Bermuda and Pennsylvania bluegrass, and Scull actually stirs an excitement in us when we find that it produces an inviting, velvety surface which not only pleases Harvard's sinewy scholar-athletes but receives compliments from many of the steroid-swollen hulks on visiting teams who roll around on it.

In Part Two, Scull takes us on the curious journey of what happens to the artificial turf after it is dismantled. He finds some of it being utilized as carpet in the home of Dr. Louise Screemer, the Harvard professor who is highly regarded in academic circles throughout the nation for her lectures that call for the death of capitalism, free speech, and most white male heterosexuals. The author discovers that another portion has been fashioned into dining room drapes in the apartment of Dr. Seymour Blight, the Harvard professor who has become another idol in the academic world as a result of his impassioned lectures that call for the death of Western civilization.

Finally, Scull tracks down the last pieces of artificial turf. They have been woven into a topcoat that's worn on chilly days by Dr. Arnold Rude, now a Harvard professor but once on the faculty at the University of Wisconsin, where he first became known as "the high priest of political correctness." Yes, the author reminds us, this is the same Dr. Rude who constantly accuses the federal government of being sexist, racist, and disablist, and vows to continue his violent demonstrations until the president of the United States is a one-legged black lesbian.

O.K., that's it — I have to stop having all this fun and get on with some important business.

The important business is to welcome an extremely gifted group of laptop fondlers into this collection, and tell them their consistent excellence at what they do makes me proud to say I'm a member of the same profession.

Having had something to do with the selection process, I naturally think they comprise the strongest lineup of working-press sports writers I've ever seen bunched into a hospitality suite of this kind. I make no apologies for the fact that several of these laptop wretches, who used to be ink-stained wretches, are old friends of mine, some older than others, or that one of them even happens to be my own daughter. They're all in here on the strength of their obvious talent — they had no trouble obtaining their own clubhouse badges. I don't know that some of them came under the same influences I did. We've discussed it enough times over milk and cookies, or maybe it was whiskey and cigarettes. Depends on the era.

As a youth who often prowled through journalistic anthologies and biographies, trying to learn something, I naturally found it easy to be dazzled by Damon Runyon. Of all his gems, my favorite lead is this one from 1931: "Al Capone was quietly dressed when he arrived for court this morning, bar a hat of pearly white, emblematic, no doubt, of purity."

Henry McLemore's attitude appealed to me instantly, no sooner than the day I stumbled upon the following lead from the Berlin Olympics in 1936: "The Olympic marathon was run on Tuesday, and while it is now Thursday, I'm still waiting for the Americans to finish."

Of course, the boss sports writer of all time was John Lardner, no contest. A son of Ring himself, John Lardner died in 1960, far too soon, at the age of 47. But when a lot of us old guys congregate to speak of such things as good writing, we still quote him more often than we quote anyone else, even ourselves.

Just to pick one of John Lardner's nuggets at random, here

follows the lead from one of his *Newsweek* columns in the early 1950s: "Take yacht racing, now. Why does it fascinate the sporting public so much that crowds will stand all night outside a newspaper office in Terre Haute or Des Moines waiting to hear the result of a regatta for F-Class Butterfly Sloops off Throg's Neck, Long Island? For that matter, who was Throg?"

As for where to put our sports events and our sports heroes in the large scheme of things, I think I can speak for most grizzled veterans of the press box society when I say that over the years we have been too concerned with meeting deadlines to give it much thought.

Actually, a close friend of mine, who has also been making his living as a deadline slave for the past three or four decades, may have said it best for all of us a few months ago. Somehow, he got dragged kicking and screaming onto one of those silly panels that universities like to arrange where huge issues are discussed. My friend found himself to be the only sports writer present, and was further alarmed to be surrounded by various professors and psychologists on the panel, where the big question to be taken up was "Why are sports important?"

For a couple of hours, he did his best to listen to the professors and psychologists as they fell deeply in love with the sound of their own voices. Finally, the question was put to my friend, the sports writer. Why did *he* think sports were important?

"I really don't know," he said. "Can I go home now?"

DAN JENKINS

Baseball's Troubles Could Play Out to Be No Routine Comedy

FROM THE CHICAGO TRIBUNE

ABOUT 50 YEARS AGO, the legendary comedy team of Bud Abbott and Lou Costello performed a baseball routine for Broadway audiences. It was called Who's on First? Here's an updated version, Nobody's at Home.

LOU: Heeyyy, Abbott!! Here it is the middle of August, and I go to the ballpark today and it was empty.

BUD: Strike.

LOU: Strike? What are you talking about, strike? I didn't see a strike or a ball or a single or a home run. I went to see a ballgame and nobody was there.

BUD: Oh, and did you introduce yourself to the commissioner?

LOU: Commissioner? How could I say hello to the commissioner if nobody was there?

BUD: Because I'm sure he'd have been happy to meet you.

LOU: Who?

BUD: No, he's on first base. Or at least he used to be before the strike. But I'm not sure the commissioner would have said hello to you.

LOU: What?

BUD: Second base.

LOU: Wait a minute. Who were we talking about?

BUD: Nobody, until you brought up first base and second base.

LOU: That's right. Nobody. I went to the ballpark and saw nobody.

BUD: Exactly, the commissioner of baseball.

LOU: Nobody is the commissioner of baseball?

BUD: Now you're starting to make some sense.

LOU: Make sense? I don't even know what I'm talking about. You must think I'm dizzy.

BUD: No, I already know Dizzy. He's in New York running the union. His people average $1.2 million a year to play baseball, but it's not enough, so he's the one who called the last strike of the *1994* season.

LOU: You mean the players make that kind of money and they stopped playing? Is he goofy?

BUD: No, I already told you he's Dizzy. But Goofy is the guy who made Dizzy do it. Goofy works for the owners. He's their chief negotiator. Not a bad guy. Here's a picture of him.

LOU: What kind of a hat is that?

BUD: Salary cap. That's what all this is about. That's why there's no more baseball and there might not be for a long time.

LOU: But isn't somebody in charge to stop the strike?

BUD: I thought I told you that Nobody was in charge. Somebody will be brought in, probably from Washington, to take over for Nobody. But it isn't a job for anybody now, so Nobody is going to do it until Goofy and Dizzy get the strike settled.

LOU: Amazing.

BUD: Oh, he's out of it now. Amazing started the players union more than two decades ago, but he beat the owners like a rug so often he retired and turned it over to Dizzy. Have you got it all figured out now?

LOU: I don't know.

BUD: He's the president of the National League. He has nothing to do with anything. Now, what have you got to say for yourself?

LOU: I'm confused.

BUD: No, you're not. Not unless you're the president of the American League.

LOU: I Don't Know and Confused are the presidents of both leagues?

BUD: Why do you care?

LOU: I don't care.

BUD: He runs the White Sox. He says it doesn't matter to him. He could be a hawk or a dove.

LOU: Now we're talking birds.

BUD: That's all they do in Baltimore, where the Orioles sold for $175 million and you can't get a ticket. But then the owners say they're going broke, which is part of the reason for the strike.

LOU: Nonsense.

BUD: He bought the Giants for $100 million to keep them in San Francisco, then spent $43 million on one player, then said baseball is a mess financially.

LOU: Heeyyy, Abbott!! If you're in the entertainment business like we are, and we sell seats to a movie or show and we leave in the middle of it, then aren't we selfish?

BUD: No, Selfish owns the Yankees.

LOU: What I mean is, wouldn't our fans be entitled to their money back? All their money back. I mean baseball fans buy season tickets on the promise that there'll be a season. Where can I complain?

BUD: This is baseball, so Nobody's home. Try him there.

LOU: Smart.

BUD: Smart? I don't know anyone by that name in this game.

DAVE KINDRED

A Hitter First, A Hitter Always

FROM THE SPORTING NEWS

TED WILLIAMS IS HITTING. Always has been, always will be. Ted
Williams is sitting by his pool on a sunny Florida day. He has an
imaginary bat in his hands, and his fingers are moving, as if the
phantom stick of wood were a musical instrument under his touch.
He twists his hands on a thin bat handle that only he feels. There
comes to his old hero's handsome face a look of boyish delight, for
he sees, and only he sees, a baseball coming his way. Oh, my. The
joy of putting good wood on a baseball is eternal, and here is Ted
Williams about to have fun . . .

"Hoyt Wilhelm's pitching. And Hoyt Wilhelm's all time for me.
I'd get up against Hoyt Wilhelm and his first knuckleball, you could
see it good but it was moving. The second one, it's moving more
and you'd foul it off and you'd say, 'Geez, *that's* a good knuckleball.'
And now he throws you the three-strike knuckleball. It's all over
the place, and you're lucky if you don't get hit with it because you
don't know where the hell it's going. You could swing at it *AND
GET HIT BY IT!*"

Ted Williams is 76 years old, and his voice is a kid's. He talks in
italics and explosions of italics. The words become an actor's mono-
logue given texture by gestures and sound effects and body language so precise that when he flutters a hand, doing a butterfly's
flight, you, too, can see the Wilhelm knuckleball on its way. Oh, my.
Williams bites his lower lip. He turns his hands around the bat. He
narrows his eyes, and the game is on. A half-century ago they called
him The Kid. Perfect.

When Ted Williams is hitting, as he is at this moment by the pool, every nerve ending in the kid is alive to the precious possibility of a line drive off a distant fence. He calls them blue darters and scorchers. Now he is hitting against Hoyt Wilhelm, whose knuckleball confounded hitters for twenty years.

"I was always looking for Wilhelm's knuckleball because, geez, you were going to get it. I never will forget this one day. It was in Baltimore. And the ball got halfway to the plate. And I said —"

The kid's eyes pop wide open. Astonishment.

"I said, *'Fastball!'*"

Williams all but leaps from his chair to get at it.

"BOOM! LINE DRIVE TO RIGHT FIELD!"

Then comes a smile soft with pleasure.

"I don't think I ever saw another fastball from Hoyt Wilhelm."

Ted Williams calls. Says come on down. Says he has chosen the twenty best hitters of all time. In February they'll go into the Hitters Hall of Fame adjoining the Ted Williams Museum in Hernando, Florida. He says come on down. Says he has chosen two men from each league for the Ted Williams Greatest Hitters Award, to be an annual award, the hitter's equivalent of the Cy Young.

Come on down. Let's talk.

So . . .

The curving road toward Ted Williams's house stops at a wrought-iron gate. On the gate, his uniform number: 9.

Williams no longer moves with an athlete's ease. He tugs and pulls himself into position to get out of a car bringing him home from a workout.

Somewhere in the house a dog barks, and Williams calls out, "Slugger! Where are you, Slugger? Come here, boy, come here, Slugger."

And what else would you call Ted Williams's dog?

The slugger himself walks with the unsteady gait of a man on a rolling deck. He has one hand on a cane. A pair of glasses hang by a cord around his neck. He wears khaki shorts, a yellow golf shirt and brown deck shoes. There are spikes of gray in his thicket of black hair. Tall and erect, the lion in winter conjures the splendid splinter of the 1940s who for two decades and in two wars did a hero's work.

One morning in February of this year, Williams falls in his bedroom the way old men often fall. A blood vessel in the brain breaks open; the brain loses some part of its ability to govern the body. Williams has had small strokes, one in December 1991, another a few months later. The latest is more serious.

It costs him strength in his legs. His left arm and left leg go numb and weak. He can see nothing, this man who had been a fighter pilot with vision once measured at 20-10.

But on this sunny day nine months later, Williams no longer needs a wheelchair, no longer needs a walker, needs nothing, really. He carries a cane just in case. His sight came back, though the peripheral fields of vision remain a blur.

He counts his health as a marked improvement from February's weakness and darkness. He is even sly about it. "The only thing I'm concerned about," he says, "is my mental deficiency . . ."

Someone begins to mumble something about memory loss, only to be interrupted by Williams laughing: "I'm *kidding*, I hope.

"I'm thinking pretty good. I don't see quite as well as I'd like to. If I look at you, I can see most of you but not distinctly. If I look at your head, it gets down to your chest.

"I'm exercising. My strength is pretty good. I work out three times a week, walk a mile three or four times a week. On the exercise bicycle four times. I do sit-ups. I take five-pound weights and work on my arms, twenty times up with each arm. I'm getting now [to] where they're giving me 35-, 40-pound barbells to lift.

"My legs are strong. Used to be they could hold my leg down if I'm sitting in a chair. They can't do that no more. My left arm and left leg are still a little bit numb, but I'm getting better down there all the time. My appetite, geez, I can eat. I drink gallons of fluids."

Williams's eyes are watery and without sparkle. Even when he becomes animated in conversation, as he does for most of two hours, his voice an enthusiastic explosion of delight, his eyes seem to be somewhere else.

One day this summer, not long after the stroke, he told Dave Anderson of the *New York Times* about a dream he'd had in the hospital. He was working in the spring with Red Sox hitters, as he always did. Somehow the fearsome lefthander from Seattle, Randy Johnson, was on the mound. The Red Sox hitters say to Williams, "Why don't you get up there and take a few cuts?"

Only Ted Williams dreams this way: "I tell them, 'I haven't hit in years and I just had a stroke and I can't see too well,' but they kept teasing me and I say, 'Yeah, I'll do it.' But as I'm walking to home plate, I'm thinking, 'I'm not going to try to pull this guy because he can really throw.'

"The first pitch, he laid one right in there. I pushed at it. Line drive through the box for a base hit."

He laughs loud and long, the old man young again, made young by hitting, and you wonder if any great performer ever had more fun doing his work than the kid from San Diego who in 1935 put his eye to a knothole and saw, at a great distance, a left-handed hitter with style and, no way the kid could know this, a .349 lifetime average in the big leagues.

"Fun? The most fun in baseball is hitting the ball," Williams says. "That's all I practiced. That's all I did. That's all I could do for twenty years of my early life. If I had not become a pretty damned good hitter, there was something wrong. I had the opportunity; I had energy-plus, enthusiasm-plus, to want to do that very thing. And I certainly must have had some ability, being quick and strong."

And he put his eye to a knothole one day: "A kid copies what he sees is good. And if he's never seen it, he'll never know. I remember the first time I saw Lefty O'Doul, and he was as far away as . . ."

Ted Williams turns his head, looking across the pool, and his eyes become instruments of measure. ". . . as far away as those palms. And I saw the guy come to bat in batting practice. I was looking through a knothole, and I said, 'Geez, does that guy look good!' And it was Lefty O'Doul, one of the great hitters ever."

"Gods don't answer letters," John Updike wrote. He meant Ted Williams wouldn't tip his cap for fans. This is also true: Gods will talk all day about hitting.

Ted Williams, who dreams hitting, who lived hitting, who looked through a knothole sixty years ago and saw his future at-bat, who can see Hoyt Wilhelm's knuckler with a kid's vision after an old man's stroke — Ted Williams will talk about DiMaggio with two strikes, will tell us what Hornsby taught him, will tell us he wishes he could talk to Michael Jordan.

Williams will talk about hitting and hitters. He'll tell us he could, sometimes, smell the ball. He'll say there were nights he couldn't sleep for wondering why he couldn't hit. For an hour Williams will make music that if put into one piece would sound like this . . .

"Don't swing level and don't swing down. Swing slightly up at the ball because it's coming slightly down. Get it in the air. Ground balls are a pitcher's best friend, so you gotta get it in the air with power.

"Two strikes, choke up a little. Hit the ball hard through the middle. Like the great DiMaggio. Two strikes, Joe just didn't want to strike out. So he'd hit it somewhere. Trouble with hitters today, they swing from their butt with two strikes because if you hit thirty-four home runs, even if you hit .260, *Whew, BIG PAYDAY!*

"Mickey Mantle was one of the greatest ever in the game. Had the almighty home-run stoke. And fast, he didn't even have to hit a ball good to get a hit. The year he hit .360-something, I hit .388, everything falling in. I couldn't run a lick. I had 8 or 9 infield hits, and Mantle had 49. But he hit 50 home runs, too, even if he didn't know the difference between two strikes and no strikes. Had no idea, just swung from his butt. But what a player, what a guy.

"Hank Greenberg was a little on the Mantle side. Never saw Greenberg reach out and punch a ball, half-fooled, and still get a base hit with it.

"Now, the great Mr. Musial would go the other way with two strikes. Every time I saw Stan Musial, he went *five for five!* I saw him two different days. *Five for five both days!* I had it once in my life, and I saw him get it twice. So, anyway, he could run like hell, and he could slap it all around, and he had a great park to hit in, and in the last ten years of his career he hit with power.

"Power is it. I'm picking the twenty greatest hitters ever. Power. The concept of my list is that the major ingredients of the complete hitter are, number one, power, and, number two, getting on base. Why is getting on base so important? Here I hit .340 and he hits .340. But I hit 40 home runs and he hits 20. Now, I've got more total bases. He walks 38 times, and I walk 138. Getting on base is how you score runs. Runs win ballgames.

"I walked a lot in high school, and in the minors I walked one hundred times. It didn't just start in the big leagues. You start swinging at pitches a half-inch outside, the next one's an inch out and pretty soon you're getting nothing but bad balls to swing at. Rogers Hornsby told me, 'Get a good ball to hit.' Boy, that's it. *Get a good ball to hit.*

"I could see the spin on a pitch. If you're looking for breaking stuff, you see it's spinning twenty-five feet out there. Anticipation. I knew what was going to be thrown before I ever swung. I knew what the count was, what they got me out on, what the pitcher's out-pitch was, where the wind was blowing.

"And if they'd made me look bad on something, *boy, would I lay for that son of a bitch*. I was a good guess hitter. A *real good* guess hitter. And when they came back with the pitch that made me look bad, *BOOM!* It would cost him then.

"Somebody asked me, if you can see the spin, you ever hear the ball? No, but I smelled it. Took a big cut at a fastball. Didn't get but about four-sevenths of it, just nicked it back. I could smell the wood burning. I told this to Don Mattingly and Wade Boggs. Boggs looked at Mattingly; Mattingly looked at Boggs, like they're asking each other: What's he smoking? But I smelled it. And Willie Mays and Willie McCovey told me they smelled it, too.

"Good hitters today. You gotta think about Barry Bonds, Matt Williams, Jeff Bagwell. I love to watch that Frank Thomas hit. That's one big, strong guy. He can inside-out 'em like that and hit 'em outta there. Ken Griffey Jr. hits 'em in almighty clusters.

"I wish, I wish, I *wish* that I could have had a chance to talk to Michael Jordan. I am convinced that had he been a baseball player instead of a basketball player and had the baseball practice with the right surroundings he'd have been a hell of a player. He had to have the opportunity to *hear* all the things that can be involved in baseball, and he didn't hear any baseball.

"He's got a pretty good swing. He's got things that could be helped. I would just talk to him about the science of hitting. It's fifty percent mental. Why? Because of anticipation. Thinking who the pitcher is, knowing whether I'm strong or weak on a high ball and practicing that.

"Hitting is a correction thing. Every swing you're changing. Every thought you're correcting. Every time up you're thinking.

"My whole life was hitting. Hitting, nobody ever had more fun. I'll tell you, though, I'd like to tell you how many nights I couldn't sleep because I wasn't hitting good. I'd look up at the wall and I'd think, 'Holy, geez,' and I'd always be able to come up with some answer or some situation that started off the trouble.

"It was always more mechanical than anything else. And the biggest mechanical thing that I did was swing too hard. And when you swing hard, you're swinging big. And when you swing big, you have to start earlier. So you're fooled on more pitches. And how'd it all start? Because I went *whoosh* at a ball and, *boy, did it go!* Just a little flick and look where that ball went.

"So I get to thinking, with a little bit longer swing, it'll go a little bit farther. Then I'd start pulling. And when you start pulling, you start bailing out a little bit early — until I'd stop that and just go back to flicking the bat at the ball, just getting the bat on the ball, and then everything'd be O.K. again for a while."

Ted Williams has a bat in his hand. It's a real one, a Louisville Slugger with his name burned into the barrel, the burned wood reminding him: "What a thrill, the first time you get a bat with your name on it."

That happened for him fifty-eight years ago.

On this sunny day by the pool, a photographer has given Williams the bat and asked him to pose with it: This way, Ted, that way, hold the bat like this, lay it on your shoulder, rest your chin on it. The photographer is bending and crouching and moving, looking for a better angle, the camera shutter clicking, asking Ted for another smile.

Gods don't answer letters.

Neither do they smile seven times on request.

Williams growling to the photographer: "That's enough. You got enough for a book."

It is the fall of 1994, just past the great man's seventy-sixth birthday, not a year since the stroke. He talks about the therapy center where he met a girl whose name is Tricia. She's twelve or thirteen and wants to be a lawyer. She, too, has had a stroke. Williams tells you about her intent little eyes watching you. He did a little something for her, he says, and she wrote him a nice little note. He says he plays checkers with little Tricia.

He wants to go fishing, Ted Williams does. For fifty years he has taken rod, reel and fly against every fish worth the fight in any water anywhere. He wants to get back to it.

He says, "No kidding about this: I didn't think I could ever use a cane by itself. Geez, now I can walk by myself. The only thing that bothers me is I don't see quite as good, and I wouldn't see something down on the ground. But I'm accommodating all the time, getting better all the time. I'm never going to be able to run. I never thought I'd be able to . . ."

He's about to say he never thought he'd go fishing again.

But enough.

He has heard enough of this never stuff.

Now his voice is rising. His chin comes up two clicks of defiance. He's The Kid again.

"I never thought I'd be able to go fishing again, but I know *damn well I CAN SIT IN A CANOE!* And I can strip my line down here . . ."

His hands are moving as if on a fishing line at his feet in a canoe on a silvery stream somewhere. He sits straight up in his chair, tall and erect, now making a phantom cast, now whistling, *"Whish, whoosh,"* the sounds of a reel whirring and line slicing the air.

"And I can throw it damn near as far," Ted Williams says. His face is warm with hope. "Maybe next spring. Maybe next spring I can go salmon fishing. I just feel like I'm going to be able to . . ."

STEVE RUSHIN

1954–1994:
How We Got Here

FROM SPORTS ILLUSTRATED

The Titan of Television

HISTORY HAS THROWN a thunderous combination. Blacks are voting in South Africa today; Richard Nixon awaits burial tonight. In the office of the president of ABC News, nine muted televisions, recessed in a mahogany wall, monitor global events. Nine TVs, arrayed in a grid, frame the faces of Clinton, De Klerk, Mandela: They look like the Hollywood Squares of high office.

"It is so striking," says Roone Arledge, the owner of this louvered window on the world. "You look at Nelson Mandela and you look at Muhammad Ali. I can't help but see one in the other. The indomitability of spirit that both men have. You know, with the exception of the pope, Mandela may be the most famous man in the world today. Ali was that for many years."

Nixon's face pops onto a screen, like fruit in a video slot machine. True story: When Arledge was the president of ABC Sports in 1971, he hired the anvil-headed Frank Gifford away from CBS. Gifford's first assignment at ABC was to announce the Hall of Fame exhibition football game in Canton, Ohio. But when Nixon decided to drop in on the game, suddenly — horrifically — Gifford's first assignment was to interview the president.

Minutes before the broadcast Nixon told Arledge what a fan he was of the New York Giants in those days when Gifford embodied that team. In fact, when Nixon practiced law in New York, he often attended postgame parties at Giff's place. And then the president of the United States said a most curious thing to the president of ABC Sports. RN told RA: "I'm sure Frank would remember me."

Sometime in the second half of this century, sports became an axis on which the world turns. The most famous man on earth was a heavyweight fighter, the Leader of the Free World boasted fretfully of his friendship with Frank Freaking Gifford. Earlier this day, in his ABC office, Arledge had mentioned the name of Michael Jordan, an American export as ubiquitous and profitable as Coca-Cola, and was asked how in heaven's name this had all come to be. How and when, exactly, did the globe become an NBA-licensed, Charles Barkley–signature basketball spinning madly on God's index finger?

Resplendent in a navy blue suit, Arledge considered the question as an aide brought coffee, which was placed on a coffee table, next to a stack of coffee-table books: one on the Dalai Lama, one on Abraham Lincoln, one on Muhammad Ali.

"There have been comparable times in history when sports have been at the center of a culture and seemed to dominate the landscape," Arledge began. "Whether in Greek society or in what used to be called the Golden Age of Sports. But everything . . ." Pause. Sip. ". . . *everything* is magnified by television."

And Roone Arledge returned to his coffee. And nine muted televisions fairly lit the room.

American scientists solved the conundrum in 1954: How might mankind minister to its own sustenance — without missing a minute of *Mr. Peepers?* An Omaha company developed technology by which a meal of turkey, cornbread dressing, peas and sweet potatoes could be frozen, boxed, sold, thawed, cooked and safely eaten without an ounce of effort by the consumer. Swanson & Sons called this 98-cent mealsicle the "TV Dinner," to be eaten on a "TV tray," in front of, of course, the "TV." Godless Soviet scientists, meanwhile, frittered away their time developing the earth-orbiting satellite.

Nineteen fifty-four was a dizzying breakout year for television. Steve Allen starred in the network debut of *The Tonight Show* on NBC. Johnny Carson starred in the network debut of *Earn Your Vacation* on CBS. The Army and Joe McCarthy starred in the Army-

McCarthy hearings on all four networks — NBC, CBS, ABC and Dumont — as Senator Joe rooted out Reds through the riveting summer of 1954.

In that same summer Roone Pinckney Arledge Jr. was a 23-year-old corporal waiting at Aberdeen (Maryland) Proving Grounds for his imminent discharge from the Army, at which time he could begin to transform television, and television could transform sport into something truly stupendous. Upon graduation from Columbia University in 1952, Arledge worked briefly at Dumont, and ever since, though his duties in that job had been menial, TV had coursed through his veins.

In 1954 a New York attorney named Howard Cosell left the practice of law (and his $30,000 salary) to embark on a career in sports broadcasting (for $250 a week), despite the fact that he had turned 36 years old that March, his receding hairline in need of reseeding.

In 1954 a twelve-year-old child in Louisville had his red Schwinn bicycle stolen. "I'd walk out of my house at two in the morning, and look up at the sky for an angel or a revelation or God telling me what to do," the boy turned man would later tell biographer Thomas Hauser. Cassius Clay learned boxing to avenge the theft of his bike.

Soon all of these celestial events would confluent, meeting before the world on television, which stood poised to dwarf every other communication medium in 1954. That year Jack Warner forbade the appearance of a television set in the home scenes of any Warner Brothers movie, the film industry futilely attempting to wish TV away. It was too late.

"By 1954," wrote David Halberstam in *The Powers That Be*, "there were 32 million television sets throughout the country, CBS television's gross billings doubled in that single year, and CBS became the single biggest advertising medium in the world. The real money, money and revenues beyond anyone's wildest dreams, was in television and above all in entertainment. The possibilities of nationwide advertising were beyond comprehension; afternoon newspapers quickly began to atrophy; mass-circulation magazines, which up until the early fifties had been the conduit of national mass advertising — razor blades, beer, tires, cars, household goods — were suddenly in serious trouble; within little more than a decade they would be dead or dying — *Collier's, The Saturday Evening Post, Look, Life*. Television was about to alter the nature and balance of American merchandising and journalism."

Amid all the withering print, 1954 also saw the birth of a mass-circulation magazine. The launch of *Sports Illustrated* on August 16 was especially propitious, for television, beginning almost that very year, was going to infuse sports with fabulous wealth, beam iconic images of athletes through space and around a wired world, push the major leagues to realize their manifest destiny in the American West, elevate interest in games to unprecedented heights and attract the professional interest of some vastly talented men and women, not to mention Rudy Martzke.

As Corporal Arledge riffled through those first issues of *SI*, the magazine seemed to encompass all that interested him about sports. "It incorporated art and journalism in a way that was totally compelling," he says now, and he wondered then why TV couldn't do the same. He and friends lived a Sunday-to-Sunday existence as followers of the National Football League. Looking at photographs of these *warriors*, their hands gauze-wrapped like burn patients', steam clouds bursting from their mouths, he wondered why you never saw *that* on a telecast?

A magazine could offer a tight, clear photograph of Y. A. Tittle at the instant he stepped out-of-bounds. Why couldn't television? A scribe could write what he saw happening on the field, no matter how unflattering. So why couldn't a television announcer . . . *tell it like it is?*

Despite the wild success of its all-octogenarian talk show, *Life Begins at 80,* the Dumont network went telly-up in 1955. When the newly discharged Arledge found a job that year, it was as a stage manager at NBC, where he would soon become a producer for a Saturday-morning children's show. The program, hosted by Shari Lewis, was prophetically titled *Hi Mom,* a phrase that would resonate in NFL end zones some ten years later when Arledge took the NFL to prime time.

Hi Mom brought Arledge his first Emmy, in 1959, and within two years he was producing sports at ABC, where everything he touched turned to gold statuettes. There was really little hope of competing with him when you think back on it; after all, the man had won an Emmy producing *a puppet show.* What would he do with the Olympic Games?

Before he made the Olympics Olympian, fathered *Wide World of Sports, The American Sportsman, Monday Night Football, The Superstars, Nightline, 20/20, This Week with David Brinkley, Prime Time Live* and Howard Cosell; before he pioneered and/or perfected the use of instant replay and handheld cameras and isolation cameras and sophisticated graphics and underwater video and split screens and field microphones; before he miked a dead zebra so that *Sportsman* viewers could better hear its being devoured by lions; before this ruddy-faced man named Roone fashioned a grand, safari-going, desk-dodging, expense-vouchered, limo-driven life for himself, he wrote a famous memo to his superiors at ABC telling them he was going to do all of that. The year was 1961.

Nineteen sixty-one happened also to be the year that FCC chairman Newton Minow famously called television "a vast wasteland." Television's presentation of sports, specifically, was something worse altogether.

"The prevailing attitude was summed up by baseball commissioner Ford Frick," wrote Marc Gunther and Bill Carter in their book *Monday Night Mayhem.* "'The view a fan gets at home,' Frick once said, 'should not be any better than that of the fan in the worst seat of the ballpark.'"

Turnstile-obsessed baseball owners agreed, and the networks fulfilled their wishes with primitive coverage. It would be uncharitable to say what your typical baseball owner was at the time, but it rhymed with Frick: If you wanted to *see* a ball game, went their shortsighted thinking, you would simply have to buy a ticket to the ballpark.

None of this mattered to ABC, which had no pro football and only a piece of baseball when Arledge arrived. But the development of videotape and the DC-8 — cassettes and jets — allowed him to go "spanning the globe to bring you the constant variety of sport," which was really a fancy, Roone-ified name for auto racing.

To be fair, *Wide World of Sports* also brought heavy coverage of figure skating and gymnastics, sports that would stir a quadrennial appetite for ABC's coverage of the Olympics and vault a few female athletes into the ether of superstardom: Olga Korbut and Peggy Fleming, Nadia Comaneci and Dorothy Hamill, Mary Lou Retton and Katarina Witt, *Tonya and Nancy*. Nevertheless, it was a measure of television's meager interest in the Games that ABC paid $50,000 for the 1960 Winter Olympics in Squaw Valley and then skittishly reneged on the deal. But the space race was on, the cold war was at its hair-trigger, missiles-in-Cuba, shoe-pounding peak, and, says Arledge, "it became apparent with the Olympics in those days that if you had an American against a Russian, it didn't matter *what* they were doing, they could have been *kayaking* and people would watch it."

Soviet cosmonaut Yuri Gagarin had been shot into space, and U.S. pilot Francis Gary Powers and his U-2 spy plane had been shot *out* of it. So eager were Americans to see vanquished Russkies of any athletic stripe that even twenty years later, when the host nation would finally beat the Soviets in ice hockey at Lake Placid, the U.S. would go bananas over a sport about which it knew precious little. The victory would be consecrated by many as the greatest sporting achievement of the second half of this century, and the moment of triumph would be punctuated by announcer Al Michaels's asking in all sincerity, "Do you believe in miracles?" The game was brought to Americans by Roone Arledge and the American Broadcasting Company, which had been serving the cold war hot for two decades.

In the mid-1960s the Olympics and a new college football package were ABC's only familiar showcases, which meant that *Wide World* lavished extraordinary attention on exotica, Arledge flying around all creation to buy the rights to anything that wasn't already owned: the Twenty-Four Hours of Le Mans, golf's British Open, the Japanese All-Star baseball game. While in Tokyo to negotiate the rights to that extravaganza, the peripatetic Arledge took in a Japanese film. The action often occurred at half speed, in the grand tradition of the bad martial-arts movie. Not for the first time Arledge wondered: Why couldn't this be done on television?

His return to New York included a layover in Los Angeles. In a bar called Julie's, Arledge asked ABC engineer Bob Trachinger how TV could become master over time itself. Trach sketched it all out on a sodden cocktail napkin — how an image could be taken off an Orthicon tube and replayed at half speed and . . .

ABC first used slow-motion instant replay on Thanksgiving Day of 1961. The most scintillating play in the game between Texas and Texas A & M was . . . a field goal. The network replayed the chip shot as if it were historic, just as they would replay the scene two Novembers later when Ruby shot Oswald. But on this November day, as Arledge recalls, "the earth did not shake."

The temblor came one weekend later. Syracuse was at Boston College, whose quarterback, Jack Concannon, scampered 70 yards for a first-half touchdown, a black-and-white streak across the television set. But when ABC replayed it, defenders could be seen clearly missing tackles, key blocks were suddenly thrown into sharp relief, and announcer Paul Christman was able to narrate every nuance of the run. The screen flickered like hell, but Concannon was balletic at half speed, and any Ban-Lon-wearing, Ballantine-swigging, Barcalounging viewer at home could see the whole field opening up before him. Look closely, and you could see much, much more. "You could see," says Arledge, "a whole new era opening up."

The National Football League was not always a vaguely sinister and monolithic American institution, something like General Motors, the single biggest advertiser on the league's Sunday-afternoon telecasts. But then came December 28, 1958, when CBS broadcast the enervating NFL championship game between the Baltimore Colts and the New York Giants, starring friend-to-Nixon Frank Gifford. From that day on, NFL games would be presented as if they were somber pursuits of grave national importance.

"CBS was the paragon of professional football broadcasting," notes Arledge. "Ray Scott was its voice, and it treated every game as if it were played in a cathedral. The CBS style was very sedate, always has been: Pat Summerall followed in that tradition. But Ray Scott — Ray Scott was a voice from behind the altar."

ABC, meanwhile, began televising something called the American Football League. What was it about using the word *American* in its name that always seemed to render a corporation second-rate? The American Football League and the American Broadcasting Company were to the early 1960s what the American Basketball Association and the American Motors Corporation were to the 1970s, the latter two producing some ugly Pacers and seemingly little more.

Eventually, however, the underdog ABC and AFL would elevate each other. Because AFL players were largely unknown, Arledge ordered up omnipresent graphics: When Don Maynard of the New

York Jets caught a pass, his name would immediately materialize on the screen. Three plays later, when he caught another pass, his name would appear again, with an interesting factoid to let you know that this was the *same guy* who caught the last one and perhaps you should keep an eye on him.

"Before ESPN and CNN and talk radio, we only had the time of the game to tell all of these stories," explains Arledge as if talking about the Bronze Age. (In fact, at a production meeting on the day of Nixon's funeral in April, Arledge demanded that his staff acquire a list of everyone who would be in attendance at the ceremony in Yorba Linda. "If Alexander Haig shows up," he said, "I want to put on the screen ALEXANDER HAIG, NIXON'S CHIEF OF STAFF.") The technique of on-screen graphics began in earnest with those first ABC broadcasts of the AFL. Alas for Arledge and ABC, after four years the league sold its broadcast rights to richer NBC and then, four years later, merged with the NFL.

By 1969 the NFL had played five games on Monday nights, the first of them in 1966. All five were carried by CBS, to mediocre ratings. But with ABC the odd web out on pro football games, Arledge of necessity approached NFL commissioner Pete Rozelle about playing a game *every* Monday night beginning with the 1970 season. The idea had always appealed to Rozelle, who had loved the night exhibition games the Los Angeles Rams played when he was their publicist in the early fifties. "There was something special about the spotlight hitting the players when the starting lineups were announced," Rozelle has said. "It created a different aura than day football. It was decidedly more dramatic."

Once persuaded of the idea, though, Rozelle maddeningly offered the Monday-night games to his loyal networks, CBS and NBC. But CBS took a pass: They had a hit in *Mayberry RFD* on Monday nights, and besides, God intended for you to go to church on Sundays, not on Monday evenings. (And make no mistake, the NFL *was* church: To his lasting regret Rozelle ordered the league to play on the Sunday after the Kennedy assassination, in part because a landmark television contract was in the works and in part because the league was feeling a thou-shalt-keep-holy-the-Sabbath inviolability.)

In any event NBC, which had its popular *Movie of the Week* on Monday nights, also spurned the offer. So ABC had football for the fall of 1970 with one condition: Arledge insisted that he be able to choose his own announcers without interference from the NFL. Television contracts in that day called for approval of network announcers by the leagues; indeed, it was only four years earlier that CBS broadcaster Jack Whitaker was thrown off the Masters' telecast by tournament officials for impudently calling the Augusta National gallery a "mob." But Rozelle agreed to give a free hand to Arledge, and the first person Arledge hired for his new *Monday Night Football* was Howard Cosell.

A few years earlier Arledge had signed Cosell to appear as a boxing analyst on *Wide World* and to cover the sport at the 1968 Olympics. Cosell instantly seized a high profile with his interviews of Muhammad Ali, whom Cosell insisted on calling . . . Muhammad Ali. This was deemed outrageous and deliberately provocative, even though Muhammad Ali was the man's legal name and had been for four years. "We've forgotten how weird some people's opinions were," says Arledge. Indeed, when ABC asked Ali — who had been stripped of his heavyweight title for resisting the Vietnam draft — to commentate on its boxing coverage, it did so despite warnings against the idea from the U.S. State Department.

In those first giddy days following those first Monday nights, Arledge had to dance a conga to his desk, sidestepping bushels of letters and telegrams tottering in piles throughout his office. He could peel one off a stack at random and invariably the missive would read, "Get him off the air!" Of course, "him" was Cosell, who later estimated that half of his mail began with the cheery salutation "You nigger-loving Jew bastard . . ."

The essence of the outcry was clear. "We were desecrating something," says Arledge. "CBS had Ray Scott, and now we had this loudmouthed Howard on TV questioning *everything*, yelling about what a *dumb* trade that was, and asking, 'Don't football players have rights?' And a lot of the owners just couldn't deal with it."

It was clear, too, that television could create a collective national experience, could unite a country in something, if only in its distaste for this toupeed boor spouting polysyllables in a broadcast booth. By the fall of 1971, 30 million viewers were tuning in to ABC on Monday nights.

With those kinds of numbers, it became a fait accompli: Within four years the World Series was made a primarily prime-time affair, and by 1978 the Super Bowl had also encroached on that rarefied space. Don't blame television or him, says Arledge; blame baseball and football owners: "Because they want to get more money, and the way to get more money is to play your games in prime time."

Sure, advertising dollars were wallpapering the networks' Sixth Avenue offices as well, but before long those dollars would return to the NFL as $10 bills. CBS paid $14 million a year to televise the NFL in 1964 and '65. By 1982 the three networks paid a combined $2.1 billion to televise NFL games for five years. By 1990 five networks paid $3.6 billion for three years. And in 1993 Rupert Murdoch and the Fox network paid $1.58 billion for the rights to televise just the National Football *Conference* for four years.

Football would be played no more in the CBS cathedral but in a Fox-hole where coverage will likely owe more to ABC and Arledge. In 1974, when he hired Fred (the Hammer) Williamson to briefly join the *Monday Night* lineup — a position that in 1983 would be filled by a more glamorous football entity, O.J. Simpson — Arledge noticed, on a chain around the Hammer's neck, a clenched black fist and a solid-gold penis, two items of jewelry seldom worn by Ray Scott of the CBS television network.

His ABC press-kit biography used to end with the unbecoming (and highly dubious) boast that Roone Arledge holds the records "for shooting the largest leopard and Cape buffalo — the latter considered the most dangerous animal in the world — on an African safari." How could anyone *know* that those two animals were the largest of their kind *ever* shot on an African safari? As for that clause between dashes — the most dangerous animal in the world — it seems a rather subjective and gratuitous flourish, does it not?

Arledge has occasionally been accused of creating yards of his legend from whole cloth. Tony Verna, a former director at CBS, will tell you that he and his network were first on the air with slow-motion instant replay, on an Army-Navy football telecast on New Year's Eve in 1964, though the historical record is obstinately unclear on the matter.

Certainly Arledge *has* known virtually every world leader and athletic giant of our time as head of the News and Sports division at ABC, and his is the world's grandest TV résumé. But even among his myriad achievements, one stands above all as the Cape buffalo of his accomplishments. It happened in Munich in 1972.

Arledge produced ten Olympics, and they are collectively the pride of his twenty-five years at ABC Sports. But the prices were dear, and he can tick off each of them to this day: Innsbruck in 1964 cost $250,000. Mexico City in 1968 cost $3 million, and that one really got to him. His colleagues thumped him on the back after he won the rights to those Games, but Arledge felt like vomiting. "Why are you *congratulating* me?" he asked. He was sick and remorseful, bedeviled by the buyer's guilt you and I might get after shelling out for a Chevette.

Munich ran $13.5 million, and four years later the '76 Games in Montreal cost $25 million, and suddenly it was all insane. "It used to be in those days," says Arledge, "that you'd rebuild an entire city if you had the Olympic Games." Montreal got new roads, a refurbished infrastructure and a soon-to-be-domed stadium for its two weeks before the world.

Still, there were two sticking points with the Montreal Olympic Organizing Committee as Arledge was negotiating the rights to those Games in the middle of a Quebec night. The MOOC-a-mucks demanded 1) that Cosell not be assigned to the Olympics and 2) that no mention be made of the Munich Games in ABC's coverage of the opening ceremonies.

Arledge calmly responded with a question of his own, not out of anger but with a bemused, almost clinical detachment: "Are you out of your mind?"

The Montreal rights had drawn such a high price precisely *because* of what had happened in Munich. For starters, the 1972 Games had been the first to take over the whole of a network's prime-time schedule. (The Mexico City Games had been shunted to ABC's worst time-slot ghettos.) What's more, those Olympics had been a riveting athletic success: When they were over, Mark Spitz had more gold hanging from his neck than Fred (the Hammer) Williamson, and the U.S. men's basketball team had had its own gold stolen by those villainous, still-invincible emissaries from the Evil Empire in an epic final.

Yet the lowercase games themselves had become but a jot on history's seismograph after the events of September 5, when eleven Israeli athletes were taken hostage by Palestinian terrorists in the athletes' village at 4:30 that morning.

Jim McKay, ABC's Olympic studio host, was preparing to take a dip in the hotel pool on his only day off in the fortnight when he was summoned to duty. He would be on the air for the next eighteen hours, anchoring field coverage from Cosell and from Peter Jennings, the network's Beirut correspondent, who was in Munich for the Games. Citizens of the world sat gathered around their televisions, the electronic hearth hissing and spitting bad news like sparks. In the end even some relatives of the hostages themselves received the sickening news from McKay, who, wearied and wan, could say little more than, "They're all gone."

Within a day Arledge and his staff had produced a forty-minute instant documentary on the murders, featuring reaction from Willy Brandt and the Munich chief of police and members of the Israeli Knesset and Golda Meir. He was puzzled when, Rozelle-like, Avery Brundage ordered the Games to go on that day; he was puzzled, likewise, when ABC News told him it did not want his documentary, that this was somehow still about sports. So Arledge moved *all* of his commercial spots in that day's Olympic programming to the beginning and middle of his show and ran the damn documentary in his own time, forty minutes uninterrupted at the end of the Olympic program. And don't think he forgot the slights when he took over last-place ABC News (in addition to Sports) in 1978 and made it the More-Americans-Get-Their-News-from-ABC-News-Than-from-Any-Other-Source king of Broadcast Row.

Arledge's coverage from Munich "changed television itself," wrote Gunther and Carter. "From then on, whenever a catastrophe struck, viewers no longer were content to wait for film at eleven; they expected television to afford them a chance to be eyewitnesses to history." In short, these "viewers" were about to become voyeurs, a phenomenon that would seem to reach its apocalyptic apotheosis on a Friday night in the summer of 1994 when 95 million Americans stayed tuned to several networks to see if O. J. Simpson would commit suicide on the San Diego Freeway.

ABC won twenty-nine Emmys for its Munich production. Even the president of archenemy CBS, ABC's own Evil Empire, approached Arledge at a post-Olympics luncheon in New York and congratulated him, something that just doesn't happen on the graceless weasel farm of network television. "It was," Bob Wood told Arledge, "like the nation was reading the same book together."

You can hear it. Power thrums through the corridors like traffic through the streets of Gotham, five stories below. Roone Arledge became president of ABC News exclusively in 1986, and from his elegant office here he can now look at sports as a father might look at somewhat disappointing children who have left the nest.

He sat by, gaping like the rest of us, as CBS overpaid for baseball by half a billion dollars in 1990. He calls the NFL's most recent television contract "a stroke of luck," after watching the league stuff Rupert Murdoch's money down its pants like a frenzied participant in a Dash for Dollars contest.

Arledge worries that these price tags may one day hang like toe tags on American sports. "The basic ill in sports today has got to be money," he says, "and it's ultimately going to corrupt everything. You have owners who can't control themselves giving all this money to players. You have twenty-five-year-old kids making several million dollars a year and thinking they're *entitled* to it: They argue that rock stars and movie stars make that kind of money, and they're performers just like athletes are. But I would like to think there's a difference between an athlete and a rock star. Unfortunately, it may well be that as new generations come along, they won't miss the virtues that used to be at the center of sport. They may see sports only as a means to a sneaker deal."

With all these chickens coming home to roost, doesn't this television executive feel a little like Harlan Sanders? Arledge acknowledges his and TV's place in "the feeding chain." But network execs — and team owners and athletes, for that matter — are entrepreneurs who can do as they please. Arledge makes $3 million annually, but he also made his sports division, traditionally a loss leader for a network, eminently profitable.

It is state-sponsored sports fanaticism that he finds particularly vexing, all of these modern-day ancient Romes across America, obsessed with gladiators and lavish Colosseums. Think of all that a new NFL team will do for Charlotte, Arledge says — wonderful, inestimable things — but also think of all that a new NFL team will *not* do for that city.

"I think a question that has to be asked is, In a time of poverty and homelessness and crime and all the other problems this society has, should we be building $400 million stadiums with public funds?" he says. "In most cases these stadiums are publicly financed but privately profitable. And there are very few other places where that is true. It is not true of the Metropolitan Opera. We are notorious in this country for not subsidizing the arts and politics and things that we should. And yet, we do it in sports without even thinking about it. In fact, it's a hallmark. If you *don't* do it, you're somehow second-rate."

In other words, you're not . . . major league. Up-and-coming cities need major league franchises to be considered *major league,* and they need gleaming new stadiums to attract the franchises. It is the magical mantra of the film *Field of Dreams:* If you build it, they will come. One man understood this better than any other. Nobody built a bigger field from bigger dreams than Judge Roy Hofheinz, who was himself as big as all of Texas.

Home in the Dome

The Judge smoked twenty-five cigars a day, great tobacco-filled dirigibles that befit a man of his dimensions: the 57-inch waistline, the cuff links as big and loud as cymbals, the long Cadillac limousine in which he drove himself through Houston. It was said that Judge Roy Hofheinz could not find a chauffeur willing to work his hours, which were roughly the same as a 7-Eleven's.

Sleep, and you cannot graduate from high school at 16 (as the Judge did), pass the Texas bar at 19, be elected to the state legislature at 22 and to the judgeship of Houston's Harris County at 24. To the Judge life was a Whitman's Sampler of possibilities. He devoured the legal profession, politics, the slag industry, real estate, radio, television and professional sports — licking his fingers clean of each career before plucking out a new one.

The son of a laundry-truck driver, Hofheinz was also at various times Lyndon Johnson's campaign manager, the mayor of Houston, the builder of the Astrodome and the owner of the Ringling Bros. and Barnum & Bailey Circus. The last two roles best suited the Judge's personality, though a Houston contemporary named Willard Walbridge once found it insufficient to equate Hofheinz with P. T. Barnum. Said Walbridge, "He made P. T. Barnum look like fourteen miles of bad road."

Thus in the early 1960s, when the Judge was planning sport's first domed stadium, he insisted that the dugouts be an extravagant 120 feet long. This was done not as a pioneering concession to player comfort but so that as many ticket buyers as possible could be obliged when they asked for seats behind the dugout.

When those seats, fully upholstered, theater-style, were installed, their various colors formed a garish palette that the Judge (whose garb ran to canary-yellow pants and test-pattern blazers) thought profoundly beautiful. "I'm inclined to think the Lord agrees with me a little bit," he explained, " 'cause I've never seen the flowers of the fields all one color." It is instructive to note that the Lord agreed with the Judge, not the other way around.

After all, it was the Judge, not the Lord, who carved out the modern physical landscape of professional sports, a terrain blistered by domes and green with the fungus of artificial turf. Both were the brainchildren of Judge Roy Hofheinz.

Even as baseball emerges from the architectural dark ages of the 1960s and '70s, marked by the blight of the multipurpose stadium, and begins once again building traditional parks like Camden Yards and The Ballpark in Arlington, these — and *all* big-time sports stadiums and arenas constructed today — are designed around the luxury skybox and the elaborate electronic scoreboard. Both are the intellectual offspring of the Judge, who changed the very way Americans attend their games.

"We combined baseball with a cocktail party," says Fred Hofheinz, 56, the Judge's younger son, himself a former mayor of Houston and his father's right-hand man in the first years of the Astrodome. "You can wander around your box with a drink in your hand and sell some guy some insurance. And I promise you, there are people all over sports now who never look at the sports event. The whole time, they're selling. I was at a Rockets game last Saturday, and I don't even remember who won."

On an April night in 1965, the Astros flew from their spring training home in Cocoa, Florida, to Houston, where they bused directly to the brand-new Astrodome to drop off equipment. Larry Dierker, an eighteen-year-old rookie pitcher on that club, bounded from the clubhouse into the concourse-level seats that night, taking in the multiple miracles before him: the air conditioning, the grass growing indoors (artificial turf was not laid until the following year), the translucent roof (greenhouse by day, a planetarium by night) — the whole otherworldly quality of this $32 million marvel on the Texas prairie. To this day, Dierker recalls the moment exactly. "It was," he says, "like walking into the next century."

As the story of Los Angeles begins with irrigation, so the story of the Astrodome begins with air conditioning. Willis H. Carrier was the Edison of the air conditioner, a mechanical engineer who predicted in 1939 that man would soon live beneath climate-controlled bubbles, with God powerless to impose weather on his creatures. To many of his contemporaries, Willis H. Carrier was, well, downright daft.

But was he? The globe is now goitered with domed stadiums, everywhere from Tokyo to Toronto. In Carrier's native upstate New York, Syracuse Orangemen play basketball and football in the Carrier Dome, an eponym that suggests Carrier was right after all. He *was* right. But it was the Judge who made good on the prophecy.

Roy Mark Hofheinz began relieving Texans from the sun — and of their money — as a nine-year-old during Prohibition, when he set up a refreshment stand in his front yard, displaying a hand-lettered sign that read NEAR BEER SOLD HERE, BUT NO BEER SOLD NEAR HERE. He was still cooling customers in the 1970s, when his AstroWorld amusement park hummed with the sound of that ultimate Texas extravagance: It had *outdoor* air conditioning.

At home in the dead of a Houston summer, the Judge would often turn his own AC up high enough to frost the family room; when he had the house feeling like a refrigerated boxcar, he would build a fire in the fireplace and bask in its crackling warmth.

Yes, sir, air conditioning could bring Christmas in July. So together with Houston oilman R. E. (Bob) Smith, who had a bigger pile than God, the visionary Judge decided to build the world's largest air-conditioned indoor shopping complex, just off Westheimer Road in Houston. That was the late fifties. The word today is *mall*.

About that time a group of local investors was trying to land a major league baseball team for Houston. Frustrated in its efforts, the group began planning a third big league, the Continental League. "This was the heyday in ownership profitability, in control of ballplayers," Fred Hofheinz points out. "The reserve clause was still in place. Most baseball clubs were privately held by rich individuals. Baseball was a *club* — an inside club. And the Continental League was designed to put pressure on everybody to expand the American and National leagues."

In little more than a decade, baseball's reserve clause would be challenged by Curt Flood of the St. Louis Cardinals, and the mahoganied country club of owners in the other three major professional sports would be gate-crashed by a couple of California hepcats named Gary Davidson and Dennis Murphy. But in 1960 the baseball Establishment forestalled these events by simply allowing two more members beyond the red velvet ropes, granting National League franchises to New York and Houston. The latter team would be called the Colt .45s. And the Colts would be owned by Judge Roy Hofheinz, who abandoned his plans for a shopping mall when he alighted on a better, more colossal use for the cool, gentle breezes stirred by the man-made miracle of air conditioning.

Understand that the Judge blew a lot of smoke, and not all of it came from a lighted corona: He always said that he was inspired to build the Astrodome after a visit to Rome with his wife, Dene. "Mama and I were standing there looking at the Colosseum," he would say of the ancient arena, which was at times roofed by a tarplike velarium in inclement weather. "It was a large, round facility, and most of the stadiums in the U.S. had been built to conform to the shape of the playing fields. Rectangular."

And indeed, the Astrodome would be round, built to fit baseball and football and basketball and boxing and tractor pulls and concerts and what-have-you. So would the four undomed ballparks that would follow rapid-fire in the late 1960s and early 1970s: the abominations of Busch Stadium in St. Louis, Riverfront Stadium in Cincinnati, Veterans Stadium in Philadelphia and Three Rivers Stadium in Pittsburgh. Those parks are called octorads, or rounded rectangles, and it was precisely that kind of esoterica — architectural and otherwise — that had a dead-bolt lock on the Judge's imagination.

For his intellect was as sharp as the crease in his trousers. The Judge wore a gold watch, but it concealed a tiny slide rule, which says a lot about the man. "I remember vividly a stack of books on the kitchen table," says Fred. "All of them about domes."

Convinced that man could raise a dome higher than man could hit a baseball, the Judge and R. E. (Bob) Smith purchased 494 acres of scrubland, empty save for a lone mesquite tree, from the Hilton Hotel Corporation. The city had already planned fourteen lanes of freeway to run past the site, and ground was broken for the Harris County Domed Stadium, to be opened in 1965. For three seasons the Colt .45s would play outdoors in a temporary, low-budget ballpark called Colt Stadium: By day fans would be hotter than bejesus and by night would be buzzed by Cessna-sized mosquitoes.

The name Colt .45s evoked the old Houston, whereas the Judge was looking to help shape the new, Space Age city, which was already home to NASA. So he telephoned a friend, astronaut Alan Shepard, one evening in the winter of 1964 and asked him if the Mercury Seven crew would like a ball club named for them. Of course, replied Shepard, who was such a sports fanatic that he would carry golf clubs to the moon on his trip there in 1971.

Thus the Colt .45s would become the Astronauts, a name the Judge preemptively clipped to Astros, knowing that newspaper-headline writers would do so anyway. (Defiantly, newspaper-headline writers briefly referred to the Astros as the 'Tros, and to this day they are often the 'Stros.) The Harris County Domed Stadium would become the Astrodome, and the Judge would become master of what he called his Astrodomain: the Astrodome and the Astros, the Astrolite scoreboard and the Astrotots puppet theater, the Astro-Bowl bowling alley and the AstroWorld amusement park and the AstroHall exhibition arena. They were enough to make you AstroSick, but the names took root.

The Astrodome was paid for with municipal bonds, but the Judge built fifty-three luxury boxes with $2 million out of his own silken pocket. "It was done," says Fred, "to attract people who used baseball games as a backdrop to sell their products."

And the Judge could sell nasal spray to the noseless. When players refused to appear on the Astros' pregame radio show because they weren't receiving watches or lube jobs or golf shirts or gift certificates in compensation, the Judge made an impassioned clubhouse speech to his charges: "Radio is the only link that a *blind man* has to his beloved Astros, for God's sake, and . . ."

"I don't even remember what all he said," recalls Dierker, "but for weeks after, players were lining up to do that show."

So the Judge had no trouble renting his luxury boxes, which he said were inspired by, of course, a trip to the Colosseum. "I found out that the emperor and all the bigwigs sat at the *top* of the stadium," he used to say. The truth is, the bigwigs did not sit at the top of the Colosseum, and the Judge did not set foot in the old arena until 1967, when he flew to Rome to purchase the circus from John Ringling North. For publicity purposes the papers were signed in the historic showplace. When the Judge's photo-opportunists tried to move a large stone into the picture, Colosseum guards went berserk. The stone had been in place for two thousand years, having been laid there by the emperor Vespasian.

When the Astrodome opened for its first exhibition baseball game, on April 9, 1965, it was proclaimed the world's single largest air-conditioned space. When the first home run was hit that day, by Mickey Mantle of all people, the 474-foot-long scoreboard flashed TILT! If an Astro hit a homer, on the other hand, the scoreboard (with the world's largest screen) would produce a smoke-snorting bull, American and Texas flags flying from its horns like the flags on the fenders of a presidential limousine. (All of which would soon prompt Chicago Cub manager Leo Durocher to say, portentously, "Houston is bush.") On this day of the first exhibition, in fact, the President himself was in rapt attendance; the Judge's close friend Lyndon Johnson watched the 'Tros beat the Yanks 2–1.

"There was a *mania* to get inside the Dome that first year," says Astrodomophile Chuck Pool, a former Astro publicist who is now media-relations director for the Florida Marlins. "There was a Boy Scout Circus in the Dome in 1965. Ordinarily the Scouts would sell 50,000 tickets for these things, but maybe 3,000 people would attend. People bought tickets as a donation. But in 1965 they sold 60,000 tickets, and everyone with a ticket showed up to watch the Boy Scouts, with thousands more outside screaming to get in."

Sixty thousand people paid to watch a Webelo tie a slipknot. Millions of tourists would pay $1 apiece to enter the Dome and watch nothing at all. Fifty-three thousand would watch UCLA and Houston — Lew Alcindor versus Elvin Hayes — play on January 20, 1968, the night college basketball came of age. And 19 million worldwide watched five years later as Billie Jean King and Bobby Riggs caricatured the battle of the sexes by playing a preposterous tennis match in the Astrodome. While King's 6–4, 6–3, 6–3 victory that night was trumpeted as a sporting milestone, her triumph would prove fleeting, as two decades later only a handful of women in golf, tennis and Olympic sports would be able to match the handsome incomes of their male counterparts. But on this night of spectacle in the Dome, King made her testosteroned tormentor look ridiculous.

Nothing was quite so ridiculous, though, as that week the Astrodome opened, when baseballs fell like baseball-sized hail on the

Astros and the Yankees and the Baltimore Orioles and the Philadelphia Phillies. The Dome's translucent roof panels created such a
glare during day games that Baltimore's Boog Powell took the field
in a batting helmet. The league tried different-colored balls — red,
yellow, *cerise* — to combat the problem, which was basically this:
The Astros were in danger of becoming the first team to call a game
on account of sunshine.

The club immediately painted over the roof panels, banishing
sunlight. "And that was the death knell for grass," says Fred. The
grass, Tifway 419 Bermuda, had been specially developed by scientists in Tifton, Georgia. But without sunlight the grass was going,
going, gone. And yet the death knell for Tifway Bermuda 419
would be the life knell for another kind of turf being developed by
scientists at Monsanto — as well as the life knell for knee surgeons
for decades to come.

For the remainder of the 1965 season, the Judge simply painted
over the dead grass and dirt in his outfield, mixed in some sawdust
with it and *called* it grass, though it was essentially a sandlot.

"I think he suspected all along that the grass wouldn't work," says
Pool. "Artificial turf was developed in 1964 through a Ford Foundation study that indicated city kids entering the Army had lower
coordination than suburban and rural kids. The study concluded
that it was because city kids had no play areas. The first artificial turf
was installed at Moses Brown Playground in Providence. And Hofheinz had installed a patch at spring training in '65."

Before sealing the deal to introduce artificial turf into the year-
old Astrodome, the Judge procured a 30-foot-long sample of the
wonder-stuff from Monsanto, installed it at old Colt Stadium and
assaulted the surface in sundry Hofheinzian ways that would never
have occurred to the manufacturer. Among the durability tests
administered by Hofheinz: Rented elephants urinated on the nylon
rug while trampling over it — approximating the kind of abuse a
Lenny Dykstra might one day deliver to the surface.

In March 1966 carpet was laid in the Dome. In the first major
league baseball game played on AstroTurf, a Los Angeles Dodger
rookie named Don Sutton got his first major league win. The Astro
starter was Robin Roberts, who was headed for the Hall of Fame,
and it appeared that AstroTurf was headed there as well. Busch
Stadium in St. Louis, which opened later that year, would forsake

grass in 1970 for low-maintenance AstroTurf. By 1973 five more stadiums would have synthetic surfaces, and AstroTurf welcome mats would join lawn jockeys and pink flamingos as staples of American exterior decorating.

As would be expected of a man who knows where to rent an incontinent elephant, the Judge traveled widely in life. The 1970 stroke that left him in a wheelchair (until his death, in 1982, at age 70) did little to slow him. No, the Judge smoked life down to the butt end, as if it were one of his Sans Souci Perfectos, the cigars he snuffed out in gold ashtrays shaped like upturned fielder's gloves.

Aides would simply *carry* the Judge up to the Parthenon, like the potentate he was, on a visit to Athens. Like Lord Elgin, the Judge assembled all sorts of curiosa — unsightly statuary, antique furniture, garish baubles — to cart back to Texas. The crates piled up at his Houston homes, not unlike in the last scene of *Citizen Kane*.

"I'm surprised they haven't made a movie about this man," says Pool. "He was truly larger than life. At the end he had grown a beard and looked like Orson Welles. And his voice, it had this . . . *riveting intensity.*"

What was the epigraph that began *Kane?*

In Xanadu did Kubla Khan, a stately pleasure dome decree . . . The Judge had moved into his Dome following the death of Dene in 1966, into his famously sybaritic apartment above the right-centerfield-pavilion seats.

Behind the odd-shaped windows the Judge lived for eight years, surrounded by a billiard parlor, and a minigolf course, and a beauty salon, and a barber shop, and an interfaith chapel, and a children's library, and a presidential suite reserved for LBJ, and bathrooms with gilded toilet seats.

The Judge had another sometime residence, the Celestial Suites at the AstroWorld Hotel. A bathtub there was so large, it required an indoor-pool permit. In fact, the $3,000-a-night Celestial Suites penthouse was listed in *The Guinness Book of Records* as the planet's most expensive hotel room. Elvis stayed there, though rumor has it that *he* found the place, decorated with the detritus of the Judge's European shopping sprees, too gaudy.

On weekends the Judge relaxed at his bayfront retreat, called Huckster House. The great man unwound there by clanging a locomotive bell he kept in the front yard, ringing the thing like

Quasimodo at ungodly hours of the night "just to let the neighbors know we're around."

Alas, it is all lost now: Huckster House, the Celestial Suites, the apartment at the Astrodome. Pool took the media through the Judge's chambers for one last tour before the Astros gutted the residence in 1988. It had been fifteen years since the Judge lived in the Dome, but parts of his crib remained spookily intact. Pool, rummaging through the rooms alone, opened one door in the dark, flipped on a light and was greeted by a disembodied head falling off a shelf: It was the overstuffed noggin of Chester Charge, the Astros' first mascot.

It is all lost now, but in its day the Judge's Astrodomain was a spectacle the likes of which the world had never seen, nor will likely ever want to see again. "I've stayed in some pretty good places," columnist Art Buchwald said after a night in the Celestial Suites, "but nothing quite so ridiculous as that joint."

There will never be another Judge. There will never be another Dome. French ambassador Herve Alphand visited Houston in 1965 and compared the steel-girdered roof of the Astrodome to the Eiffel Tower. "The Eiffel Tower is nice," agreed the Judge, "but you can't play ball there."

They all came: Bob Hope and Billy Graham, Buchwald and Buckminster Fuller. Lyndon & Lady Bird. Huntley & Brinkley. Princess Grace & Prince Rainier. When the (Astro)world was young, a Houston Astro might meet anyone upon arrival each day at the park.

On the eve of the 1967 Houston Champion International golf tournament, there was a pregame closest-to-the-pin contest: Various Astros drove golf balls from home plate to a flagstick in center field, competing against a team composed of PGA veterans and . . . Lawrence Welk. "I can still remember, [Astro infielder] Doug Rader kept calling Lawrence Welk *Larry*," recalls Dierker wistfully. "Hey, *Larry* . . ." The Astros were brash and young, and expected to remain so forever.

But time passes. Huntley & Brinkley split up, Princess Grace was killed in a car wreck, and sometime in there the Astrodome went flat, like a sunken soufflé. The Camelot optimism that ushered in the 1960s — that ushered in the Astrodome — had long before gone flat, like old champagne. Or the champagne music of Larry Welk.

The erstwhile Eighth Wonder of the World is now another dreary pitcher's park, albeit one that gave us fake grass and turf toe and rug burn and corporate boxes and those infernal cartoon clapping hands that tell us when to cheer. But happily, the legacy of the Astrodome is more than that, as the legacy of the 1960s is more than Vietnam and assassinations.

"I think what has happened to professional sports since 1960 is what I call the *gentrification* of it," says Fred Hofheinz, who chooses his words carefully, as if selecting tomatoes at the market, turning each possibility over in his head before speaking. "Up until then, there were sports fans and there were sports pages and a lot of people who followed sports. But beginning about the time that my dad and other promoters around the country became involved — with the advent of television — sports became something that *everybody* followed.

"Enormous new markets opened up, and the Dome was part of that: If you were to go to a Houston Buffs minor league game, you would have seen the die-hard fans, the people who kept scorecards and read the box scores every morning. That guy was in the minority at the Dome. At the Dome the wives came. The children came. Suddenly it was a whole new milieu of fans. The Dome greatly broadened sports' appeal for these people. In Houston it became a social event to go to the Astrodome. Women went to the Astrodome in *heels!*"

Indeed, the Judge created an entire press box for women society-page writers. The "hen coop" produced Astrodome stories that turned on such questions as "Is it proper for a man to wear his hat indoors?" Of course, the hats in question were cowboy hats, this being Texas; other American men had stopped wearing snap-brimmed fedoras to ball games (or anyplace else) after John Kennedy went bare-noggined on Inauguration Day in 1961.

Let the word go forth: The 1960s were to herald a new, hatless era. The Space Age. In Living Color. If the new decade wasn't exactly a new century, well, you could *see* a new century from there — from a concourse at the Astrodome in Houston, Texas. That city, it should not be forgotten, would fairly redeem the violent 1960s, just 165 days before the decade expired, by landing Americans on the moon with a bronze plaque. WE CAME IN PEACE FOR ALL MANKIND.

As for the stadium named for the astronauts: When the Judge was still living in his famously sybaritic apartment above the right-field bleachers, an electrician named Don Collins had cause to work in the Astrodome at all hours. In the middle of some nights, in the vast, empty, dark arena, Collins could look up to a window of the Hofheinz residence and see only the glowing ember of a cigar, floating there like a firefly, high above the synthetic playing field.

The Judge is gone from this life some twelve years now, but the ember still glows, a spectral stogie. Its blue smoke hangs like a spirit above every arena in the land.

The League Leader

Gary Davidson has a lot of balls: gold-and-orange-striped footballs that flew like kited checks in the World Football League, and red-white-and-blue basketballs whose pigmented leather was hard to grip in the American Basketball Association. He has dark blue hockey pucks held over from the World Hockey Association, smart little slabs of rubber that look alarmingly like those urinal-disinfec-tant cakes.

To be fair, Davidson had originally lobbied for a less subtle fire-engine-red puck for his new WHA to use, but that notion was angrily shot down by the general manager of the Alberta (eventu-ally Edmonton) Oilers, Wild Bill Hunter. "That is the most ridicu-lous thing I've ever seen," Hunter said when first affronted by the proposed scarlet puck. "Our players will never be able to see that puck."

Why not?

"Because," said Wild Bill, "they'll be looking for a *black* one."

The word *ridiculous* comes up often when speaking of the spawn of Gary Davidson, who made his way through only slightly fewer leagues than Jules Verne and turned out more acronyms than the New Deal of Franklin Roosevelt. This is the man who was the first president of the ABA, a cofounder of the WHA and the founder of the WFL. In the 1970s Davidson's rebel leagues were designed to be the *mod* alternative to the *square* professional sports Establishment, or at least the 1974 WFL media guide would have you believe that. "The Detroit Wheels are a 'now' team," grooved the guide. "The World Football League's twelve teams are 'where it's at.'" When the Wheels later went defunct, Detroit was somehow . . . de-funked.

It wasn't just the Wheels. Most of Davidson's teams and all of his leagues would eventually go south, metaphorically emulating the Toronto Northmen of the WFL, who became the Memphis Southmen before playing the first game in their unspeakable "Burnt Orange and Old Gold." But while the leagues lived fast, they also died young, leaving creditors and historians to sort through the bad checks and ridiculous nicknames left behind. (It is doubly instructive that one of the first checks ever written to the WHA was the initiation fee for the Miami Screaming Eagles. It bounced.)

The leagues were sublimely ridiculous from day one, literally from the moment that the formation of the ABA was announced in 1967. Davidson's autobiography is entitled *Breaking the Game Wide Open*. He calls it "a terrible book," and indeed it has more dead spots than the floor of the Boston Garden. But the book's account of the press conference held to launch the ABA, at New York's ultratony Hotel Carlyle, is enlightening.

"The buffet was loaded with delicacies of every description," Davidson wrote. "The whiskey flowed like water. A free ABA basketball was given to every writer and broadcaster in the place. Naked dancing girls circulated everywhere — well, they weren't really naked, and they weren't really dancing girls, but you get the idea. I don't know what they were or what they were doing there. . . . We spent $35,000 and we got a circus for our money. Everyone had fun, but no one took us seriously. It was a joke, and it made us look ridiculous."

It also made them look prophetic. You want to know what the *most* ridiculous thing was about Gary Davidson and his rebel leagues? It was this: In many ways, they weren't ridiculous at all.

"Gary Davidson," noted this magazine in 1975, "has been one of the most influential figures in the history of professional sport."

"What man, more than any other, has had the greatest impact on professional sports in America?" asked an editorial in *The Sporting News* in 1977. "You'd have to say Gary Davidson. . . ." In the months that passed between those two pronouncements, sports were undergoing a Davidsonic boom — and yet the name Gary Davidson, to hear it now, has little resonance for Joe Fan.

He was a Ted Turner who colorized the games even as he terrorized the existing salary structures. He and a team of fellow attorneys unshackled athletes from their restrictive contracts in the established National leagues: the NHL, the NFL and the NBA, the latter a league whose average player salary quadrupled, to $109,000, during the ABA's nine-year life span. In the Davidson lexicon, those leagues and the three TV networks made up the professional sports Establishment. "Never met Roone," Davidson says, "because I was never part of the Establishment."

Of course, Davidson also helped professional sport to establish itself, to realize its manifest destiny in North America. He spread franchises like fertilizer to all corners of the continent as he scattered his sales pitches (like fertilizer) to prospective owners in San Antonio and Winnipeg and Indianapolis, cities that became *major league* the instant a local millionaire industrialist said yes to Davidson's alluring offer of sporting eminence.

This is the primary legacy of Davidson's leagues. "A lot of new cities that had never had teams proved they could carry teams," says Tim Grandi, the former associate general counsel for the WFL. "And certainly, whether Gary intended it or not, players acquired new freedoms and prosperity that didn't previously exist. He wasn't Moses, but he did take control of professional sports away from a clique of owners and opened it up to more people and more cities."

"Walter O'Malley and Horace Stoneham are viewed as being extremely important in the evolution of modern pro sports," says Max Muhleman, a former vice president of the WFL. "What they did was induce other owners to view the sporting landscape in much larger terms. I can see a lot of that in what Gary Davidson did."

"I was probably responsible for more benefits to the players than Pete Rozelle or any other commissioner," Davidson says quietly today, "but I don't think that that will come up much anymore."

It won't come up because Davidson has been forgotten. His was a colorful streak across the 1970s sky, but one that ultimately fell short, like Evel Knievel at the Snake River Canyon. And yet his improbable story is worth reviving: Raised by a divorced mother, he worked his way through his first year of UCLA Law by picking up freshly murdered corpses at the coroner's office while on the night shift of an L.A. mortuary. Not many years after graduation, having established himself as a tax and finance attorney in Orange County, Davidson got in on the ground floor of something called the American Basketball Association. Once again, and for many years to come, Gary Davidson would be working with stiffs.

*

"In the 1950s," Davidson notes in his autobiography, "men who had been unable to obtain major league franchises formed the Continental League. It never got off the ground, but the threat of it forced expansion which brought some of the Continental League members into baseball's major leagues."

Spectator sports never much interested Davidson. Professional leagues captured his imagination only when he realized they could be used as a Hofheinzian financial lever. Only then did he find fifty ways to love his lever.

As the Continental League gave us the New York Mets and the Houston Astros, so are Davidson's rebel leagues responsible for the Edmonton Oilers and the Denver Nuggets and the Hartford Whalers and the Indiana Pacers and the Quebec Nordiques and the San Antonio Spurs and the Winnipeg Jets and the New Jersey Nets; for three-points shots and goalposts in the back of the end zone; for Julius Erving and Wayne Gretzky.

Wayne Gretzky. Davidson had never seen a hockey game until he cofounded the World Hockey Association in 1971. Before the league began play in '72, three potential franchise owners visited California from the hockey Holy Land, Canada. The idea was to get better acquainted with the 37-year-old Davidson and his 45-year-old colleague, Dennis Murphy — who had founded the ABA — by attending a Los Angeles Kings game with them.

"I'll never forget," says Murphy. "We're all sitting there in a row, the game is about to start, and the linesman goes to center ice and is about to drop the puck when Gary says, 'What are they doing?'"

Wild Bill Hunter, a profane, white-haired frontiersman who conjured images of Yosemite Sam, looked at Murphy and barked, "Who the hell is this guy?"

"Later," says Murphy, "Gary would fall asleep during the game. But in fairness to him, he never purported to know anything about hockey."

Well, he purported to know *something*. When the WHA named Camille Henry, a former star with the New York Rangers, to be coach of its New York Raiders, Davidson made the announcement at a press conference in Manhattan. He confidently began, "I'd like to welcome Henry Camille . . ."

As waves of laughter washed up to the podium, Davidson reddened like one of his prototype pucks. "No, no," he pleaded with

the media hyenas, desperate to correct his mistake. "I mean . . .
Hank. Hank Camille!"

The whole point was to make money, and to make money you had
to make headlines, and for this pursuit Gary Davidson was perfectly
appointed. He possessed what imaginative reporters called "Robert
Redford good looks," and his habitual speech impediment magically evaporated when the camera lights came on. Davidson was a
Skippy-smooth pitchman in a new era of sound bites, an era when
there was no government undertaking, however massive, that could
not be expressed in an insipid little slogan: *Think metric. Whip inflation now. Fifty-five saves lives . . .*
    In both the WHA and the WFL, Davidson personally took a
franchise as his own, for free, as if by birthright. He then sold them
immediately: In the WFL he got $690,000 for his franchise, which
became the Philadelphia Bell, whose offices routinely fielded complaints from citizens unhappy with their telephone service. Davidson would also draw a hefty salary to run the leagues from his law
office — that is, once he had sold enough franchises to *form* a league.
    Along the way Davidson was abetted by his old friend and law
partner Don Regan, and by Murphy, a former marketing executive
and former mayor of Buena Park, California, an Irishman from
County Flimflammery with a winning smile and a world of energy.
Together the trio played magnificently the egos of small-town, big-
money megalomaniacs throughout the continent, men who simply
couldn't resist owning their own pro team.
    "Back then there were guys who had made millions making wid-
gets in Omaha, but the only guys who knew them were maybe their
bankers and the guys at the country club," says Grandi. "But with a
sports franchise, they recognized an opportunity to be known in
L.A. or Detroit. Maybe 90 percent of them were flakes, but . . ."
    "Dennis Murphy would go into a town," says Davidson, "and call
an accountant or call a lawyer, and ask if he had any clients who
were interested in professional sports. He wasn't saying, 'Do you
have any interest in a vinyl-dye factory?' Within two days he would
have gotten enough leads for us to have someone to talk to. We
would then come in, and the line would be, 'Would you rather be
known as the owner of the Detroit Wheels or as a manufacturer of
brassieres?'"

"Pick a city you have never been to before," says Regan. "Say Quebec City. We flew into Quebec City during the WHA days. We had the mayor, the governor, the biggest businessmen in town. . . . We'd fly in, they'd run a bloody carpet out to us, they'd drive us away in Rolls-Royces, they'd treat us like we were the potentates of the world. And the whole reason was, the existing Establishment then was so monopolistic and arrogant."

The monopolistic and arrogant Establishment of the NHL and the NBA and the NFL drove the rebel leaguers, fueling them with a loony motivational paranoia. "We fought for everything we got," says Murphy, "to the point where we had bugs in our chandeliers. I'm not accusing the NHL or the NBA, but who the hell else would put them there? Before we'd go into our meetings, we'd have guys go in there with debugging devices. It was war."

Though it may sound like Murphy has bugs in *his* chandelier, Davidson corroborates these theories of industrial espionage. "We thought," he says ominously, "that Al Davis had our office bugged."

Installing a surreptitious listening device at any rebel-league meeting would have been a logistical challenge; the league drafts, for instance, always had a quintessentially 1970s mind-if-I-crash-here spontaneity to them. They were held in just about any joint that could provide an impressive dateline. Thus, World Team Tennis — which Murphy helped found in 1973 with the staunch support of Billie Jean King — conducted its first draft in New York in the auditorium of the Time & Life Building, home of *Sports Illustrated*. (To this day in our editorial meetings, we mind what we say about Al Davis.)

To be fair, there *were* grounds for genuine suspicion in the days of the WHA. Gordie Howe, a luminary with that league's Houston Aeros during the 1973–74 season, was a member of Team Canada '74, a squad composed entirely of WHA players. An eight-game series with the Soviet national team included four games in Moscow. "The Soviets put us all in this real ratty hotel," recalls Murphy, who adds that Howe was particularly appalled by two seedy chairs in a corner.

Howe strolled over to the chandelier in his room. "Colleen," he said loudly to his wife, "I wish these people in Russia would recognize what a great star I am and give us a couple of nice chairs." The

Howes left to attend practice, and they returned two hours later to a new pair of beautiful chairs. "Thank you very much, my Russian hosts," Mr. Hockey told the light fixture.

"We were known," swears Murphy, "as the Bug League." You don't have the heart to tell him that *everyone* was bugged in the Soviet Union, that the KGB did not target the WHA specifically — but then you suspect that Murphy already knows this.

Such self-important self-delusion was vital to the rebel leagues. When Davidson was trying to sell a franchise in a strange city, he arrived with a manufactured air of centuries-old regality.

"You'd created this story, this image, this mirage, but all of a sudden you begin to have value," recalls Davidson. He gestures across his office; in a trophy cabinet sits a mounted replica of the check for $1 million made out to Robert Marvin Hull from WHA Properties, Ltd., dated June 27, 1972. Winnipeg owner Ben Hatskin was given the WHA rights to Bobby Hull because he was willing to kick in an additional $1.75 million in salary to lure the NHL's premier scorer. This was an unheard-of sum in 1972 — Hull's 1971 salary with the Chicago Blackhawks had been $150,000. "We weren't sure Bobby could even play," says Davidson. "But that check created so much publicity around the world that even though Winnipeg hadn't played a single game, that franchise had value."

Davidson wasn't sure the Golden Jet could play in Winnipeg because the NHL had filed suit to retain Hull and all the other players who had signed with the WHA. The WHA, in turn, filed an antitrust suit against the NHL and was granted an injunction to play its games while the court cases were pending. In the mid-seventies the NHL abandoned its reserve clause — the legal absurdity that bound players to a team perpetually after their contracts expired — and in 1979 agreed to absorb four teams from the WHA. The lawsuits were dropped, but the WHA was rendered extinct.

By this time Davidson had already resigned from the WHA and turned his attention to his dream of a world football league. He was going to do nothing less than conquer the globe. Says Regan, "We were young enough and naive enough that we didn't know there were limits, that the world has finite boundaries."

These men were feeling immortal, the success of the WHA standing as a monument to themselves. Of course, there were other, smaller monuments: In the WHA's first season of existence, Andre Lacroix won the W. D. (Wild Bill) Hunter award as scoring champion, J. C. Tremblay was honored with the Dennis A. Murphy award as best defenseman, and Bobby Hull was the Most Valuable Player and proud recipient of the Gary L. Davidson trophy.

As Davidson prepared to breathe life into the WFL beginning in 1974, athletes' eyes were on a bigger prize. The prize would be won in baseball, the one major sport that Davidson had not challenged. In 1973 a former steel-union boss named Marvin Miller, the executive director of the Major League Baseball Players Association, had secured salary-arbitration rights for his constituents. Two years later an arbitrator's decision would grant "free agency" to pitchers Andy Messersmith and Dave McNally.

In the year between those two milestones, egregiously ill-timed plans were revealed for a new rebel baseball league, an opera buffa that would have nothing to do with the Davidson clique. Emboldened by the impact of the WHA and by the gaudy promises of the proposed new football league, a man named Sean Downey announced in April 1974 the imminent formation of the 32-team World Baseball Association, to play in the U.S., Latin America and Asia. "Baseball as presently played and structured," said Downey, one of several original owners of the New Orleans franchise in the ABA, "is a bore." He would have known: Sean Downey was himself an insufferable gasbag with an ego like a detonated self-inflating raft. In the 1980s he would create his own abrasive, right-wing television talk show with himself, using his middle name, as the host. Morton Downey Jr. presumably figured that the show was the next best thing to owning a baseball team — and not all that different, as Marge Schott would one day demonstrate.

There is a remarkable photograph in the May 1, 1974, edition of the *San Francisco Chronicle*. Gary Davidson is shown "discussing matters," according to the caption, with tight end Ted Kwalick, formerly of the San Francisco 49ers but newly signed by the Honolulu Hawaiians of the World Football League. Kwalick is indoors, but he is wearing Foster Grant sunglasses. His spectacular dress shirt bears stripes so wide that there is room for only two of them. *Two stripes.* His shirt collar resembles a pair of pterodactyl wings. The knot in his tie is slightly larger than a baby's head. As for the tie itself, it is

STEVE RUSHIN   43

simply enormous, as if Kwalick were still wearing the napkin he had
tucked into his collar at lunch.

The WFL's promotional literature boasted that this was a "now"
league, which may explain why the league now looks so "then."
Nineteen seventy-four turned out to be the WFL's only full season,
but that season somehow began with bold promise in that summer
of the Watergate denouement. Play began on Wednesday nights in
July, as striking NFL players were printing T-shirts emblazoned with
a fist and the slogan NO FREEDOM, NO FOOTBALL. The new league
had the look of a high-salaried land of milk and money, flush with
the wealth of men like Hawaii owner Sam Battistone, the czar of
Sambo's Racially Insensitive Family Restaurants. The future was a
grand boulevard, as wide as a Kwalickian lapel, and the King himself blessed the new endeavor: Elvis sat in a skybox on opening
night in Memphis. The Philadelphia Bell drew a reported 120,000
fans to its first two home games.

Tax records, however, would show that only some 20,000 tickets
in Philly had been sold at full price. John F. Kennedy Stadium was a
paper house, filled with fans in free seats. In fact, the entire league
was a heavily mortgaged paper house, losing $20 million in its first
twenty-week season. Members of the Florida Blazers were not paid
for the final *ten* weeks of the season. Paper house? Coach Jack
Pardee personally bought toilet paper for the Blazers' home locker
room. "You've heard of hungry football teams?" his wife, Phyllis,
once told a reporter. "The Blazers really *were* hungry."

Somehow the Blazers still managed to make it to the optimisti-
cally named World Bowl I, which historians have since renamed
World Bowl I-and-Only. Their opponents in that game, on December 5, 1974, were the Birmingham Americans, whose uniforms
were confiscated on behalf of a creditor by sheriff's deputies the
day after their 22–21 triumph. As for the losers, well, at least they
didn't go home empty-handed: Legend has it that following the
opening coin flip, a Blazer captain put the silver dollar in his sock.

Gary Davidson exhumes his past from a sad little grocery sack. "I
didn't want to lose all this," he says while dipping his hand into a
paper bag full of brittle press clippings. "I don't think too much of
this stuff is preserved in people's memories."

Seated in his Orange County real estate office, he lets his fingers alight on a yellowed piece of newsprint. "Here's a *Los Angeles Times* story about 1974, with pictures of Agnew, Nixon and Davidson," he says with a sigh. "A bad year." He lifts his photo to the light, regarding himself as if in a mirror. "Good god," he mutters softly.

Good god. The Me Decade was supposed to have been his, and 1974 was to have been the most glorious year yet for him. He began writing his autobiography that February. He was photographed for the April 15 cover of *SI*, flanked by Kwalick and Calvin Hill of the Hawaiians. He confided to friends that he was thinking of running for the U.S. Senate in '76. He had everything, and *People* magazine came to photograph it: the millionaire at home in exclusive Emerald Bay, with four handsome children and a wife named Barbie, a former cheerleader at UCLA.

Trouble was, the man's life was a shimmering mirage. Where to begin? Hank Aaron hit his 715th home run on April 8, and Davidson was bumped from the front of *SI*; a copy of that unpublished cover hangs in his office, near the check to Robert Marvin Hull. (Says Davidson's secretary, beholding these mementos, "He had fifteen minutes to evacuate his home during the Laguna Beach fires last fall. What do you think he went back for?")

The glamorous Hawaiians turned out to be a hollow coconut, struggling to survive like every other team playing the hollow-sounding game of "WiFfLe ball," as sports writers called it. "I remember when Dan Rogers was hired to be the first general manager of the Hawaiian franchise, and he was given a lifetime contract," says Grandi. "It wasn't too long after that, the owner called and said, 'I'm sorry, Danny, but I'm afraid you're dead.'

"So Dan came back and worked for the league, and during those final days he was talking on the phone at his desk. The desk and chair were rental furniture, and the league had fallen behind on its payments. Sure enough, the rental company comes by and takes away the desk and chair. But Dan kept right on talking on the phone."

By the end of 1974 there had been the indignity of World Bowl I-and-Only, Gary and Barbie had begun divorce proceedings, Davidson had wrecked his Jaguar, and he had been knifed in the parking lot of a Newport Beach restaurant, Woody's Wharf, while arguing with some drunk. Our Redford double got seventy stitches in his face from the last two incidents. Nineteen seventy-four literally scarred him for life.

"I turned forty," he says, continuing to recite this litany. "I ended

up upside down about $4 million, and that did not make for a good
year." Nixon was exiled to San Clemente in August. And you begin
thinking that maybe that old *L.A. Times* story got it right, that
Davidson's photo belongs on the same page with Nixon and long
lines at the gas station and those WHIP INFLATION NOW but-
tons, just another relic of an American gone bust in the mid-1970s.

If you think it is a stretch to connect Watergate and pro football,
consider this: A sign in the war room of CREEP — the Committee
to Re-elect the President — at the time of the Watergate break-in
read WINNING IN POLITICS ISN'T EVERYTHING, IT'S THE ONLY
THING. Nixon knew Frank Gifford. He surely knew Vince Lombardi.

Since 1974 Davidson has been as elusive as Bobby Fischer, the chess
prodigy who went into his own self-imposed exile that summer. "I
think Gary went to live in Haiti," said a friend when asked recently
about Davidson. Whispers another friend, "I heard he tried to
commit suicide."

Even as his autobiography was shuffling off the presses two decades ago, Davidson had begun taking drives into Baja, cruising
from village to dusty village in search of a place to start over. By
1976 he was spending much of his time on a sisal plantation in
Haiti. Ten thousand people on 40,000 acres. Among his investment
partners in Dauphin Plantations was Baby Doc Duvalier, who did
not believe in a liberal profit-sharing plan. The plantation was
eventually sold to a group of Haitians, and Davidson was back in
Orange County — not far from San Clemente. "All the people on
the plantation," says Davidson as a footnote, "probably ended up
starving to death."

His story was supposed to end here, horribly, but a funny thing
happened on his way to obscurity. Unlike his basketballs, Gary
Davidson bounced back. He found God and a new wife, and revived
his real estate career by developing retirement communities. At
sixty he remains the same picture-of-health fitness freak who used
to encourage his employees to climb five flights of stairs instead of
using the elevator. He now says grown-up things about professional
sports, like "Today's player salaries are a bit distorted" and "The
owners have let things get out of control" and "The fans are paying
too much." He has become a bona fide millionaire. Like that Screaming Eagles check, it turns out Gary Davidson was made of rubber.

"There's a famous line in Shakespeare," Davidson says. "In *King*

Lear the Fool says to King Lear, 'Too bad you grew old before you grew wise.' And so the theory is, maybe I started to get wiser as I grew older."

Davidson's Shakespeare is in need of Rust-Oleum, but the important thing is that he got here, that he got to Wise. Some men go their whole lives, can't find Wisdom with an AAA road atlas. Three days after meeting Davidson, you stand in front of a Santa Monica hotel. You are waving goodbye to Dennis Murphy, who now runs a professional roller-hockey league. Abruptly, Murphy comes back to you. There is *one more thing*.

Smiling, he says, "You don't think Gary's interested in getting back into the sports business, do you?" No, you say. No, he isn't. Gary Davidson would rather manufacture brassieres than get back into the sports business.

The Long, Hard Run

"Got a pencil?" Jim Brown asks when you call to arrange a visit. "Here's what you do. Call 310-652-7***. Ask for Rockhead Johnson. He has my calendar. You two work out the date."

"I'm sorry," you respond. "What was the first name?"

"Rockhead."

"Rockhead?"

"Rockhead. Rockhead Johnson."

So you dutifully dial the number and wait for Rockhead to answer, but instead you get a receptionist at Amer-I-Can, Brown's public-service organization. Summoning the most businesslike voice that circumstances will allow, you ask, "May I please speak to Rockhead? Rockhead Johnson?" A long and awkward pause follows, after which you're told that *Rock* is out of the office. *Rock* will be back in an hour. Can *Rock* return your call?

"This is Rock," Rock says when he phones back later. "Rock Johnson."

By now the full horror has hit you: You've been had — suckered, as Brown likes to say. The man's name isn't Rock*head* at all. Only one person calls him that, and only one person gets away with it. You've just been juked by Jim Brown.

*

He is still a familiar presence on television, an imposing bust on the small screen: His square head sits on square shoulders, a square hat sits on his square head. At fifty-eight, he remains an enormous Rock 'Em Sock 'Em Robot of a man. His arms are crisscrossed with scars, his fingers veer off at each joint in unexpected directions, remnants of the cartoon-violent NFL of the 1950s and '60s.

But that vision of a massive, muddied Brown begins to evaporate in your head while you drive, high above Sunset Boulevard, on a serpentine street that runs like a stream through the Hollywood Hills, Benzes and BMWs docked bargelike on both curbs. You turn off and plunge down into Jim Brown's driveway, where a young, besuited chauffeur, who has been dispatched by a local television studio, takes it upon himself to try to shoo you and your sorry blue Pontiac from the premises.

Moments later you are rescued, and Brown is amused. "I live in a *bool*shit world," he says of Hollywood. "But that's cool. When I go out, it's like, 'Put on your suit, baby, you're going down into the *circus*.' You go to Roxbury's, you know what you're going for: To see the stars and the girls and the *bool*shit — 'Hey, what's goin' on, babe?' 'Aaaaay, Big Jim, what's happenin', man?' There's a time and place for that, as long as you don't buy into it. My way to cut through the *bool*shit is with simplicity. And when I stay here, everything is simple."

Jim Brown tolerates no *bool*shit. It is practically his credo. Ask him why he so unabashedly admires Muhammad Ali, and Brown tells you straight up: "He has the heart and courage to stand up for beliefs that are unpopular." Bill Russell? "Exceptionally smart, exceptionally principled, no *bool*shit." Conversely, in his autobiography Brown calls O. J. Simpson a "phony" and adds: "The Juice likes to pretend he's modest, but that's just the Juice *being* the Juice. O.J. is extremely smart, man knows how to make a buck, and his 'aw shucks' image is his meal ticket. He's not about to jeopardize it by being honest." And: "I never look at him the way I do a Bill Russell, or a Walter Payton. I talk to those guys, see them speak, I know what I'm hearing is the real man. Too often, I can't say the same about O.J." The book was published five years ago.

Today, just down the hill, lies the circus, Los Angeles, a scary riot of Simpson hearings and Menendez shootings and King beatings — an apocalyptic place of fire, earthquake, mudslide and pestilence that only four decades ago was an Eden to Walter O'Malley. But up here at the Brown residence, all appears to be placid and predictable simplicity. He has lived in the same house, driven the same car, had the same telephone number since 1968.

That was the spring when the Reverend Dr. Martin Luther King Jr. was assassinated in Memphis. A framed portrait of King hangs in Brown's foyer. But nowhere on display in the house is a single personal memento of Brown's own varied careers — as a football superstar, as a film actor, as an activist in what he calls "the movement for dignity, equality and justice."

Toward that end Brown has opened his immaculate home through the years to an astonishing cross section of humanity. Recently, Brown says, former Secretary of Housing and Urban Development Jack Kemp and the head of the Nation of Islam shared the couch on which we now sit. "I can have Louis Farrakhan here, you, fifteen Jews," he says. "It don't make no damn difference."

Never has. As a child he was thrown in with all races and generations, almost from the time his father, Swinton (Sweet Sue) Brown, a fighter and a gambler, abandoned him at birth. Jim Brown was raised by his great-grandmother, whom he called Mama, on St. Simons Island, off the coast of Georgia. He went to school in a segregated, two-room shack, went to the toilet in the backyard. When he was eight, Mama gave him a box lunch, buttoned him up and put him on a train for Manhasset, New York, where his mother worked as a domestic. In that white and wealthy community Jim Brown became an athletic prodigy. At Manhasset High he was a kind of ward of a group of white professional men, doctors and lawyers and teachers, who demanded that he study and run for student government.

"Without Manhasset, without Dr. Collins and Ken Molloy and Mr. Dawson and Ed Walsh, it would've been impossible," Brown says of his remarkable existence. "These people actually saved my life, man. I would never, ever have been anything without them. And it was so pure. If kids can see honesty and interest from people of that age, that's what builds, man. So you can't *fool* me with all of the other *bool*shit, 'cause I've got an example for the rest of my life. You wanna see what goodness is? I look at those people. I know what love is. I know what patience is. I know what consistency is. I know what *honesty* is."

Ken Molloy was a Manhasset attorney and a former Syracuse lacrosse player who insisted that Brown select Syracuse over the dozens of schools that were recruiting him for football, basketball and baseball. It was only after Brown arrived on campus, housed in a different dorm from the rest of the football team, eating on a different meal plan, that he first fully encountered discrimination. It made him miserable in that freshman year of 1953–54.

You have asked Jim Brown to look at his remarkable life. You are seated in his living room, which overlooks the pool, which overlooks the yard, which overlooks Los Angeles. You have come to take in the view: of race, celebrity, the real world and the star athlete's obligations therein these last four decades. Brown has seemingly lived every issue in sport and society since he left home for Syracuse so long ago. He continues to work in places like South Central and San Quentin. You ask Jim Brown to assess this public life he entered forty years ago, and he says, "I am oh, so tired."

Just before 1 P.M. on May 17, 1954, the chief justice of the Supreme Court of the United States began to read the unanimous decision in *Brown* v. *Board of Education*. Legal segregation was ending. In Harlem that year Malcolm X was appointed the leader of Temple Seven for the Nation of Islam. And across the river in the Bronx, the great New York Yankees of Mantle and Berra and Stengel had still not dressed a black player.

"I came up at the crossroads of segregation," says Brown. "There were still colleges where black players couldn't play. There were teams that would go south and black players had to stay in private homes. These were very difficult times. It was a blessing on the one hand because there were opportunities, but it was demeaning because you were still looked on as inferior. It was almost as if you'd been given a *favor.* And you always felt you had to perform much, much better."

And so Jimmy Brown, the only black on the freshman football team at Syracuse, went from fifth-string halfback to the best player in the nation in his four years of playing for a coaching staff that — save for an assistant named Roy Simmons — initially begrudged his presence there.

But by the time Brown graduated in 1957, Syracuse was eager to recruit black halfback Ernie Davis and then Floyd Little, both of whom wore Brown's number 44. Syracuse won a national football championship in 1959 and now regularly fills that dome named for Willis H. Carrier, and much of that is directly attributable to the heroics of James Nathaniel Brown. It is more indirectly attributable to Simmons, the kind assistant football and head lacrosse coach who took Brown under his wing; with Simmons's guidance, Brown used his spare time to become, many would say, the greatest lacrosse player in history before going on to do the same, many more would say, in football.

Jim Brown scored 38 points a game as a high school basketball player. He was drafted by the Syracuse Nationals of the NBA in 1957 even though he had stopped playing basketball after his junior season in college. He received a letter of inquiry from the great Stengel of the Yankees — even though, by Brown's own admission, "I wasn't that good."

On his final day as an athlete at Syracuse, Brown won the discus and shot put in a varsity track meet, returned to the dressing room to change for a lacrosse match and was called back to the track by a student manager. *Could he throw the javelin?* Brown threw the javelin 162 feet on one attempt. Syracuse won the meet.

The man belonged to a higher species. Jim Brown was built like a martini glass, with a 46-inch chest and a 32-inch waist; he was an exceptionally fast man who looked slow in motion on the football field: gracefully slow, a man running in a swimming pool.

Pulling out of his stance and bursting through the line, he accumulated would-be tacklers, men hopping a moving train, until he slowed and finally collapsed eight or 10 or 12 yards upfield, buried beneath a short ton of violent giants. One didn't really try to tackle Brown; one tried only to catch him, as one catches the 8:05. "All you can do is grab hold, hang on and wait for help" is how Hall of Fame linebacker Sam Huff put it.

Brown rose slowly from the scrum after every carry and hobbled back to the huddle in apparent pain before bursting through the scrimmage line on the next play for another eight or 10 or 12 yards. This was the earliest hint of Brown's acting aspirations, for he wasn't really hurt, or at least not hampered. No, in his entire nine-year professional career, he never missed a game. He played all of the 1962 season with a severely sprained wrist just this side of broken. He did not wear hip pads, ever. And so it finally became apparent to opposing defenses that Brown wasn't ever *going* to be hurt by conventional malevolence.

He was simply that rarest kind of competitor, who made men and women gape, whose performances each Sunday displayed the pure athlete in his prime. Jim Brown is why we love sports in the first place, the reason we tolerate the big dough, the crybabies, the *bool*shit.

He joined the Cleveland Browns in 1957, a year before pro football came of age with the Baltimore Colt–New York Giant overtime championship game. His coach, the progressive Paul Brown, just gave him the ball and let him run, which is all Jim Brown really wanted. "But you could never just play and *not* be cognizant of the social situation in the country," he says. "Every day of your life, that was in your mind. You had to question why they only put black players at certain positions, why there were positions that blacks weren't smart enough to play. They had a whole *bunch* of rules. You always had an even number of blacks on the team so they could room with each other. You always had six or eight. You couldn't have . . . *five*." Brown laughs, then immediately turns stern.

"So I was very conscious of the civil rights movement," he continues, "and very active in what I call the movement for dignity, equality and justice. In fact, it superseded my interest in sports. Sports gave me an opportunity to help the cause. And so I did that."

He made certain that his black teammates wore suits and ties, urged them to be fiscally responsible and saw to it that they were at all times protective of their own dignity. Whenever Brown uses the word, as he does often, he says it slowly, carefully enunciating all three syllables: DIG-ni-ty.

In the mid-1960s he enjoyed trolling the black community of Cleveland in his Cadillac convertible or walking the streets of Philadelphia with the former Cassius Clay, greeting the people in barbershops and record stores, the two greatest athletes of their time just saying hello to folks, their very presence bestowing DIG-ni-ty on a depressed and unsuspecting neighborhood.

The night Clay beat Sonny Liston in Miami for the heavyweight championship in 1964, Brown sat with him for two hours afterward in Clay's hotel, with Malcolm X waiting in the next room, as Cassius confided to Brown that he had embraced Elijah Muhammad and the Nation of Islam and had taken the name Muhammad Ali.

Brown was in London two years later, filming *The Dirty Dozen,* when Ali refused induction into the U.S. Army. "A Muslim who was managing Ali told me that they wouldn't mind him going into the service," recalls Brown, "but they couldn't tell him that." So Brown flew to Cleveland, where a group of fellow black athletes were gathering to hear Ali out in a much-publicized summit meeting. Brown, Lew Alcindor, Willie Davis, Bill Russell and John Wooten listened as Ali said, "My fate is in the hands of Allah." The group then announced support for their friend, whose religious convictions were all they had to hear . . .

The story continues, but Brown cannot be heard over the whine of a weed whacker, wielded by a man trimming the lawn out back. "See that man right there?" Brown asks when the noise recedes. "He's a gardener, and he's one of the best men I've ever met. I respect that man as much as I respect anyone. He does his job. He's fair. He doesn't complain. He's considerate. He's a family man. He's got *principles.*"

The weed whacker is wailing again, but no matter. You already know how the Ali story ends: Brown flies back to London from Cleveland, never to return to football. In nine seasons he had gained a record 12,312 yards and won a championship. He got out at his peak, just before the epochal 1966 season, just before the NFL-AFL merger and the Super Bowl and the hype. His final salary in football was $65,000.

The Dirty Dozen established Brown as an actor. And while Gloria Steinem called him "the black John Wayne," his thespian talents were better described by Lee Marvin, who said that Brown was "a better actor than Olivier would have been a fullback." Brown always played the same character, essentially himself; even the names didn't change much: Fireball, Slaughter, Gunn, Hammer, Pike. After five years the Industry tired of Brown, and Brown tired of the Industry — "I began to wonder," he says, "do I have to be called nigger in *every* script?" — and he fell back on the work he'd been doing all along.

In the late 1960s the Ford Foundation had given more than a million dollars to the Black Economic Union (BEU), an organization that Brown had helped form to promote black entrepreneurship through a network of athletes and MBAs. More than four hundred businesses were touched by the union, whose motto is splayed across the top of a battered newsletter that Brown fishes from a file in his den: PRODUCE, ACHIEVE, PROSPER, declares Volume I, Number I of the publication, dated April 1968. Among the items inside is the photograph of eight black high school students in Cleveland. The BEU would be funding their college educations, much as those men in Manhasset had done for Brown fifteen years before.

"It's only a drop," says Brown, suddenly putting away the file, "because what's happened is, there has been no follow-through with black athletes today."

"If I had the participation of the top twenty athletes in this country, we could probably create a nationwide gang truce," Brown is telling you, as well as a professor from the University of Iowa who is visiting Brown's house while researching a book on gangs. "These athletes represent such a great amount of resources and influence. These kids would be *flattered* to have their lives changed by them."

It may be little more than an accident of geography, but a trip to Brown's hillside home, up the winding drive that requires one to climb and climb, has the quality of a visit to some mountaintop guru, a man offering solutions to intractable problems. And among the most intractable of those problems — a fly in the rich soup du jour of sports and TV and money — is the notion that sports is now eating its young.

"You give the kids athletes to follow, and you give them false hope," Brown is saying. "You take the emphasis off just being a good student, getting a job and having a family. Instead, it's 'I want to be Michael Jordan. I want to have those shoes.' Kids in this area also look to the drug dealer, the gangster, the *killer* as a hero, which is something we didn't used to have. So these are the two sets of heroes, and both of them are bad."

Which is something we didn't used to have. Ask Brown what happened in the seventies and eighties to create these problems, and he'll tell you it was the seventies and eighties themselves. The seventies, the Me Decade, the Decade of Free Agency, and the eighties, with alliterative icons, Michael Milken and Gordon Gekko, and its alliterative mantra, Greed is good. Back-to-back decades of decadence.

"The rich got richer, didn't they?" Brown says. "Well, who suffered? If *you've* got all the money, *I'm* gonna suffer. When executives are paying themselves $500 million, that's tyin' up a lotta dough. Take anything to an extreme, it will self-destruct. That's why the destruction of the Soviet Union was inevitable. . . . And this country has festered; there's an underbelly: Prisons are overcrowded, recidivism is at an all-time high, the education system is going downhill, there's this new culture of drugs and gangsters and killing without *any* thought. Kids are shooting each other at thirteen and fourteen, and all of a sudden it's not gonna stay in the inner city."

As if on cue, a thirteen-year-old boy from Brown's neighborhood appears at the front door. Brown says hello, asks the boy how his father has been, asks him where his mother is, then lowers the boom. "I heard you got a beeper now. You got a beeper?" he asks the kid, referring to the new totem of the urban street criminal. The boy nods shyly.

"For what?" demands Brown.

"Messages."

"Messages? What do *you* need messages for?"

By now two other kids have arrived with a parent, and the whole group walks through the open house and out back to the pool. Brown sighs tremendously, and it sounds like the air brakes decompressing on a city bus.

"The other culture's taken over," he says. "The gangsta culture. Everything is gangsta rap, the gangsta attitude, gangsta body language. Car-jackings. Drive-bys. Red, blue, Disciples. Snoop Doggy Dogg has more influence on kids than Bill Clinton does." Brown yawns enormously, like the MGM lion.

"So the teacher no longer gets any respect," he continues. "The teacher used to get respect. Athletic programs on the lower levels no longer have an effect on the general populace of schools. It used to be that athletic activity was healthy. You played, but you weren't playing to become a pro. Now, if you don't have pro potential, sports are a waste of time. Agents are now looking down to high schools to find potential prospects. So it's no longer fun. Even the Olympics are no longer fun.

"When I was playing, you weren't gonna make a whole lotta money. But you were *playing the game,* and playing the game at the highest possible level. *And you liked that.* That's why the greatest sporting event I see today is the Ryder Cup. It's about nothing

except caring about competition. You can see that it means something to those guys. You can *see* them choking on short putts, it
means so much. I don't see that in other sports.

"Now, money, period, has *become* the game. So the game suffers.
An individual will go anywhere. The day after a team wins the World
Series, the team is changed. Sure you gotta make money, but how
much money, and at what cost? A person couldn't buy my house
right now for *any* amount of money. Because it's my *home*. I'm
comfortable here. Quality of life is what's most important."

This much is certain: By 1994 too many athletes, teams, entire
franchises have long forgotten the concept of home, and too many
children have never known it. As the millennium nears its end,
home is just that place where you pause and pose after hitting a
baseball out of the park.

"When I was growing up in Georgia, I guess we were supposed to be
poor," Brown says. "But we weren't poor. We had all the crab and
fish and vegetables that we could eat. The house was small and
weather-beaten, but hell, I lived *well*. Because there was so much
family there, a whole community of people who cared about each
other. See, that was my foundation. I'd *hate* to have to come up
without that."

And so, in places like Trenton and Canton and Compton, Brown
teaches rudimentary life skills to gang members and soon-to-be-
released convicts through his Amer-I-Can program. He directs a
staff of fifty street-credentialed "facilitators," who help people learn
to do things like read and get a job and manage their personal fi-
nances — which isn't to say that Brown's role is hands-off.

A visitor to one symposium on gangs in Brown's home tells the
story of a punk who kept disrupting the host's efforts to establish a
dialogue. After Brown repeatedly asked the young man to excuse
himself, the young man challenged Brown to step outside with him.
Well, Brown and the gang-banger wound up rolling out the back
door in a comic-book ball of dust. Shortly thereafter they reappeared and shook hands, and the meeting resumed.

One of Brown's charges — "one of my gangsters," as Brown calls
them — recently got out of his gang, got a job and got married.
The wedding was held at Brown's house.

*

O. J. Simpson was himself a gang member made good. He now stands charged with double homicide, having been cheered by "fans" on live television while fleeing police on the L.A. freeways. It's said we like to build our stars up just to tear them down, and in fin de siècle California, the state may deem it necessary to *execute* one of the greatest athletic stars it has produced. When Simpson was charged in June, Brown unbecomingly appeared on national TV to offer the opinion that Simpson was a cocaine user. In football they call what Brown did "piling on."

They are both former running backs and actors who make their homes ten miles apart in Los Angeles. Simpson eclipsed Brown's single-season NFL rushing record in 1973. Both men have histories of domestic-violence allegations. The Los Angeles Police Department has released tapes of a 911 call that Nicole Brown Simpson made when her enraged ex-husband broke down a door to her home and entered, screaming obscenities. Brown has been accused at least four times of violence against young women, most notably in 1968, when he was accused of throwing his girlfriend from a balcony. None of the charges were proved in court, and Brown denies them all. "I like sex . . . I mess with young women," he says. "I know it's bad, but I'm bad."

Riinnnnnnggg. An end-table telephone springs to life.

"Hello?" says Brown. "Mm-hmm? Oh, I'm sorry, but I'm finished. Yeah, I can't explain anything anymore. Well, I'm so sorry, but I can't. Mm-hmm . . . I wish I could . . . No, I don't have anything to say . . . Yeah, but I'm not interested in all that. I've said my piece, and I'm gonna let that roll. I'm gonna watch and see what happens. See, the public has to get educated. I'm already educated. I know what's goin' on. I deal with *real life.* I don't get into things that I don't know about. But thank you. Thanks for calling."

Yet another caller asking Brown to handicap the upcoming Simpson preliminary hearing? "Yeah, because I brought the whole cocaine thing up," says a weary Brown, who claims somewhat dubiously that he was just trying to bolster an insanity plea, that cocaine could provide a devil-made-me-do-it defense for Simpson. "They criticize me. They say I'm against O.J. I'm for him. I'm for *truth.* You and me and O.J., we all have our negatives and our positives. I know this is America and we like to have our heroes, but hell: Martin Luther King screwing around — people are still in denial about that. The Kennedys, Bobby and John, they womanized. I look at the good and at the bad. Do *I* like a lot of women? Hell, yeah. What bothers me is when people hold on to the falseness of something. "Did you hear the [911] tapes?" he asks, by way of explaining why he has no interest in the elaborate pas de deux of the courtroom. "There's this whole emphasis on who leaked the tapes, not on the *truth,* not on whatever is *real,* not on resolving this in a *real* manner. Everyone is interested in the courtroom and what happens there. Well, hell, all kinds of crazy things can happen in the courtroom, and this is not necessarily going to get resolved.

"I looked at the Rodney King beating and said he got the crap kicked out of him, and I don't care *what* you say, I'm finished with it," says Brown. "But they turned *all* that around in court." Brown laughs. "Y'all can go on and talk *all* that *book*shit; I saw the beating. That thing was *ridiculous.*" Brown's laugh gains momentum, a ball rolling slowly downhill. "Those guys suckered that case so bad, they got everyone in doubt." Brown imitates himself watching the King tape on TV, stroking his chin reflectively: "Well, maybe he *didn't* get beaten . . ."

And Jim Brown sputters one more tired laugh.

Ask him how he will be remembered, and Brown offers his own epitaph. It isn't much: "On the popular level, they'll say, 'He was a football player. Controversial. Threw a girl out the window.' I don't care. *Maybe* they'll say, 'He was honest.'"

But he does care, all of us do, and so Brown tells one final story. When his friend Huey Newton, the former Black Panther leader, was shot to death on an Oakland street in 1989, Brown was asked to read a memorial poem at the funeral. Standing at the podium, Brown had a look at the faces sprouting from the pews: H. Rap Brown, William Kunstler, a whole team photo of sixties revolutionaries. He had an epiphany: "That these people were just like me," Brown recalls. "Different methodologies, but the same goal: to make this a better country."

His body creaks massively as he rises from the sofa and says goodbye. As you're leaving, as you approach the drawing of MLK in the foyer, you sense again that little has changed in this house since 1968. There is one thing, though. "I'm stiff," you hear Brown saying, with a laugh, as you exit the room. "I'm gettin' *old.*"

And then Jim Brown heads for the patio, still looking for daylight.

It's All in the Mall

In a painting, there's a spot at which the parallel lines — a river or a ribbon of road — appear to converge. Artists call this the vanishing point, that place in a drawing where things seem to disappear into the distance, often creating the illusion of a horizon. And so I find myself at the vanishing point of this story: I am standing, atremble, before the largest shopping mall in America. This is the horizon. All lines converge here.

So vast is the Mall of America in Bloomington, Minnesota, that the area in which I've parked is labeled P5-WEST-BLUE-NEVADA-D-6, a mantra I have desperately repeated since abandoning my rental car in the world's largest parking complex. Even by itself this would be the consummate postwar American dream: the 13,000-car garage. But the aptly named Mall of America says so much more than that about the desires of modern society.

The Megamall, as it is known locally, is built on seventy-eight acres and occupies 4.2 million square feet, but publicists prefer more grandiose international imagery to convey its knee-weakening scope. The mall, therefore, could comfortably contain all the gardens of Buckingham Palace, is five times larger than Red Square and contains twice the steel of the Eiffel Tower. Most telling of all, it is twenty times larger than St. Peter's Basilica in Rome. For its visitors, who have come from virtually every country in the world and number 100,000 a day on average, the Mall of America is indeed the One True Church.

Mind-boggling sports analogies have also been employed to describe this edifice. "Seven times the size of Yankee Stadium," said the *New York Times,* adding that it has "eighty-eight football fields worth of [floor] space." Such comparisons are especially apt at the Mall of America, which was built on the site of the former Metropolitan Stadium, longtime home of the Minnesota Twins and the Minnesota Vikings. In 1982 the teams moved from the Met to the Metrodome in downtown Minneapolis. Ten summers later the mall opened, constructed as a square doughnut, at the center of which is an indoor, seven-acre amusement park called Knott's Camp Snoopy.

In the northwest corner of Camp Snoopy, embedded in the faux-stone floor, is a five-sided plaque that evokes home plate at the Met. In fact, it more closely resembles a tombstone, bearing as it does the legend METROPOLITAN STADIUM HOME PLATE 1956–1981. Five hundred and twenty feet away, in the southeast corner of the amusement park, affixed to a wall three stories above the floor, is a fold-down seat, looking down like a lifeguard's chair. The seat is in the approximate spot where Harmon Killebrew deposited the Met's most prodigious dinger, on June 3, 1967. If Killebrew were to hit the home run today, it would carom off Hooters.

Next to the mall lies the derelict rust-hulk of Met Center, erstwhile home of the Minnesota North Stars, who now play in Dallas — a hockey team in the buckle of the Sun Belt. Minneapolis officials, in the wake of the Stars' departure, are trying to lure another NHL team to the gleaming downtown arena in which the NBA Timberwolves now play. In June the NBA denied the Wolves permission to move to New Orleans, where they would have been owned, in part, by a Houston attorney named Fred Hofheinz. You will recall that he is the son of the Judge, who built the Astrodome, which spawned the Metrodome, to which the Twins and Vikings moved, thus clearing property for . . . the Mall of America.

Of course, before building the Astrodome, the Judge had planned to build an air-conditioned shopping mall on Westheimer Road in Houston. Instead he sold that property, which was developed in 1970 as the Galleria, a mall that thrives to this day with what once seemed a wonderful novelty: an indoor ice-skating rink at its center. The Mall of America, meanwhile, was developed in part by brothers Mel and Herb Simon, owners of the Indiana Pacers, late of the American Basketball Association, the first rebel league of Gary Davidson.

In America's Original Sports Bar, on the Megamall's fourth level, patrons watch games on the fifty-five televisions that pull in action from around the planet. But the most telling snapshots of sports and society today are to be seen in the mall's more than four hundred stores: in Kids Foot Locker and Lady Foot Locker and World Foot Locker, in Footaction USA and The Athlete's Foot and Athletic X-Press, in Sports Tyme and Team Spirit and The Sportsman's Wife, in No Contest and Golf for Her and Mac Birdie Golf Gifts, in Big Leagues and Going to the Game and Wild Pitch. A friend once counted nearly two dozen Megamall stores in which one can purchase a Starter jacket. There are, meanwhile, two bookstores in the place.

In sports-addled ancient Greece, citizens created the agora, the marketplace as a center for social exchange. Socrates said, "Having the fewest wants, I am nearest to the gods." In sports-addled post-war America, citizens created the shopping mall, the marketplace as a center for naked commerce. Social exchange? An official Mall of America T-shirt says SHUT UP & SHOP.

It is fitting, and perhaps inevitable, that last winter's most unrelenting sports story unfolded each day from a shopping mall in America. For what are big-time sports today if not a boundless marketplace? And so there was Tonya Harding, week after stupefying week, blithely turning triple Axels for the television cameras on a skating rink at the Clackamas Town Center mall in Portland. She was preparing for the Olympic Games, another invention of the ancient Greeks, suitably adapted for our times.

"Who told you you can't have it all?" So goes a lyric from the Mall of America theme song, voicing a notion as unmistakably American as the mall itself. "In our collective discourse," writes David Guterson in *Harper's*, "the shopping mall appears with the tract house, the freeway, and the backyard barbecue as a product of the American postwar years, a testament to contemporary necessities and desires and an invention not only peculiarly American but peculiarly of our own era too."

It was, fittingly, a man named Victor who developed America's first fully enclosed shopping complex, vanquishing the suburban landscape of Edina, Minnesota, in 1956. Southdale, as it is named, remains a staggering success four decades later, apparently unfazed by the Mall of America, a mere ten-minute drive to the east. Victor Gruen's creation was quickly loosed on other inclement cities: The modest Gulfgate soon went up in Houston, and Judge Roy Hofheinz was thus inspired to explore the limits of air-conditioning for his own gargantuan mall.

Come 1960, when the Judge was newly smitten by sports and Roone Arledge was arriving at ABC, Melvin Simon & Associates, Inc., built its first shopping center, Southgate Plaza, in Bloomington, Indiana. Today the firm's $625 million Megamall is the third-largest tourist attraction in America — at least according to the mall's own press kit, which claims that only Walt Disney World and the country-music capital of Branson, Missouri, are more visited.

And yet, far more than Mickey Mouse or Mickey Gilley, it is the

mall that is emblematic of our age: from the thirteen-year-old girl
who went into labor here to the trailer-park marriages performed
at the Chapel of Love on Level Two to this now familiar little
postwar irony: The Mall of America was financed by the Mitsubishi
Bank of Japan.

Distinctly of our time and place, the mall is also entirely otherworldly. While strolling about the mall's four levels, I fall in behind
two businessmen, one of whom produces a bleating cellular phone
from his jacket. "If it's for me," says the other guy, "tell them I'm not
here." In fact, no one is here, because here is . . . Nowhere, a place
of perpetual seventy-degree days and hospital cleanliness, a self-
contained city that serves all needs, but one in which only Willis H.
Carrier could feel comfortable.

At the same time the mall is . . . Everywhere, with its 14-plex of
movie theaters and its Cholest-o-Plex of fast-food counters. In the
Mall of America, as in the United States of America, there is the
ubiquitous Raider cap on every head, a pair of Nikes in every store
window and the presence of professional athletes everywhere — in
person, on packages, in electronic pictures. They wink as we walk
past, and whisper, "Who told you you can't have it all?"

It is National Fragrance Week at the Megamall, and promotional
literature promises six days "filled with activities designed to stimu-
late your nose." There is, for example, a Smelling Bee for children.
And at Bloomingdale's, "Michelle McGann, top-ranked LPGA player,
will host a breakfast and speak about what fragrance means to her."

I follow my nose to Oshman's Super Sports USA, a sporting-
goods concern so breathtakingly vast that one hardly notices the
basketball court, the racquetball court, the batting cage or the
archery range on its premises. Not far away, the 11,000-square-foot
World Foot Locker is tiny by comparison. Every NFL, NBA, NHL
and major league baseball jersey is available here. World Cup jer-
seys are on display. Every icon of international sports appears to be
represented. "We sold a lot of Astros caps this spring," general
manager Dan Peterson tells me. "The Brewers, the Tigers — just
about any team with a new logo sells pretty well." Which is why
teams now change logos like they're changing pitchers? "Yes," agrees
the affable Peterson, who is attired in a referee's shirt.

On display at Field of Dreams, a sports-memorabilia store, is the

cover of *SI's* 35th-anniversary issue. Framed — and autographed in
the enfeebled hand of Muhammad Ali — the cover can be yours
for $149. A 1954 Topps Hank Aaron baseball card from his (and
our) rookie year goes for $900. This same week, on a home-shop-
ping channel, I have seen Stan Musial peddling his signature for
$299.95, "or three monthly payments of $99.98." Children once
got Musial's signature on a game program. Now they get it on the
installment plan.

An Orlando Magic jersey signed by Shaquille O'Neal is available
for $595 at Field of Dreams. I want to ask the manager how many of
those the store sells, but I am reminded of the advice proffered by
the mall's T-shirt: SHUT UP & SHOP. The shirt sells, if you're interested, for $14.95.

Beneath the fronds of a potted palm, a doleful black man waits on a
bench. His is the hundred-yard stare of the mall widower, a man
whose wife was swallowed by Macy's much as sailors are claimed by
the sea. The mall has a two-story miniature golf course to alleviate
the widower's ennui, but this potbellied man is a good mile away
from Golf Mountain. And so he waits, in his replica NFL jersey, a
three-quarters-sleeve Cleveland Brown shirt of a 1960s vintage. The
number on his chest, naturally, is 32.

This corpulent Jim Brown reminds me of the corporeal Jim Brown,
who would probably not be surprised to learn that six months after
the Megamall opened, gunplay crackled in Camp Snoopy and three
people were wounded in a struggle for a San Jose Shark jacket. This
was an address on the appalling state of society, to be sure, but the
shots were more than that: They were literally a ringing endorsement, a one-gun salute to the San Jose Sharks and the wild, worldwide popularity of their logo.

I am reminded of the fact that this hockey team in San Jose is a
direct descendant of Gary Davidson. So is the hockey team in
Orange County, California: The Anaheim Mighty Ducks are the
first postmodern pro sports franchise, a mere merchandising venture owned by Disney, a logical line extension derived from a film.
And as the Pepsi Ripsaw roller coaster ratchets up a hill overhead, I
am further reminded that *The Mighty Ducks* sequel was filmed, in
part, here in Camp Snoopy.

A columnist once described Davidson as "always eager to meet the demand for something nobody asked for," and it occurs to me now that the same might be said for the Megamall: You can buy a synthetic human skeleton here or a sign that reads PARKING FOR LITHUANIANS ONLY or the children's book *Everyone Poops*. In this state of reverie I find my reflection in a beer at America's Original Sports Bar, 20,000 square feet of tavern, fifty-five televisions flickering like lightning through windows at night. As ESPN parcels out the evening's highlights, I recall something Roone Arledge said as we sat in his network office. "It used to be common practice in tennis that if a tough call went against your opponent, you hit the ball into the net on the next point if you were a gentleman," he had said. "You didn't want to win because of a bad call. I can't *conceive* of a top tennis player doing that today. Could you see McEnroe? Connors? *Andre Agassi?*"

And while watching *SportsCenter,* I cannot conceive of a player today hitting a home run and running the bases with his head down. Or imagine a halfback simply handing the ball to an official after a touchdown. Why would a man merely lay the ball off the glass when he could dunk on some fool and then bark into the baseline camera, sure, like Narcissus, to see his own reflection on the cable network that night?

Only a few weeks have passed since Chicago Bull captain Scottie Pippen refused to enter a playoff game when his coach designed a play giving someone else the last-second shot. Pride and insecurity, the prospect of embarrassment and the perception of disrespect: It is why children shoot children for their Shark jackets; it is why Derrick Coleman turns down a $69 million contract offer from the New Jersey Nets; it is why Barry Bonds demands the same obsequious deference given to the supernovas of the movie and music industries. As Agassi says in a famous TV commercial, "Image is everything."

All of which makes it devilishly tempting in 1994 to look beyond the beauty of athletic competition and see only the off-putting backdrop of marketing and money, money in amounts unimagined in 1954. "Everyone is more interested in money in most cases than they are in sport," Arledge said. "And a lot of fun has gone out of it. The original motivation a lot of us had for wanting to be a part of sports — that no longer exists." Pause. Sigh. "On the other hand, the level of performance is so high today, who could have ever imagined *that?*" And it became clear as he talked enthusiastically about the Stanley Cup playoffs that the harried Arledge hadn't shaken sports at all, and couldn't if he wanted to. "I'm so happy to see him talking about sports again," his assistant said while ushering me out. "I really think he misses it."

Cynicism is a sine qua non of modern citizenship, and as I continue pacing the mall's terrazzo floors, past the Carolina Panther beach towel beckoning from the window of Linens 'n Things, I am given to seeing sports only as the multinational business that it is. But then I think of the unfailingly upbeat baseball writer I know. He checked into a drafty old hotel in Cleveland at three o'clock in the morning a few years ago, preparing to cover the miserable Indians that afternoon. "Business or pleasure?" the desk clerk asked him, and the scribe was forced point-blank to describe the sports industry. "Business," the writer finally said, smiling, "but it's a pleasure."

Sports are a swirl-cone mix of capitalism and entertainment (it occurs to me at Freshëns Yogurt), and forty years after the Army-McCarthy hearings, fourteen years after Lake Placid, four years into the post-Soviet nineties, America remains the world's leading exporter of both commodities. Ray Charles opened the Mall of America by singing a single song: *America, the Beautiful.* His rendition raised gooseflesh. His reported fee for doing so was $50,000.

America, the Beautiful, indeed.

They stand as twin towers of postwar American ingenuity — the fast-food emporium and the suburban shopping mall — and the two concepts are conjoined in connubial bliss in a Mall of America food court, where I am ingesting a Pepsi-Cola: "The Official Soft Drink of the Mall of America," the press kit reads. "2.6 million cups served in 1993." My "cup" is roughly the size of a nuclear-waste drum.

Pensively sipping, I cannot help but recall the two Pepsi spokespeople I had seen a day earlier, two tall-drink celebrities conversing on MTV. Orlando Magic center Shaquille O'Neal was sitting for an interview with supermodel-journalist Cindy Crawford. Shaq was demonstrating the different smiles he will rent to interested advertisers. "This is the 2.9," he began. And though a small fissure appeared across his face, Shaq was speaking not in Richter-scale figures but in millions of dollars. "This is the 5.3," he continued, grinning amiably. "And this is the 8.9." O'Neal beamed enthusiastically.

"And if somebody offered you $20 million?" asked Crawford.

A ridiculous smile-for-hire engulfed O'Neal's head; he held the pose, a ghoulish grinning Shaq-o-Lantern.

You can't spell Shaquille without the letters S-H-I-L-L. Stoked by this realization, I take a stroll, attempting to count the stores in which one can purchase an item bearing the euphonious name of the seven-foot spokescenter. When the toll hits nineteen (stores, not items), I realize the laughable inadequacy of my count: I have not looked in video-game stores or in department stores. A pasty fat boy wearing an O'Neal road jersey pads past me in Shaq Attaq shoes by Reebok. I have even neglected, somehow, to count the shoe stores.

How could I have forgotten? An unmistakable size-20 Shaq shoe stands sentry in front of World Foot Locker. One cannot handle the autographed shoe, for it reposes under glass like the Star of India. What the shoe really is, is the star of Bethlehem, drawing mall-walking magi into the store. "Shaq," the manager needlessly informs me, "is quite popular."

In Babbage's, an electronics store, I ask the manager, "Is there a video game that Shaquille O'Neal —"

"The rumor is they're *working* on one," the guy says, anticipating my question. "Look for it the beginning of next season." I am given to understand that the much-awaited game will have a martial-arts mise-en-scène and that it will be called . . . Shaq-Fu!

Fu, Fi, Fo, Fum: Sam Goody stocks the rap album. *Shaq Diesel,* while allegedly unlistenable, is nevertheless available on cassette and compact disc. At Toy Works, I adore the Shaq action figures by Kenner. Shaq's film debut, *Blue Chips,* has come and gone at the movieplex. *Shaq Attaq!* and *Shaq Impaq* beckon from bookstores. Shaq-signature basketballs line the shelves at Oshman's. Field of Dreams stocks wood-mounted photos of O'Neal: Shaq-on-a-Plaque. I stagger to The Coffee Beanery, Ltd., looking for Swiss Shaqolate Mocha, vacuum-Shaq-Packed in a foil Shaq-Sack. The mall's walls are closing in. T-shirts seem to be telling me to SHUT UP & SHAQ.

In addition to harvesting these golden eggs, Shaquille O'Neal is paid $48,000 per game to play a fearsome brand of basketball in Orlando. Fifteen thousand fans happily pay to watch him do so forty-one nights a year. He may yet revolutionize the game. *Who told you you can't have it all?*

"You can't have everything," comedian George Carlin likes to say. "Where would you put it?" It appears they've put everything here, in Champs Sports. Surrounded by officially licensed merchandise, seated in a director's chair embossed with a Mighty Duck, thirty-two televisions arrayed before me and each one of them playing NBA highlights, I rest my Niked feet at last.

For weeks I've been wondering how we got here in sports — from primitive to prime time, from the invention of the wheel to the invention of Shaquille — without pausing to ask, "Where *are* we, anyway?" But the information kiosks at the Mall of America make it perfectly clear. "You Are Here," all the map arrows say. "You Are Here."

JAMES ELLROY

Sex, Glitz and Greed: The Seduction of O. J. Simpson

FROM GQ

THE SIMPSON-GOLDMAN snuffs are recognizably prosaic. Subtract the accused killer's celebrity and showbiz milieu and you've got a spur-of-the-moment whack-out equally indigenous to Watts, Pacoima and Dogdick, Delaware. The intersection of fame, extreme good looks and pervasive media coverage has blasted a common double slash-job to the top of the pantheonic police blotter of our minds. The Leopold-Loeb, Wylie-Hoffert and Manson Family cases — replete with complex investigations and psychological underpinnings emblematic of their time — cannot compete with the Simpson Trinity. A botched hack-and-run caper has become the Crime of the Century.

On Sunday, June 12, 1994, O. J. Simpson did or did not drive to his ex-wife Nicole Brown Simpson's pad and slaughter her and a young man named Ronald Goldman. He did or did not wear gloves and a ski mask; he did or did not butcher his victims with a bone-handled knife, a bayonet or an entrenching tool. He did or did not split the scene and drive to his own home, a few minutes away.

Nicole Brown Simpson was or was not a devoted mother, a cocaine addict and an airheaded party girl. She was or was not an anorexic, a bulimic or a nymphomaniac given to picking up men at a Brentwood espresso pit. The minutiae of her life can be compiled and collated to conform to almost any sleazy thesis. She is most unambiguously defined by this heavily documented fact: O. J. Simpson beat the shit out of her over the last five years of her life.

Ron Goldman was either a waiter who wanted to be an actor or an actor working as a waiter — a very common L.A. job euphemism. He was or was not Nicole Simpson's lover. He did or did not borrow Nicole's Ferrari on occasion — which did or did not piss off O.J. no end. Forensic evidence indicates that Goldman fought very hard for his life.

Forensic evidence is utilized to supersede interpretation and conjecture through the application of impartial, empirically valid scientific methods. Forensic evidence is used to place suspected felons at crime scenes. Forensic evidence is a counterweight to gooey pleas for mitigation.

The gathering of forensic evidence is a conscious search for the truth. So are legitimate attempts to debunk scientific fallacies and sloppy applications of long-established forensic procedures. The analysis of forensic evidence may prove to be the adjudicating bottom line in the O. J. Simpson case. The flip side might be logical chaos — a verdict or the absence of a verdict spawned by the numbingly protracted cross-media extravaganza that has deluged all would-be jurors and indeed the entire American public with an accretion of contradictory details both densely pertinent and superfluous — a huge shitstorm of information, misinformation, innuendo and disingenuously reported rebop that backs you into a corner like a date rapist you can never escape until you shut down your electronic and printed-page access to the world, move to the South Pole and start fucking penguins.

O.J. did or did not shed his own blood outside Nicole's pad. He returned from an overnight trip to Chicago sporting a fresh cut — which might have been caused by his slamming down a glass upon hearing the news of his ex-wife's death or might have been caused by his slashing at the woman a bit too close to his free hand. Blood trajectories are primarily matters of forensic and hard legal concern. They lack the mass-market appeal inherent to hearsay accounts of an attractive woman's sex life and attempts to portray a career misogynist as a lost brother to the Scottsboro Boys, and until the blood-oozing interactive O.J. CD-ROM hit stores, we just might have to view where that blood was spilled as a literal indication of Mr. Simpson's guilt or innocence — a niggling restriction to keep us tenuously open-minded as data rains down and inundates us.

The O. J. Simpson case is a gigantic Russian novel set in L.A. The extravaganza occurred in L.A. because the major characters wanted to suck the giant poison cock of the Entertainment Industry. It's a novel of metamorphoses — because L.A. is where you go when you want to be somebody else. It happened in L.A. because it's the best place on earth to get breast and penis enlargements. It happened in the Brentwood part of L.A. because homelessness, crack addiction and other outward signs of despair appear at a minimum there.

O. J. Simpson wanted to be white. Ron Goldman wanted to be an actor — an equally ridiculous ambition. Nicole wanted a groovy fast lane and the secondhand celebrity that comes with fucking famous men.

Her second-tier status extended to her death. She became the blank page that pundits used to explicate her husband's long journey of suppression.

Nicole bought a ticket to ride. The price was nakedly apparent long before she died. Her face was pinched and crimped at the edges — too-pert features held too taut and compressed by too many bouts with cocaine, too many compulsive gym workouts and too much time given over to maintaining a cosmetic front. Her beauty was not the beach-bunny perfection revered by stupid young men and the man who may or may not have murdered her. The physical force of Nicole Brown Simpson is the glaze of desiccation writ large on her face. The lines starting to form might have been caused by inchoate inner struggles, or the simple process of aging, or a growingly articulate sense that she had boxed herself into an inescapable corner of obsessive male desire, random male desire, and a life of indebtedness to things meretricious and shallow.

Nicole's relationship with O.J. was deceptive and collusive from the start. He bought the hot blonde that fifty years of pop culture told him he should groove on, and an unformed psyche that adapted to his policy of one-way monogamy. She bought a rich, handsome, famous man possessed of infantile characteristics, which led her to believe that she could control him.

He bought a trip through his unconscious and a preordained mandate for horror. She abdicated to an inner drama that would ultimately destroy her.

They both bought a trip to Hollywood. O.J.'s athletic career was phasing out at the time they met; he sensed that he could continue his nice-guy impersonation and ease himself into plum acting roles with his long-perfected chameleon aplomb. He had made a second career out of disarming people with smiles and self-effacing gestures, and if he failed to hit the level of transposition that quality acting required, he could always play his familiar old ingratiating self, lower his cloning-sights from Laurence Olivier to Sly Stallone, get a mojo going as an action-flick hero, make big bucks and score beaucoup poontang in the process. He knew a shitload of wimps and tough-guy wanna-bes in the Biz — geeks who subscribed to the ruthlessness-as-strength-of-character ethic that pervades Hollywood but had never been in a fistfight and loved to tell jokes about their wives leaving them for well-endowed *shvartses.* He knew these guys; they knew him; he got a symbiotic groove going with guys like that. Guys like that could make him a *biiiiiig* movie star.

O.J. miscalculated. His powers of sociopathic seduction were best exposited in five-second sound bites and best received by callow young women. It should be noted that O. J. Simpson is not the smartest motherfucker ever to walk the earth. He is a man of great physical gifts, superficial charm and limited cunning, who segued from football to Hollywood with an impressionable girl in tow. He nested in a place where marriage is a shuck and a smoke screen for hidden sexual agendas; he brought a woman into the Inside World that the Outside World has been brainwashed into believing is the World Most to Be Coveted. He got her hooked on celebrity the way pimps get whores hooked on dope.

O.J. brought Nicole into a world where he was a second-class citizen. He got small roles in doofus comedies — but the tough-guy wanna-bes had no serious use for him. He would never be a movie star because he possessed the expressive range of a turtle. He'd transformed himself into a confirmed ass-kisser who could never appear truly heroic or dangerous onscreen.

Nicole witnessed O.J.'s long downward slide. She saw the essential bifurcation of his fame: He was a big cheese to the outside world and small potatoes to the world he sucked up to. She came of age in lavish surroundings and reveled in insider perks. She had a front-row view of her husband cracking under the weight of his emptiness.

O.J. got his racial-identity wires crossed up a long time ago. He must have figured his choices narrowed down to white man's shill or glowering rape-o. He never figured out that the vast majority of black men do not fall into either camp. His appeal transcended race because he was an equal-opportunity con artist capable of snow-jobbing blacks and whites alike. He fit into Hollywood because he had looks and name value, fawned and joked to the correct degree and zinged some pseudo-egalitarian heartstrings. If his trial becomes a referendum on African-American rage and its inevitable consequences, a minute cause-and-effect examination of his life will reveal no overt instances of personality-forming trauma directly attributable to specific acts of white racism. To offer the historic oppression of blacks as a salient factor of mitigation in an adrenaline-fueléd double lust homicide is preposterous. O. J. Simpson will have *truly* transcended race at that moment when blacks and whites get together and recognize him as a cowardly piece of shit who may or may not have murdered two innocent people and left two black *and* white children devastated for the rest of their lives.

Of course, it won't go down that simply. This is one gigantic L.A.-set Russian novel that exceeds the most extreme visions of Los Angeles as a bottomless black hole of depravity. This is a bottomless meditation on celebrity that will not eclipse until someone more famous than O. J. Simpson is accused of murdering two people sexier than Nicole Brown Simpson and Ron Goldman in a considerably more outré manner. This is a story told in a thousand voices — one of those microcosmic, kaleidoscopic, multiviewpoint jobs that sum up a time and place with interlocking subplots that go on forever.

This novel teems with grotesque characters and roils with unhinged incidents. The multimedia creators of this novel are grateful for the opportunity to regroup in the wake of a major disappointment: The Michael Jackson scandal diminuendoed before they got the chance to exploit its full sleaze potential and work up a hypocritical load of bile over the plight of butt-fucked children. They've got their teeth in the O.J. case now — they're pit bulls with a standing order for more, more, more — and verisimilitude and dramatic viability outgun outright veracity as the criteria for determining the thrust of their reportage. Thus a longtime informant who says he heard two white men do the snuffs gets screaming national coverage before being dismissed with footnote-like shrugs; thus A. C. Cowlings cavorting at a porno-industry winging militates against O.J. with an inference of "check this lowlife jungle bunny out"; thus Valley-girl model Tiffany Starr pitching a boo-hoo number about her two-date relationship with Ron Goldman implies that any man who'd pour the pork to this bimbo deserved to get whacked.

Thus freedom of speech has given us a hybrid extravaganza that rests somewhere between haphazardly proffered obfuscation and willfully evolved fiction. The exploitability of the case intersected with ascendance of tabloid television and created a phenomenon of great magnitude, and to censor it or attempt to curtail it in any manner would be unconscionable. The O. J. Simpson case is a collective work of performance art that has to play itself out before it can be assessed, structured, deconstructed and dissected for moral meaning.

It may boil down to issues of public disclosure and legal ethics. It may boil down to an outcry for journalistic circumspection and objectivity at all costs.

The art of fiction hinges on subjective thinking. Novelists must assume the perspectives of many different characters. Some months ago, the Simpson defense team assumed O.J.'s perspective and realized that their client was flubbing his performance as an innocent man unjustly accused. O.J. never screamed "Let's nail the shitbird who killed my wife!"

The defense team worked up some belated damage control. They took their strand of this gigantic Russian novel interactive via a toll-free tip hot line. O.J. offered a fat reward for information leading to the apprehension of the real snuff artists — cash he might or might not have after his lawyers bleed him dry. The Los Angeles Police Department canvassed the area surrounding Nicole Simpson's townhouse in a search for witnesses to confirm or refute O.J.'s guilt, and got nowhere. The defense team, eager to cast the LAPD as both incompetent and racist, put out their public appeal — in case potential witnesses missed the canvassing cops and the media coverage attending the most publicized crime of all time. This was a move of epic disingenuousness — specious in its logical structuring and wholly cynical in its application.

The post–Rodney King LAPD would prefer not to hassle high-profile blacks. Popping a low-profile white killer for the job would vibrate their vindaloos no end. The Simpson defense team understands the tortured history of the LAPD and Los Angeles blacks —

both its historical validity and the level of justified and irrational paranoia that it has produced. They put out a magnet to attract misinformation, fear and outright madness — and some of the more presentable bits they receive may show up in court as fodder to further confuse an already informationally swamped jury.

And the LAPD will be exhorted to check out "leads" that they know will lead nowhere, or risk a barrage of courtroom recriminations that will further obscure the facts of the case, serve to excite racial tension and contribute to the cause of general divisive bad juju.

The defense team's probably thinking they can sell the hot-line tapes for big bucks. The LAPD's probably wishing they framed some random pervert for the job.

If O.J. is guilty, he should cop a plea behind exhaustion. His 2,033 yards in one season rate bupkis when compared to his post-football sprint.

Second-rate acclaim and the pursuit of empty pleasures wear a guy out. Beating up women is a young man's game. Attrition narrows your choices down to changing your life or ending it.

Change takes time. It's not as instantaneous as a few lines of coke or some fresh pussy.

Suicide takes imagination. You've got to be able to conjure up an afterlife or visions of rest — or be in such unbreachable pain that anything is preferable to your suffering.

O.J. went out behind a chickenshit end run. He didn't have the soul or the balls to utilize his first two options.

SALLY JENKINS

The Sorry State of Tennis

FROM SPORTS ILLUSTRATED

TENNIS IS spoiled rotten. If you are wondering exactly when a wonderful game became such a lousy sport, the answer is, the first time a corporate executive gave a fourteen-year-old a stretch limo to play with.

To the average sports fan tennis played by pampered, insolent children, run by overtanned businessmen and governed by quarrelsome organizations, and every one of these parties is hopelessly out of touch with the real world. While prize money spirals ever upward — this year the men are competing for $58.6 million and the women for $35 million — the players seem to do less and less to earn it.

The public might stand for such excess if tennis weren't so boring. In fact, to many sports fans it's irrelevant. When was the last time it led the evening sportscast? John McEnroe and Jimmy Connors are all but gone, Chris Evert is retired, and Martina Navratilova will soon follow. Andre Agassi and Boris Becker are oft-injured phantoms, and Monica Seles, the victim of a stabbing a year ago, is on indefinite sabbatical. Steffi Graf and Pete Sampras can't hold the sport up alone.

On those rare occasions when a player with a recognizable name takes the court, nothing happens. If you want action, go to a basketball game. In the average men's hard-court match the ball is in play less than nine minutes per hour, and on grass it's less than four minutes. The rest is toweling off, ball-bouncing, pacing and griping about calls. Meanwhile the umpire is saying, "Quiet, please," and if you try to take your seat before a changeover, the players glare at you. Then you find out that every player in the field at the Lipton Championships in Key Biscayne, Florida, in March was given a personal concierge, his or her own private Mr. French.

Some of the most influential officials and observers of the sport are dismayed by what they see: apathetic players reluctant to make even token personal gestures toward crowds or appearances on behalf of sponsors, whom they don't hesitate to squeeze for more prize money. "They give the least back of any athletes," says NBC Sports president Dick Ebersol.

"I think they need to examine their consciences," says Evert, who describes today's players as "unapproachable, defensive, isolated."

John Beddington, director of the $1.72 million Canadian Open, recently told *Tennis Week*, "I'm incredibly nervous of asking a player [to do something] for fear he'll knock my head off. You get an attitude of 'Why would I bother to do that for you?' It's been created by a superstar's earning lots of money."

Teenage champions turn pro too early and often burn out or become monsters while tennis authorities fail to discipline or educate them, afraid to offend the source of all that lucre. Billie Jean King, who cofounded the women's pro tour in 1970, says, "There is a part of me that wants to knock it all down and start over again."

Jim Courier spoke volumes about the state of the sport with his behavior at the ATP Tour World Championship in Germany in November. Tired after a long year and uninterested in his match against Ukraine's Andrei Medvedev, Courier pulled out a novel, Armistead Maupin's *Maybe the Moon*, and began reading during changeovers.

If the players are apathetic, why shouldn't the fans be? Attendance fell at this year's Australian Open by slightly more than 31,000. In the U.S., TV network ratings for the U.S. Open last year were off by 12 percent. In Germany, Europe's tennis mecca, TV ratings for the ATP Championship were down by 25 percent, even though it was held in Frankfurt and won by national hero Michael Stich.

The malaise extends all the way to your local tennis courts. At the height of the tennis boom, in 1978, 35 million Americans played the game. That number has shrunk to 22 million. Racket sales in the U.S., which represents roughly half the world tennis-equipment market, fell by 22.6 percent last year. As for tennis shoes, Nike suffered a 36 percent drop in U.S. sales in 1993 (though business has since picked up).

Even the hardest-working, best-intentioned tour players, cocooned by their wealth, are either unaware that their sport is hurting or unwilling to do anything about it. Graf claims she is under too much pressure already. "Look," she says, "I need to get away from tennis, not spend more time around it."

Interestingly enough, Agassi, the circuit's most famous hedonist, is among the few stars who understand that tennis is drowning in wretched excess. "It's all take, take, take," says Agassi. "There's nobody to blame except the people who can make it better, and that's the players."

In case they're listening, here are ten ways to make tennis better.

1. *Players under seventeen should be limited to eight tournaments per year.*

How many casualties will it take before parents, agents, coaches and governing bodies stop colluding in the ruination of child prodigies? Jimmy Arias and Andrea Jaeger, Top Five players in the early 1980s, were among the first members of the Teenage Hall of Flameout. Having battled a series of shoulder and wrist problems, Arias, now 29, is a mere journeyman on the tour, and the oft-injured Jaeger, 28, has effectively been out of the game for a decade. Yet the women's WTA Tour Players Association and the men's ATP Tour continue to encourage the youth trend. Girls may turn pro at thirteen years, eleven months and play fifteen events in their first year. Boys may play eight professional tournaments at age fourteen, and twelve at age fifteen.

Even the International Management Group, the agency that once represented Jaeger and now represents Jennifer Capriati — who at eighteen has already felt the need to go on sabbatical — has begun to question the wisdom of allowing young teens to follow grueling schedules that take them all over the globe. "I hate to see them get so good so young," says Bob Kain, who heads IMG's tennis division. "They go through an unbelievably tough period. Something more has to be done to help them."

Players join the tour before their bodies or their games are sufficiently developed. "There is hardly any coach who takes the time to develop good technique and physical fitness," said German coach Klaus Hofsäss in an interview with Germany's *Sports Life* magazine. "I keep hearing from players, 'My coach says I shouldn't volley!'" Brian Tobin, president of the International Tennis Federation, says, "The coaches, managers and agents who are living off the players don't want to take any risks. They just want the players to get 80 percent of the balls in the court, and the players tend to become robots."

A limit of eight tournaments a year for all players under seventeen would at least attempt to safeguard their long-term physical and emotional health and broaden their games, yet still allow for the breakthrough of a phenom. The coaching commission of the ITF — which runs the Davis Cup and Federation Cup competitions and helps oversee the four Grand Slam tournaments — won't go that far, but it has recommended that girls be restricted to four pro events at age 14, six at age 15, and twelve (plus the Grand Slams) at age 16. The WTA, meanwhile, has named a board of experts to study age and education requirements for girls. But no change is likely to occur in time to prevent 13-year-old prodigies Venus Williams of the U.S. and Martina Hingis of Switzerland from hitting the circuit this season if they choose to.

However, what better expert is there than Seles, who says she turned pro too early? "We've seen the results of playing at fourteen," says Navratilova, 37, who didn't go on the circuit full-time until she was seventeen. "It is no accident that I'm not only still playing, but I can contribute intellectually."

As Navratilova implies, the age issue in tennis is not just about youth; it's about education, too. Sampras turned pro at 16, Graf at 13, and neither has seen the inside of a classroom since. How well-rounded can they be? McEnroe, whatever his faults may be, is an articulate man with a wide range of interests partly because he had a brush with college, spending a year at Stanford. Evert was forbidden by her parents to turn pro until she finished high school. Like McEnroe, Connors spent one year in college, at UCLA, and Arthur Ashe actually graduated from UCLA.

"School is where you go through the final stages of your character development, but these kids don't," says Ebersol, who thinks that the players' lack of social skills keeps them from connecting with fans. "At age twelve they're off on the junior circuits, where every little need is pampered."

One player in particular who has suffered for his callowness is the 22-year-old Sampras. He's number one in the world but has been received coolly by the public. If Sampras plays long enough, the public may discover that he is an engaging, shrewd young man. But he might have connected with more people already if he had spent more time interacting with his non-tennis-playing peers. Sampras's existence thus far has been solitary.

"It's one regret I might have," Sampras says of leaving high school. "Going to school is part of growing up, developing. Going to parties, getting in a little trouble, all of that helps make you a broader person." He pauses. "Also, I might have a good friend. You know, I don't have a really good friend."

2. *Put a lid on the free stuff.*

True story: A top-ranked player on the women's tour, a teenage millionaire, was given a Lexus by a sponsor to drive during a tournament. She liked the car. She liked it so much that she asked if she could keep it. No, said the incredulous sponsor.

Fact: During tournaments every player on the men's circuit receives free accommodations, often in cushy resorts. Starting next year, women will receive free accommodations for at least three days during each tournament.

The practice of lavishing amenities on tennis players begins when they are children and builds from there. U.S. Davis Cup captain Tom Gullikson thinks the ever-increasing luxuries are one reason education is no longer valued by parents and coaches, who are eager for immediate returns on their investments. "Why isn't a college scholarship a good return?" says Gullikson.

Dr. Julie Anthony, a psychologist, tennis coach and former player, sees in the tour an unwholesome culture in which basic values degenerate. "There is no one teaching the players that they have a responsibility to anyone but themselves," says Anthony. "When you deal with teenagers, you're talking about essentially selfish organisms. They're obsessed with themselves, their hair, their skin, their weight. Then you put them in an environment that does nothing but feed their self-absorption. You're going to create some real prizes there."

Gullikson spent two years coaching Capriati. One day he presented her with a book. Capriati, fifteen years old at the time, glanced at the cover. It was a guide to good manners. "Read it," Gullikson said. "You could use it."

Some players have the grace to be abashed by their riches. "There's no question we're spoiled," says Courier. "It's embarrassing." Tournament directors, though, make their living by attracting strong fields. But as costs rise, the perks become increasingly questionable. The Lipton Championships cost $10 million to stage, yet for years many of the players petulantly complained about the conditions. Tournament chairman Butch Buchholz says, "We should probably ask ourselves more often what is a fair return on our investment. We've made some money the last few years. Not a lot."

Yet this year Buchholz not only gave all the players free rooms in first-class hotels but also offered those personal concierges — volunteers who picked up each player at the airport and were available throughout the tournament to "arrange a golf game or whatever the player might request," Buchholz said. Agassi, for one, was not just unappreciative but also derisive. "Let me put it this way," he said. "You want my concierge?"

To help restore a sense of reality, tournament directors should refuse to pay hotel costs for players. Golfers on the PGA Tour pay their own expenses. Why shouldn't tennis players?

3. *Hire a commissioner.*

What's all this alphabet soup? Tennis has too many authorities protecting their own turf: the ITF, ATP, WTA, WTC, USTA, etc. None of them has shown that it can make a decision for the good of the game instead of its own self-interest.

How did this come to be? Tennis was played and run by so-called amateurs until 1968, when player revolts ushered in the open, or professional, era. Suddenly several competing factions, along with a handful of powerful player agents, scrambled for control, grabbing whatever territory they could while the players formed unionlike organizations. The result is a sport that lacks any centralized governance or marketing and is rife with conflicts of interest. IMG, for example, not only manages about one hundred players but also runs tournaments, organizes exhibitions, holds broadcast rights to events and owns Nick Bollettieri's tennis academy.

ATP chief executive officer Mark Miles and WTA executive director Gerry Smith often seem more concerned with negotiating yearly prize-money increases for the players who employ them than with correcting the sport's deep-seated ills. Don't hold your breath, but the current tennis bodies should step aside and jointly appoint a commissioner for both men and women who will set and enforce

rules and will market the game worldwide — someone who will do
for tennis what David Stern has done for pro basketball.

The first thing a commissioner should do is simplify the schedules. Tennis is suffering from market clutter. For instance, during
the week beginning January 31, the men's tour featured three
tournaments on three continents: the $1 million Dubai Open, the
$514,000 Marseille Open and the $289,000 San Jose Open. Two
weeks after the eight-player, $2.75 million ATP championship con-
cludes in Frankfurt in November, the ITF stages the sixteen-player,
$6 million Grand Slam Cup in Munich. Further obfuscating mat-
ters are exhibitions or so-called special events, which only the most
die-hard tennis follower can distinguish from sanctioned tournaments and which are run concurrently with sanctioned tournaments.

Both tours are supporting too many events and too many players.
A total of 1,300 players are ranked by the ATP, 1,000 by the WTA.
Last year 1,043 players won prize money on the ATP Tour. By
contrast, only 336 golfers earned paychecks on the PGA Tour. The
one-hundredth-ranked male tennis player, Henri Leconte of France,
pulled in $277,126.

   4. *How about a little discipline?*

At the ATP championship every player has his own locker room,
a plush space with an easy chair and a glass coffee table. After
Goran Ivanisevic of Croatia lost to Stich in last year's semis, he
smashed his coffee table to pieces. He was not fined.

Trouble is, the players are above the authority of the officials.
Even McEnroe was defaulted only once in his career, at the Australian Open in 1990. A chair umpire is undermined every time a
player, objecting to a call, sends for the tournament referee, who
often sides with the player.

Tennis is the only major sport that virtually never suspends athletes for egregious behavior. During a match against Petr Korda at
the '90 U.S. Open, Agassi, enraged over a line call, cursed at chair
umpire Wayne McKewen and then spit at him. The two men then
argued over whether Agassi had spit intentionally, and Agassi sent
for Grand Slam supervisor Ken Farrar. After a three-way discussion
McKewen announced a point penalty against Agassi, which put him
one infraction away from being defaulted. But Farrar, who had
decided to give Agassi the benefit of the doubt, made McKewen
rescind the penalty. The match continued, and Agassi won. After

reviewing a tape of the incident the next day, Farrar concluded that the spitting had been deliberate and fined Agassi $3,000.

The next time a player smashes something, suspend him. If he acts up in a match, default him.

5. *How about a smile?*

Courier had just beaten Becker to win the U.S. Hardcourt title last August, and the crowd in Indianapolis continued to applaud him as commentator Bud Collins interviewed him before a television camera. When they went off the air, Collins gestured toward the stadium and asked Courier, "Would you like to say a few words to the crowd?"

"No," Courier said and strolled away.

When Sampras stares at his feet and Courier saunters off the court without acknowledging the fans, spectators have the uneasy feeling that they are in a vacuum rather than a stadium. Tennis, Sampras says, should be "strictly business," and Courier concurs. Yes, but it's the *entertainment* business. Otherwise, why are the fans charged $25 at the gate?

"The only thing I've always known," says Agassi, "is that people had better walk out of that stadium feeling that there's no way they'd rather spend their money."

That doesn't mean players should try to entertain at the expense of their best tennis — something of which the showboating Agassi has been guilty. It also doesn't mean that they should try to be something they're not. So Sampras isn't David Letterman. What's wrong with that? "It is sickening that someone who is down-to-earth, polite, behaves well, is reasonably clever and wears nice clothes almost has to apologize for being the way he is," says one of Sampras's admirers, Ivan Lendl, who was considered even duller during his reign as number one.

The enigmatic Courier doesn't emote either. That's fine too; Joe Montana doesn't spill his emotions all over the field. But there's a difference between not emoting and being opaque.

Nike's ad campaigns are proof that everyone can have personality. Courier has become a more accessible figure through his candid TV ads, which are part of his five-year, $16 million contract with Nike. A TV campaign will certainly emerge from the deal that Sampras just signed with Nike, which will pay him a reported $18 million over the next five years. But it's ridiculous for the public to have to watch commercials to get to know the players. Surely they can give a little more to the crowds in the stands.

Try this: At every event, spectators find lottery numbers in their programs. The winner gets to go down on the court and attempt to return a star player's serve.

"I could do that," Sampras says.

6. *Crack down on tanking.*

It happens. Everybody knows it. Sergi Bruguera of Spain, the reigning French Open champion, has given a number of efforts that seemed halfhearted at best. He was, for example, suspected of tanking at last year's U.S. Open. Trailing countryman Javier Sánchez two sets to love in the first round, Bruguera sank like a stone in the third set. Recently Ukraine's Natalia Medvedeva lost 6–4, 6–0 to Chanda Rubin in the quarters of a Virginia Slims event. Afterward Medvedeva admitted that she had dumped the last couple of games. "I didn't give up until probably 4–0," she says. She was not fined.

"I think [tanking is] becoming more prevalent," says the ITF's Tobin. As for the ATP, its ranking system practically asks players to tank. The system tabulates only a player's best fourteen tournament results over the previous fifty-two weeks, allowing him to throw out his worst results. The formula was designed to encourage players to play more; in fact, it takes the sting out of losing. What's to prevent a player from accepting a tournament's six-figure guarantee, tanking in the first round and then jetting off to appear in a lucrative exhibition the following week?

The only thing that should be tanked is the best-of-fourteen rule.

Those six-figure guarantees provide an even bigger incentive for players to give less than their all. True story: Sampras received a staggering $500,000 guarantee just to play a tournament in Qatar early this year. He cavalierly flew in the night before his first-round match and lost to a Moroccan qualifier named Karim Alami, who was ranked 205th in the world. Sampras, who is hard-working and decent, apologized for not being better prepared. Still, he didn't give the money back.

Another true story: Agassi got his own six-figure guarantee to play a tournament last year in Halle, Germany. Like Sampras in Qatar, Agassi went down in the first round. Why not? The winner's check for the tournament was only $50,000.

Guarantees should be paid only if a player reaches the quarterfinals. He doesn't make it, he doesn't get the money. (Guarantees are not such a problem on the women's tour because, with fewer tournaments, tournament directors don't have to compete for the top players.)

Some players don't bother to tank, they just don't show up. A growing problem among both men and women is eleventh-hour withdrawals. It seems that hardly a week goes by when a leading player doesn't pull out of an upcoming tournament for a suspect medical reason. On the men's tour the number of withdrawals due to injury in this noncontact sport rose from 74 in 1989 to an amazing 194 in 1993 and 52 in the first quarter of 1994. Last year the women's tour suffered a record 61 injuries and withdrawals from tournaments — 32 by Top Ten players. "They don't care," Navratilova says of the players in general. "They reap all the benefits and try to get away with doing as little as possible."

When King suggested in a year-end players' meeting that they refuse a 5 percent prize-money increase as a gesture of good faith to their sponsors and tournament directors, she was met with silence. They took the money. It may cost them.

7. *Institute pro-ams at every tour stop.*

Is it any wonder that tennis is suffering in the marketplace while golf is thriving? Most golfers can't even move the needle on the charisma meter. But they work every day at promoting their sport for their corporate sponsors. Participation in pro-ams is required on the PGA Tour. Refusal is considered "conduct unbecoming a professional golfer" and is subject to discipline. On the Senior tour, players who do not play in the pro-am are not allowed to enter that week's event.

It would behoove tennis players to take a more businesslike approach to their sport, because they could be facing a pay cut. While the ATP is wealthy at the moment, it is facing a big loss in 1996, when its television-rights deal with German TV expires. This agreement accounts for 75 percent of the ATP's worldwide TV income. The Germans won't renew at anywhere close to the current rate because of plummeting ratings caused by market clutter and viewer fatigue. The ATP is looking for a new revenue stream.

The WTA is facing a more immediate crisis. It must find a new title sponsor to replace Kraft, which pulled out of tennis at the end of last year because it had grown tired of the sport's political and financial wrangling and because it was not convinced that pouring money into tennis helped sell a single slice of Velveeta. Seven women's tournaments are without sponsorship for 1995. In short, the women could be playing a much smaller, poorer tour in the near future.

Meanwhile, corporate sponsors cite the difficulty of getting players of note to show up for a promotional effort or a cocktail party — even though the players know, as manager Ion Tiriac says, "that they get those millions of dollars not only for playing a few tennis matches but also for being available to the public." At the Virginia Slims of Philadelphia, tournament director Barbara Perry holds a meet-the-players party in the lobby of the players' hotel because the only way she can get the top women to come is by collaring them on their way out to dinner.

"Forget asking a player to do anything," says Norman Salik, a vice president of Bausch & Lomb, which helps sponsor six tournaments on the men's and women's tours. Salik cites endorsement deals with Agassi and Lendl that required them to make only one appearance — which they skipped. Bausch & Lomb will reevaluate its commitment to tennis when its contracts with the tours expire over the next two years.

8. *If a baseball player can hit a 95-mph fastball in front of 80,000 screaming people, then why does a tennis player need total silence? Let there be noise.*

Tennis needs to get hip. Imagine this: You go to a tournament, and before a match you hear rock music blasting from the speakers. An emcee gives each player a lengthy introduction worthy of a prizefighter. Two players come out in baggy shorts and Day-Glo T-shirts. They play before a crowd that moves around freely and cheers during points.

It could happen. Truth to tell, World TeamTennis has taken this kind of approach for years. After two decades of shunning King's pet project because of its commercialism, mainstream tennis authorities seem ready to steal from it. Fan ennui has driven the ATP, WTA and ITF to discuss how to give tennis more bang for the buck. The ATP has already staged promotional stunts and fan-participation events at tournaments, and it will experiment with free crowd circulation, music and on-court coaching this year. "These guys have laughed at Billie Jean for years," says Evert. "It turns out she was right."

Myth: The sound of a beer cup falling can cause a double fault.

Enough with the princess-and-the-pea conditioning. If players want utter quiet, they should play in an air lock.

As for dress codes, bag 'em. Clone the Jensens. Brothers and doubles partners Luke and Murphy Jensen, who wear bowling shirts, slouch socks and black hightops and have long hair and goatees, have become matinee idols even though they've won only one major title, last year's French Open doubles.

9. *Give it some gas.*

No sporting event should last more than three hours, particularly one that has so little live action. Why do players need twenty-five seconds between points to collect themselves? The game was better when play was continuous. Why not put a time clock on the court? If a player doesn't get his serve off in fifteen seconds, he loses the point.

Also, take away the chairs. A player doesn't need to sit down at every changeover while one ball boy holds an umbrella over his head and another pours the Evian.

10. *Spread the wealth.*

The president of the U.S. Tennis Association, J. Howard (Bumpy) Frazer, was asked what his organization is doing to promote tennis among minorities.

"Well, we have a committee," he said.

What else?

"All of our sections have committees," he said.

Anything else?

"I feel in the strongest way that minority citizens can enjoy watching and playing tennis every bit as much as I do."

Major reality check: LeGeorge Mauldin lives in South Central Los Angeles, in the heart of gangland. LeGeorge may be the best 12-and-under player in southern California, but he had to give up tennis for several months last year because funding for the inner-city program in which he played temporarily dried up.

LeGeorge is back on the courts again, thanks to a $5,000 donation from the ATP, which heard about his plight through the television show *The Crusaders*. LeGeorge takes lessons from a recently retired postal worker named Richard Williams, who for twenty years has been trying to spread the game to South Central kids on his days off.

Williams and his brother, Fred, run the California Tennis Association for Underprivileged Youth on a shoestring budget of about

$8,000 a year, which they scrape together from small donations from a variety of sources. For a year or so $800 or $900 a month came in from a neighborhood drug dealer, but in 1990 the man was sent to prison.

If tennis is to become a truly public sport and resume growing as it did in the 1970s, it must get into the inner cities. The USTA spends most of its money running tournaments. Recently, however, it combined with the Tennis Industry Association to create the USTA Play Tennis America program, under which, for $24.95, anyone can order a kit that includes an inexpensive racket, a video, a tennis manual and a series of free tennis lessons in three cities: Austin, Texas; Charlotte, North Carolina; and Tucson, Arizona. The ATP has begun funding the National Junior Tennis League, a USTA urban youth program. Still, the USTA spends only an estimated $500,000 — less than 1 percent of its annual budget of $91 million — on minority programs. And it costs $600,000 a year just to run the inner-city program in Washington, D.C.

The future of tennis may well be in the hands of people like the Williamses and Doug MacCurdy, the ITF's director of development. MacCurdy, a former teaching pro, is a veritable Johnny Appleseed, traveling to remote parts of the world to spread the game. The ITF devotes approximately $4 million a year to its global development program. Sometimes carrying only a simple kit — a couple of broad wooden bats and an old ball — MacCurdy has introduced tennis to villages from Mongolia to Benin. Today a 17-year-old girl from Madagascar, Dally Randriantefy, is the sixth-ranked junior in the world. MacCurdy has helped Randriantefy and others get training and college scholarships.

There are those who believe that the greatest tennis talent who ever lived will never pick up a racket because he or she lives in some place like inner-city Detroit or Chicago. "If you could get the racket into the hands of some of those kids," Agassi says, "they might make me look like a club player."

Back in South Central, Williams spies a bunch of kids. He approaches them with an armful of rackets and a handful of balls. "Come on over here and see if you can hit this," he says.

Meanwhile, somewhere in West Africa, MacCurdy stretches a piece of string between two trees. Then he turns to a group of village children and tells them, "Now we're going to play a little game with a paddle."

JIM MURRAY

Game Is Too Young to Die

FROM THE LOS ANGELES TIMES

ONCE UPON A TIME in this country there was a game called baseball. You would have loved it.

Green grass, bright sunshine, hot dogs, Cracker Jack. The cares of the world you left at the door. "Outta the lot, Hack!" "We're wit ya, Carl, baby!" You were a kid again. No matter what age you were.

You brought the kids. It was an heirloom sport. Passed on from fathers to sons. Generation after generation. The baseball gene ran in families.

And the ballparks! You should have seen the ballparks! Lovely old Fenway Park. That left-field fence! The Monster! The Creature that ate pitchers. Ted Williams hit here.

You ever been to Fenway Park? A pity! Everyone should spend an afternoon at Fenway Park. It's a part of Americana.

Then there was Yankee Stadium. The house that Ruth built. Opera lovers had La Scala. Balletomanes had the Bolshoi. Playgoers had the Old Vic. We had Yankee Stadium. There's a monument to Babe Ruth in the outfield. "How about that!" Mel Allen would say.

The game had stars. Walter Johnson had a fastball you could only hit by Braille. Ruth hit more home runs himself than any team in the league some years. Nolan Ryan threw two no-hitters a year.

You loved to hear the infield chattering. "No hitter up there, Sandy! Throw him the deuce! Make him be a hitter, Babe!"

Some of the best afternoons of your life were spent in a ballpark. The poet said the time spent in a ballpark, like fishing, didn't count against your life span. No one could age in a ballpark. You got younger, not older. You could live forever in a ballpark. Someone once complained the game was too slow. Not for us. I never went to a ballpark in a hurry in my life. If you're in a hurry, go to an airport, I'd tell them.

It was a game that Yogi Berra — ah, Yogi Berra! — once said ain't over till it's over. Not so dumb, at that. It's a game without a clock, is what he's saying. A football game can be over before it's over. Not a baseball game. The gun doesn't go off on you. You never run out of time, just outs.

What happened to this happy hunting ground, this magic isle in life? Where did all those summers go?

Well, it might have died in the summer of 1994. By its own hand.

No one could ever figure out quite why. It was the picture of health to the end.

It didn't run out of sluggers, southpaws, speed burners, shortstops. It ran out of love. It didn't die of old age, lack of interest, neglect. It died of disease for which there is no known cure — stubbornness.

They all said they weren't trying to kill baseball, they were trying to save it. Meanwhile, the patient died on the operating table. The tombstone should read, "Here Lies Baseball — Negotiated to Death." It was an inglorious end for such a glorious tradition.

It was the victim of the oldest feud in the annals of sport — owners vs. players. It doesn't matter what the issue is — salary cap, pensions, revenue sharing. If the owners are for a salary cap, the players are against it. If the players are for revenue sharing, the owners are against it. If the owners were against the man-eating shark, the players would be for it.

It's nothing new. It's as old as the game.

Owners were always rich men. Ownership was a hobby. But they couldn't help applying business principles — if that phrase is not an oxymoron — to their hobby. They tried to make a profit. They were, after all, capitalists.

They managed to move the game outside the Constitution of the United States early on — 1876, to be exact — when they instituted the "reserve clause," which bound the services of five players to the parent club in perpetuity. Eventually, they expanded it to include all players. The players' resistance was token at first. After all, it wasn't considered a profession then. Most of them kept their day jobs.

But the players countered by trying to form a new league — in 1890 and again in 1914. Both leagues went spectacularly broke.

The owners held unbroken sway from 1920 to the mid-1960s when the players brought up a can't-miss rookie.

Marvin Miller couldn't hit the change-up, couldn't bat .300, field .900, throw, catch or hit the curve, but he had what all the great ones from Cobb to Robinson had — a searing resentment of the Establishment verging on hatred.

The game was never the same after he joined it. Baseball's were probably the last workers of the world to unite. Miller put together a union equivalent of the '27 Yankees. They never lost a strike. Or a lockout.

Other factors played a part — most notably binding arbitration, which the owners put in themselves — but the bare facts of the matter are that, when Marvin Miller undertook to organize the players, the average big league salary was $19,000. Today, it is $1.2 million.

The even stranger truth is, even though it cost them astronomically more money to run the game, the owners ended up making more.

Most of them anyway. A whole cannot be greater than the sum of its parts and baseball is no exception. Historically, whenever a part began to threaten, the whole had a solution: Move it. There were always bright-eyed, bushy-tailed new towns slavering for big league baseball.

A lot of them have since managed to make do with pro basketball or pro football franchises. And moving doesn't always prove a solution in the long run. The portable franchise started with Boston, which moved to Milwaukee in 1953 after its attendance bottomed out at 281,276. The Boston Public Library drew more.

The Braves went to Milwaukee, where they were to draw 2,131,488 two years later. However, thirteen years later, after new ownership had announced a move to Atlanta as soon as was legally possible, they bottomed out at 555,586 and headed southeast. And there were times in Atlanta when that franchise was put in the window with a "make-offer" tag on it.

It was a great game. It's too young to die. But those who love it were not consulted, the ones who collected the bubble gum cards, peeked through knotholes, bought the jackets, ate the Wheaties, waved the pennants, and said, "Say it ain't so, Joe," and introduced sons to the game. Who cared about them?

But what's October without a World Series? Italy without a song? Paris without a spring? Canada without a sunset?

Once upon a time in this country, we had World Series. You would have loved them. Ruth pointing. Sandy Koufax curving. Pepper Martin stealing. Kirk Gibson homering.

You shoulda been here.

TONY KORNHEISER

National Pastime, Past My Bedtime

FROM THE WASHINGTON POST

WAKE ME WHEN they get to Willie Mays. After watching five full hours of *Baseball* — *and they still hadn't gotten past 1910!* — I began to wonder if I would even live through the ending. Can you believe it, *Baseball* the documentary is as slow as the game it documents.

I'm told it picks up after the first eight hours. But so did the Hundred Years' War, and I wouldn't have stuck around to see that either.

What can you say about *Baseball*? That it is lush, it is loving, and, hoo boy, is it long.

How long is it, Tony?

Do the words "consecutive life sentences" mean anything to you?

Far be it from me to suggest that Ken Burns has woven a corporate funding version of the Emperor's New Clothes — but playing the National Anthem before each episode? Pardon me, each "inning."

Pretentious?

Pretentious? *Moi?*

Oh, and Ken: Get a grown-up haircut.

It's not that I don't like baseball. I do. It's just that I guess I didn't go to the right private schools to fully appreciate it. Knowing how crucial *Baseball* is to the care and feeding of the nation's leading poets and intellectuals, I didn't want to sell it short — just because it seemed to me that it was basically an overblown chunk of baloney. So I telephoned savvy media critic Man About Town Chip Muldoon, and asked if he had seen any of *Baseball*.

"I watched the first ten minutes," he said.

"Oh, that's the part that concentrates on the spring of 1837," I said.

"Yes, I figured I had a long wait until Chico Escuela."

Let's get real. This thing is 18½ hours of slurping at the trough of baseball. If it was any more reverential, Saint Peter would be doing the narration, not John Chancellor. It opens in Brooklyn, with church bells ringing. (Baseball being the church of America, get it?) I'll bet it's set in Brooklyn, because everyone of a certain generation — the corporate funding generation — bemoans how Brooklyn doesn't have a baseball team anymore. Then again, you could have started this in Pakistan, because there's no baseball team there, either.

The first words you hear are, "In our sundown perambulations of late . . ."

And immediately you get that queasy feeling: Oh, gosh, am I gonna see George Will soon?

Right you are. You get Will, the officious George Plimpton, Shelby Foote — who's become to Ken Burns what Tony Roberts is to Woody Allen — and a parade of middle-aged white males telling you, as Bob Costas does, "What you've got to understand is: Baseball is a beautiful thing," or as the poet Donald Hall does, "There's a stillness in baseball that I love." You hear the words "pastoral," "timeless" and "renewal," and you get the feeling of the elegiac symmetry of the emerald chessboard, and it makes you wanna throw up both your hands and holler, "Hark and hot damn, I hear the rhythms of America!"

Of course just once I'd like to see Burns let someone, anyone, say, "I hate to say this, but sometimes baseball can be, uh, boring."

Like when it lasts 18½ hours.

(Let's see, *The Civil War* lasted 12 hours, and this goes 18½. I can't wait for Burns's next big score: 25 hours on *Household Pets,* beginning with the touching episode of Shelby Foote consoling a nine-year-old whose turtle fell down the disposal.)

You give me *The Natural, Field of Dreams* — without any of the Amy Madigan scenes — and *Bull Durham,* and you can take your 18½ hours and stick them in a museum.

Look, I like baseball. Like all the other old white men in the show, it's the game of my youth and the game of my father. But no matter how many quotes from Walt Whitman you dredge up —

because, hey, who'd Walt Whitman play for? — I won't think it's poetry and I won't think it's religion, and I won't think it explains the history of America. Not any more than the cotton gin, or the sunset off Monterey Bay, or a Corvette on an open highway.

Oh, Kenny, one more thing: Somewhere during the 18½ hours you're going to show me someone scratching and spitting, aren't you — even if it's Shelby Foote. Because I've been to a lot of baseball games, and I never had a sense that players sat on the bench and mused about how baseball holds up a mirror to America's soul. And, seriously, if I have to hear the haunting strains of "Danny Boy" or "Take Me Out to the Ballgame" in the background one more night, I think I may hurl. (What happened to "Thank God I'm a Country Boy"? Doesn't Ken Burns watch the O's?)

Enough with the sound of the crack of the bat.

Enough with the phony crowd noise.

Enough with the 1870s!

I sit there and watch this, and it's sort of like being in Colonial Williamsburg, forced to watch endless streams of blacksmiths make endless streams of horseshoes — because how far can picturesque get you in the 1990s? I learn things I will not ever use unless I am on *Roto Geek Jeopardy!*, such as Candy Cummings invented the curve, and a cricketeer named Harry Chadwick invented the box score, thus becoming the first Seamhead. Sometimes when I'm watching I feel like going out for a sandwich . . . like, to Argentina. Because I know that when I get home, it'll still only be the sixth inning. Kenny, sweetheart, does the word "Cut!" mean anything to you?

Three full days and we weren't even into moving pictures!

I like King Kelly as much as the next guy, but the man has been dead one hundred years. How many different photos of the man do we need to see? Ken Burns spent more time on King Kelly than William Manchester did on Robert Kennedy. (I have, however, enjoyed finding out that Evers, of Tinkers to Evers to Chance, was a complete psycho.)

Memo: Somebody tell Okrent to change that sweater already.

I am happy to report that *Baseball* continues through tonight and into the next century on PBS, which, for true baseball fans, is a virgin channel on the dial. ("Hey, MacNeil and Lehrer! Weren't they set-up men for the Brewers when Treblehorn was managing?")

If, by some twist of fate, you miss any of it, be assured you can buy the entire boxed set of tapes for a mere $179.95. What a steal! And I'll bet they throw in a lyric sheet for "Take Me Out to the Ballgame." Of course you could simply buy three blank six-hour tapes and do it yourself for nine bucks . . . and with the $170 left over, buy two football tickets.

Baseball Strike: Who Feels the Most Pain?

FROM THE DALLAS MORNING NEWS

THERE ARE THOSE in this fair land not even aware that the national pastime has shut down for the nonce. As embarrassing as this is to the Lords of Baseball, there are citizens more concerned about national spending or whether they can make it all the way across the parking lot without being conked on the noggin.

However, if you find room in your jaded heart for sympathy about the baseball strike, kindly direct it to one person more than any other. Not Tony Gwynn, chasing the first .400 average since Ted Williams. Not mom nor apple pie bakers nor even "the seamheads," a trade term for reporters who follow the baseball spoor like Apache scouts.

First, feel sorry for the manager of the Los Angeles Dodgers. Tommy Lasorda is the accident victim taken off life support. He is the experimental mouse in a glass prism with oxygen being slowly sucked out by impersonal scientists.

Mr. Lasorda without baseball is an American tragedy. Some feel the reverse is also true. Baseball without Mr. Lasorda is Thanksgiving without turkey. Or Mrs. Elizabeth Taylor Hilton Wilding Todd Fisher Burton Warner Fortensky without mascara.

Dick Williams, in his book covering six stops as a major league manager, did not treat baseball or its Lords with an overflow of reverence. But on one subject, he laid it on: "Tommy Lasorda is the best thing that ever happened to baseball."

Well, maybe not the *best* thing. That's like saying Bob Hope is the best thing that happened to the Yank war effort. But in the last two decades, no pitchman is as closely identified with baseball as Mr. Lasorda.

His critics, and they are cynical and numerous, scoff at all that "Dodger Blue" confetti he spews like a tent show evangelist. But the belief here — and I've known the fellow since he was a cunnythumb lefty four decades past — is that Tommy is a self-hypnotist. He actually *believes* all that fertilizer he spreads on the congregation. He is convinced there is a Great Dodger in the Sky, with disciples named Sandy, Jackie, Peewee and Campy.

Regardless of his agenda, Mr. Lasorda seems never too busy to sell his product in general, not just the Dodger brand. Whether he's speaking to industrial tycoons or a gang of playground kids, he's pitching the merchandise with every adjective at his command.

He choreographed a most unique act in 1978. Before one September game, the manager called a pre-game meeting.

"You are playing for the greatest organization in baseball, before the greatest fans. Today you will become the only team in history to draw *3 million people!*" roared the evangelist. "Now here's what I want you to do."

So, during the seventh inning when the attendance was announced as a record, Dodger players stopped the game, poured from the dugout, lined up with backs to the diamond and applauded the fans. That's selling trombones in River City, buster.

Sometimes, Mr. Lasorda's theatrics overshadow the fact that he is a pretty pert manager. By this modest judgment, his World Series victories over the Yankees in 1981 and over Oakland seven years later were crafted as cannily as McGraw or Durocher or Weaver or any of those immortal highdomes.

Of course, even though he has dedicated sixty-seven summers to the business, Mr. Lasorda hasn't suffered. For example, his public speaking is quite lucrative. Sometimes, lesser bookings result in commercial gifts from sponsors. He stows the merchandise away.

In fact, the Lasorda garage is legendary, stacked with refrigerators, stocked freezers, color TVs, stereos, VCRs, cameras, golf clubs, scooters, tennis equipment and sports garb of all sorts.

*

Once, after a particularly sloppy loss, the manager addressed his Dodgers almost in tears. They listened to his recital in silent amusement.

"That was the most terrible night of my forty-five years with the Dodgers," he said. "It was a disgrace to those great ones who have worn Dodger blue. Oh, how I hate for them to look down from Dodger heaven and see us perform so badly!

"Why, I'd give anything I own if we hadn't played so terribly. I'd give my house, my lot, all my furniture, my cars, my trophies, my property in the valley if we hadn't suffered that disgrace."

His voice rose to a quavering high. "I'd give up my wife's furs and jewelry if we hadn't lost that game, I'd give up my interest in the restaurant, I'd give up my boat at Malibu."

"How about your garage?" asked shortstop Bill Russell.

"No, not the garage!" snapped Mr. Lasorda.

GARY SMITH

An Exclusive Club

FROM SPORTS ILLUSTRATED

> Never join someone who eclipses you. Align yourself with one who
> increases your luster. The man who puts you in the shade because he is
> either more virtuous or vicious gains the greater recognition. He plays
> the main role, and you are relegated to support him.
>   — *Baltasar Graci, a seventeenth-century Jesuit philosopher*

SUPPOSE YOU HAD spent the best years of your life gasping for
oxygen. Suppose you had awakened each Sunday morning knowing you must run twenty-three miles to feel clean, then lie on a table
and hope someone could rub away the pain. Suppose you had
spent nights brooding over tenths of seconds, a decade of life
under the tyranny of a clock, and finally you had what you ached
for. "You're the king of the world," as one who did this said. "The
fastest miler in the world." And then, a few years later — or perhaps
only a few months or weeks — it was gone. Someone else was faster.
Someone else was king.

Suppose that one day long after this fever had passed, one day
when your hair was gray and your face was a fine web of wrinkles,
you opened the mail and found an invitation. Someone wanted you
to get on an airplane, fly fifteen hours, or twenty-eight, in order to
stand in the shade of the ones who had surpassed your sacrifice,
eclipsed your glory. No appearance fee. Would you do it? What for?

"To be the world-record holder in the mile," said Herb Elliott,
the 56-year-old Australian who was just that from 1958 until '62, "a
man must have the arrogance it takes to believe he can run faster
than anyone ever has at that distance . . . and the humility it takes to
actually do it."

What becomes of all that arrogance and humility? One by one, on the fortieth anniversary of the most famous mile ever run, the record holders arrived at the Grosvenor House Hotel in London on May 4. Shaking hands, smiling shyly, they stepped into each other's shade.

FILBERT BAYI: I don't have much money. But I have this: I'm among the greatest milers in the world. That makes me rich.

DEREK IBBOTSON: If it had been any other event, I don't think I'd be remembered now. I'd be lost.

JOHN LANDY: I was a loner, a shy young man. It opened up to live a life I never thought I'd live.

STEVE CRAM: It becomes luggage permanently attached to your name. It matters not what else you do. You'll be introduced everywhere as world-record holder in the mile. Even after you're hurt or on the downside of your career, you'll believe you can do anything. It can create great frustration.

PETER SNELL: The anchor I have is that regardless of how good you think you are, I at least have achieved something that was world class and that can never be taken away from me.

SEBASTIAN COE: I'll say it — why not? We are members of one of the most exclusive clubs in the world.

Dawn. Damp. Cool. Windy. Herb Elliott was sitting on his bed, eyes shut, mind quiet, body still. He was meditating. Jim Ryun, the world-record holder from 1966 to '75, was rousing his four children. Noureddine Morceli, the current king, was dropping to his knees, facing Mecca, murmuring his prayers. Bayi, who reigned briefly in 1975, was cooing to his fourth-born, one-year-old Cuthbert. John Walker, who dethroned Bayi and ruled until 1979, was sleeping like a stone.

The bus awaited them outside the Grosvenor House Hotel. Soon it would take them to the Iffley Road track in Oxford, where forty years ago — on a day not unlike this one — England's Roger Bannister astonished the world by running the first sub-four-minute mile. Four minutes was a barrier that had withstood decades of human yearning and anguish, a figure that seemed so perfectly round — four laps, four quarter miles, four-point-oh-oh minutes — that it seemed God himself had established it as man's limit, posted it as one quiet, subtle proof of Order against the howl of two world wars. The spectacle was seen by Americans watching their first televisions, by young lovers and ancients entering theaters around the world. At the time it seemed as improbable as . . . well, as fourteen of the world's sixteen living mile-record holders coming from Algeria, Australia, England, France, New Zealand, Sweden, Tanzania and the U.S. to celebrate it four decades later.

George Dole, a Massachusetts minister in the Swedenborgian Church who was invited to join this pilgrimage — he was one of the six runners who ran in Bannister's epic mile — climbed onto the bus before any of the record holders, full of the knowledge that perhaps no other sport had ever gathered so much of its greatness in one time and place. "Imagine," Dole said, his voice husky with reverence. "Imagine how many gallons of sweat these men represent."

Two would fail to show. Gunder Hägg, the Swede who three times set the world record (4:06.2, 4:04.6, 4:01.4) during World War II, had not come because he was 75 years old and too wearied by life for the journey. Steve Ovett, the Brit who set mile records in 1980 and '81 and now lodges guests in a renovated mansion in Annan, Scotland, had not come either, officially because he was on holiday but mostly, several who knew him said, because he is Steve Ovett. "Pathetic," growled one of the record holders. "He cheated us all," seethed another.

Slowly the bus began to fill: Michel Jazy, the 57-year-old Frenchman who held the record from mid-1965 to mid-'66 now retired from promotional work with Perrier and Adidas but still the boulevardier in his snazzy mustard-yellow sport coat. Arne Andersson, the 76-year-old retired Swedish schoolteacher who broke the record three times during World War II, in a red, yellow and blue Reebok pullover. Bayi, the 40-year-old Tanzanian, in the blue and gold native robe that his wife had crafted, clutching his one-year-old. Ryun, the 47-year-old Kansan, in a preppy plaid sweater vest, his children and wife in tow. Walker, the 42-year-old New Zealander, in sneakers, jeans and a sweatshirt. Morceli, the 24-year-old Algerian, in a mod green and purple hooded jumpsuit. Cram, Elliott, Ibbotson, Landy, Snell . . . Slowly, too slowly, they boarded, now a half hour past their scheduled departure time. "My god," remarked Elliott, "for world-record holders in the mile, they sure are bloody late."

BANNISTER: Each runner worries the others. The anxiety of being pressed and jostled increases; soon it will become too much for someone, and he will make an effort to break away from the

field. It is this controlled tension about to break down that gives
miling its great excitement. It seems to present a perfect test of
judgment, speed and stamina.

LANDY: Almost every part of the mile is tactically important —
you can never let down, never stop thinking, and you can be beaten
at almost any point. I suppose you could say it is like life.

COE: Blink and you miss a sprint. The 10,000 meters is lap after
lap of waiting. Theatrically, the mile is just the right length — beginning, middle, end, a story unfolding.

WALKER: The 800-meter record, the records in the 1,000, the
1,500, the 5,000, the relays — no one remembers them. The mile,
they remember. Only the mile.

Finally the bus headed down Park Lane, into the suburbs and then
the deep green-and-gold country meadows between London and
Oxford, the rain clouds unable to shadow the radiance within the
bus's windows or without. "Jesus!" Tony Ward, the British Athletic
Federation official who had organized this gathering, yelped every
now and then. "What a collection!" He just couldn't help it.

Mutual respect rolled up and down the aisle like marbles, rico-
cheted over seat backs, pinged off wives, as the bus chugged down
the motorway. But even among these men there was a hierarchy of
awe. Elliott, having never lost a mile or a 1,500-meter race, having
demolished the world record by the largest margin ever, 2.7 seconds, and having chucked it all at 22, had earned a special rung —
what more, they all wondered, might he have achieved? "A being,"
Jazy called him, "from another world." Ryun, having chewed 2.3 seconds off the world record on a cinder track as a skinny nineteen-
year-old — this still made them all shake their heads. Had his training, which included clusters of twenty 60-second quarter miles with
almost no time for recovery, not been so "suicidal," several milers
agreed, Ryun might well have gone down as the most prodigious
miler of all. Snell's blowtorch finishing kick was still held in awe, as
was Walker's longevity (129 sub-four-minute miles over nearly
twenty years) in an event that left Bannister bathed in sweat on the
night before each race and Elliott "incredibly, uncomfortably, powerfully, sickeningly nervous" even as he warmed up. Then, too,
there was Morceli's 3:44.39 ravaging of the record last year at age
23, entering a realm, without a rival to push him, that even these
men found almost incomprehensible.

Walker, whose career straddled track's amateur and professional eras, had to know more about Morceli. "A V-8 engine on a VW frame," he marveled. "He'll destroy so many hearts, they'll all wish they weren't born in his era. What a tough bastard." Bleary-eyed from the long flight from Auckland, Walker leaned over a seat back in the rear of the bus, trying to learn what had incubated the Algerian. Walker harbored a theory that great milers were born not on tracks but on cross-country trails, amassing heart by slogging through mud, bounding over tree roots — and yes, Morceli confirmed, that was where he, too, had begun. "What do you think of the 2,000?" Morceli wished to know, since Walker once owned that record. "I am thinking of going for that record next." The 2,000 was the son of a bitch of all races, Walker confided, the most grueling on the body.

Sir Roger Bannister, the neurologist who lives part-time in Oxford, would soon be collected and seated in the front of the bus, John Landy behind him — just as they would sit forever in track history. It was not difficult, even across the expanse of 40 years, even amid the damp fragrance of the English countryside, to catch scent of an old anguish, baked slowly to resignation. Landy, the Australian, pounding out 15- and 20-mile workouts in pursuit of the record while Bannister, the ultimate amateur, whisked off his white medical student's smock, dashed from St. Mary's Hospital in London to the tube to squeeze in thirty-minute sessions at lunch. Landy, the front-runner with the lovely economy of stride of an "Inca courier," as a writer of the time described it, hurling himself again and again at Hägg's record of 4:01.4 and at the magical number that lay just beyond it, unfurling six races of 4:03 or less between December 1952 and March 1954 and once groaning, "It's a brick wall. I shall not attempt it again." Landy bursting through the wall with a world-record 3:58 mile on June 21, 1954 . . . forty-six days *after* Bannister had smashed the four-minute barrier with his May surprise, a preemptive strike on history a full month before the summer track season was rolling. Landy finally racing Bannister to settle the question two months later in the Mile of the Century at the British Empire & Commonwealth Games in Vancouver, leading Bannister as they swept into the final bend only to see the tall, stoop-shouldered Englishman unbottle yet one more of those delirious finishes that left him all but collapsed.

"I keep rerunning that Vancouver race," said the 64-year-old

Landy, "on the theory that if I rerun it a thousand times, the results will at least once be reversed . . . but it hasn't happened yet. I've asked myself many times if I should've laid back that day, not set the pace, but I knew that would make for a slow mile and be unsatisfactory to everyone, and I didn't like the feeling of running behind someone. The trouble is, you make yourself a tangible target when you front-run, and you give yourself no tangible target. We were all the kind of men who set targets and chased them down."

Having run a faster mile than any previous human, Landy mused as the bus rolled on, had helped to transform him from a bashful loner into a man unafraid to try almost anything in life. He taught science. He helped run a cattle and sheep ranch. He worked on conservation of national parks. He became manager of the agricultural research department of the biggest chemical company in Australia, chairman of the Wool Research Corporation, technical director of Melbourne's bid for the 1996 Olympics. He wrote two books on natural history, one a bestseller, and now acts as a consultant to Australia's dairy industry and serves on committees for a hospital charity and the prestigious Melbourne Cricket Club. "The hardest thing to know, once you've taken something to the limits, as we did, is when to give something up, when to stop pushing further," Landy said. "I've tried to put a three-year limit on each of my projects. I've had a rich life."

On his lap was a sheaf of crisp photocopies, reproductions of pictures of all the world-record holders blazing around tracks in their primes. Landy straightened the stack a half-dozen times, glanced at the men around him speaking French, Swahili, Swedish and English and wondered if he dared to . . . and how it would be received if he . . .

"Michel . . . could you be so kind as to autograph these?" Landy asked. "It's not for me, of course. It's to auction them off for charity, for medical research . . . Good on ya . . . All for charity . . . wonderful . . . perfect."

ELLIOTT: Why did I run? I ran at first to remorselessly beat everyone I possibly could.

RYUN: I ran to get a letter jacket, a girlfriend. I ran because I was cut from the basketball and baseball teams. I ran to be accepted, to be part of a group.

JAZY: I ran so I would not have to fight the war in Algeria.

SNELL: I ran for recognition.

COE: I ran because I was meant to run.

LANDY: I loved to run because, in running, one's effort could be pinned down and quantified precisely.

IBBOTSON: I ran to prove to my father that I was better than my brother.

ELLIOTT: I ran later to prove that my spirit was the master of my body.

MORCELI: I run to be known as the greatest runner, the greatest of all time. I could not eat or sleep for a week after I lost in the [1992] Olympics. I have to win or die.

The bus pulled up to the Iffley Road track, where a battery of cameras four dozen strong awaited the milers. Bannister's eyes rose to the white flag with the red cross, hoisted up the pole atop St. John the Evangelist Church just for this occasion — the same flag he studied forty years ago to decide if the wind was telling him *no*. The starting pistol that commenced that race was laid in his hand, and the woman who fed him lunch that afternoon now stood at his side: Oh, do the Brits know how to do history. This was a celebration of the mile, not of himself, Bannister kept reminding everyone, but so much of the mile's magical dust was kicked up by Sir Roger's spikes on that long-ago day that it is no longer possible to sift one from the other.

The cinder track was gone, replaced in 1976 by a synthetic surface. Bannister, limping slightly from the car accident nineteen years ago that damaged an ankle and ended his weekend jogging, walked with Morceli across the last forty feet before the finish line, and the Algerian, perhaps emboldened by the rare air he was drawing in, confided to reporters that he planned to make attempts at records this year in the 800, 1,000, 1,500 and 5,000 meters as well as the mile and two miles. "You have to attempt this when you are young enough," he said softly, "and not let the chance go by."

It was Morceli, always with the shy grin, the bowed head — always showing a deference that few any longer expect from the young — whose presence most gratified his elders. But as sweet as Morceli was, Sir Roger couldn't help himself. His crusading cry as a runner had been that the athlete was just a sliver of the whole man, and the first chance he had, as he and Morceli posed side by side for photographs the day before, the doctor asked the professional runner, "Do you have any plans for after you retire? What will you do when you are thirty-five?"

"I don't know," said Morceli, all smiles and shrugs. "I have no plans."

"Will you be involved in some kind of coaching?"

"Probably, yes," said Morceli, grateful for the help. "Some kind of coaching."

In the press box above the Iffley Road track, someone asked Cram — the 32-year-old who lowered the record to 3:46.32 in 1985 and recently launched his comeback from a chronic calf injury — what he and the other record holders shared. Cram thought before he spoke, for this forum was no place for pikers. At the previous day's press conference, playing toss-and-catch with the question of how much faster a human being might run a mile, the neurologist Bannister discussed the "genetic variants" that athletes from China and India would bring to the chase, the physiologist Snell discoursed on the body's "ability to transfer oxygen across lung membrane," the Puma Australia managing director Elliott noted that the "interface between the mind and the spirit and the body" was a facet of human potential so little tapped that astonishing improvements might yet be made, and the *International Herald Tribune* writer Ian Thomsen concluded that there was more intelligence in that one group than in all of the football locker rooms in America.

"Lineage," Cram finally said. "The men here today are part of a unique lineage." A lineage cleaner, perhaps, than any other devised by mankind, neater certainly than that of kings, who were continually muddying things by fathering imbeciles or bedding with the barren, or that of heavyweights, who in the twilights of their careers were prone to pass their crowns to bums. There were no split decisions to be argued or myopic judging to be rued. Switzerland's finest watches kept score, and no man could claim the throne until he had surpassed the performance of his predecessor *on his predecessor's best day.*

Next stop for the pilgrims was Vincents Club, the fabled enclave where Oxford athletes have drunk and debated for more than a hundred years, where former Australian prime minister Robert Hawke set the world record for downing a yard of ale, in sixteen seconds, where Sir Roger himself was president during his college days and where some of the nicks in the photograph-covered walls are attributed to the celebration of his record mile. Bannister, his eloquence ever ready to combust, delivered a speech. A room jammed with old and new Oxford sportsmen toasted him with champagne and applause, and the Tanzanian army captain, Bayi, juggling his one-year-old and his glass, watched with wonder and a little sadness. "Other countries honor their history so much more than mine does," he said. "In Tanzania I am no one. Maybe one day people will understand. That will be maybe when I die."

In a private dining room awaiting the milers at the nearby Randolph Hotel, the commemorative menus lying upon the tables caught John Walker's eye. Plucking one, the New Zealand rancher began moving quietly from table to table, asking each of the record holders to grace the menu with his signature. Even with his three-inch pinch of midsection, Walker still radiated the air of a rugby player over a pint of black and tan. Of all the milers he still seemed the readiest to go out on the sidewalk and outrun anyone who dared to try him. If Walker was saying, "Sorry, Roger, but can I bother you for an autograph? . . . Sorry, Herb, but . . . ," then who, in this most exclusive of clubs, could feign to be above it?

And so the free-for-all began in earnest, the greats bustling from table to table to collect each other's scribble before the potatoes and vegetables were ladled, Sir Roger begging to bother Morceli, Morceli begging to bother Elliott, and on and on and on.

"John," said Bayi, blinking at Walker, "we've never done this before."

"This is a once-in-a-lifetime event, Filbert," said John.

"Yes," said Filbert. "Once in a lifetime." And he peered down at his page full of scrawl, racking his brain to figure out whom he had missed.

Lunch concluded, the milers splintered for an hour. Walker, Cram, Landy and Andersson took a guided tour of a few Oxford colleges; the Ryun family went to explore the old haunts of the famous Christian writer C. S. Lewis; and Elliott wandered through the bookstores in search of *Siddhartha*, the Hermann Hesse novel of a man's spiritual journey. At 56, Elliott was circling back, ready to complete the quest he had begun as a runner.

When Elliott was eighteen, sitting in the stands during the 1956 Melbourne Olympics, his hunger to run had been ignited by the spectacle that unfolded in the 10,000 meters. Vladimir Kuts, a Soviet runner who had tossed incendiary bombs at the German tanks during the defense of Stalingrad, kept surging away from

England's Gordon Pirie, then slowing enough to engage Pirie's monstrous fighting instincts, then surging away again. "It was like watching a cat play with a half-dead mouse," recalled Elliott. "Kuts utterly steamrollered Pirie. It appealed to the basic, animal part of me, the part that wanted to grind people to dust. That's what I ran for at first. But then I realized the battle wasn't against others. It was against myself. It was in defeating my own weaknesses, in demonstrating that my spirit could master my body. It's why billions of people watch people run in circles or kick a bag of leather, isn't it? It's for those moments when we realize we're not just watching bodies, when human spirit is revealed."

Kindled by Kuts, Elliott drove to Porsea, Australia, to engage the counsel of a white-haired fanatic named Percy Cerutty, who ranted of Gandhi, Christ and Tennyson, who raised drudgery to philosophy and turned a footrace into a test not of strategy or athletic skill but of human character. He had Elliott racing up and down an eighty-foot sand dune, hoisting barbells made from rusting railroad track, reading H. G. Wells's 1,200-page *Outline of History* in his camp bunkhouse at night. "He challenged my totality," said Elliott. "I came to realize that spirit, as much as or more than physical conditioning, had to be stored up before a race. I would avoid running on tracks because tracks were spiritually depleting. I never studied my opponents — they were an irrelevancy to me. Poetry, music, forests, ocean, solitude — they were what developed enormous spiritual strength. How do the modern professional runners today find that, when most everything they do would seem to deplete that simplicity, that spirituality? I'd like to talk to Morceli about that this week.

"Once I had satisfied myself in that question — that my spirit *could* dominate my body — there was no real great reason to continue. People still ask me if I made a mistake in quitting so young, but they have it all wrong. To keep having to do more, to keep being dissatisfied, what kind of man would that be? He might be called a brute."

He retired, graduated from Cambridge, grew apart from Cerutty — what role could such a Svengali play in the life of a man trying to raise six children, to climb the ladder in marketing with the Shell chemical company and then in the management of Puma in Australia? "Service to your job, your family, that's all part of human experience," Elliott said, "but my life was a spiritual desert until a couple of years ago." This time it was a Catholic priest who reawakened him with tales of life in an ashram in India, and Elliott quickly sensed that his old quest had been abandoned in its infancy, that the ultimate aim of spirituality is not so much to dominate the body as to learn to let it go. So he traveled to an ashram in India last year. Now every morning at 5:30, he awakens and reads passages from the Upanishads or the Bhagavadgita, ancient Hindu treatises on the struggle for purity and wisdom, and he meditates and tries to let all the motion and memos and meetings melt away.

Just two miles from Cerutty's old oceanside camp, Elliott bought a house on the beach, and each time he walks or jogs past the cemetery where the old prophet lies at rest, he stops and acknowledges what the old man did for his life. "We've grown back together," Elliott said. "I suspect I know what I'll do with my retirement. It won't be a rest. It'll be an adventure. The object would be to totally remove yourself from body and mind, from ego. To think I could ever do that would require total arrogance, but to do it would take total humility. Yes, kind of like . . ."

BANNISTER: I have always said that man will run the mile in 3:30 — given the human body constituted as it is, with perfect training and perfect facilities, the world remaining relatively peaceful and without too many wars, famines and disasters.

SNELL: I think I've seen the fastest miler ever. I think Morceli is the guy.

MORCELI: I think I can take another two or three seconds off of it.

COE: If you start thinking there's a limit, there is one. It's almost self-defeating. It's going to keep tumbling down.

CRAM: It won't come from training harder. It won't come from science or new techniques or new surfaces. We've exhausted those possibilities. But every ten or twenty years, the freak human being will come along. That's what will keep lowering the record.

ELLIOTT: I think I'm the only dreamer. Human beings have a huge reservoir of strength we've never tapped — we've only just begun to ply around its edges. I think there's a quantum leap there to be made. We still overprotect ourselves. It would be very unintelligent to run yourself to death . . . but I'm sure we can go a lot closer to it.

"I feel silly," said Morceli. "I feel crazy." The autograph frenzy at the Randolph Hotel had achieved several things. Now all of the record holders knew one another. Now all of them had felt silly and crazy in front of each other. There was not so much to protect. They had all stepped into each other's shade.

The chatter grew louder, the quips began to fly. "Poor Morceli!" yipped Ibbotson. "He's got withdrawal symptoms — he hasn't run in two hours!"

"I'm taken aback," said Snell. "Whenever I saw Herb Elliott before, all I ever thought of was raw aggression, this ruthless killer instinct. He's so jovial now. He's actually quite *gregarious!*"

In Snell's hands, as the bus ferried the milers back to London, was a book with yellow pages and a cover about to disintegrate. It was a seventeenth-birthday gift from his parents, the first athletic book he ever received: Roger Bannister's autobiography, *The Four Minute Mile*. Now its opening page was covered with signatures.

The musty pages smelled of memories, of an old and quiet desperation for success, of a shy, likable, big-eared, toothy-grinned boy crushed by his father's disappointment in him. The book had been given to him in the midst of two straight years in which he had failed in boarding school, smashing the teenager's chances of entering New Zealand's rigid university system, destroying his father's plan that Peter, just like Peter's dad and older brother, would become an engineer. Running became Peter's salvation. He took the 800-meter gold medal as a long shot at the Rome Olympics in 1960, eclipsed Elliott's mile record on a grass track in New Zealand in '62 and won both the 1,500- and 800-meter gold medals at the Tokyo Games in '64.

Snell had planned to run just one more year after that, to use running as a vehicle to see the world. But as psychological fuel, travel ranked nowhere near in octane to his old petrol, the need for self-esteem. At age 26 he lost nine consecutive races in less than two months and quit, but there was one reward. He found his calling that summer, becoming fascinated by the gadgets and line of inquiry of San Diego State exercise physiologists whom he permitted to run tests on him. It took years, but he slowly screwed up the courage to junk his job in promotions for a cigarette company, sell his house, leave New Zealand and stake every cent he owned on three years of study at the University of California, Davis ("I could fail quietly there," he explained), and then four more, thanks to prize money he won in Superstars competitions in the 1970s, at Washington State. His father — who suffered a stroke during Peter's last year in high school, became mute and died in '62 —

would never live to see his son's academic redemption. Today Snell, fifty-five, is an assistant professor doing research in exercise physiology at the University of Texas Southwestern Medical Center in Dallas.

"There was such pressure on an athlete then to be a complete man," Snell said. "'When are you going to do something of substance?' — I got a lot of that. Now everything's changed. It's quite respectable to be just a runner. But yet, the world record did liberate me in a way. My thrust is enjoying my work now, not publishing papers or collecting more diplomas, as many of my peers do. If I hadn't proven in running that I was the best in the world, I'd be chasing that forever in academics."

A few feet away, tiny Cuthbert Bayi was emitting ear-curdling shrieks, and Walker was peering again at the odd autograph he had received from Ryun. Above his name Ryun had written "Go with God" and beneath it "John" and the numbers "3:3–8." Other runners had written their world-record mile times beneath their names, but Ryun's figure was too fast for any twentieth-century mile; could it be, Walker wondered, Ryun's best time in the 1,500? No, it was a passage from the Gospel According to John in which Jesus declares, "Except a man be born again, he cannot see the kingdom of God."

Several seats away sat Ryun, his odd haunted look gone. He was locked in conversation with Cram, taking up the Englishman's offer to host Ryun's family at Cram's home in a week or two, agreeing how fortunate Cram was to have had countrymen Coe and Ovett drawing everyone's eyes during his years of ripening and how unlucky Ryun was to have assumed the yoke of America's hopes as a teen. Ryun is a little thicker now and wears hearing aids in both ears to correct a 50 percent hearing loss he suffered as a child, but the light in his eyes makes him more handsome than ever. His job, which takes him to schools for the hearing-impaired across the U.S. as a representative of a hearing-aid firm named Resound, allows him to appear in road races all over the country and also to tell the tale of his religious conversion before Christian groups.

Having twice set world records by age twenty, Ryun had seen his life swirl ever downward after he lost the 1,500 to Kip Keino in the high-altitude 1968 Olympics in Mexico City. He quit in the middle of several races, was savaged by the U.S. press, stopped running altogether and finally regathered himself for atonement at the '72 Munich Games. His times, as he prepared, remained erratic, the yoke yet too heavy, the joy still not there.

"I'll never forget that day after he ran a 4:19 mile and finished last in Los Angeles in the spring of '72," said his wife, Anne. "He walked out of the stadium, slammed his spikes against a tree and started screaming. I'd never seen such rage in Jim."

Brought up by a strict father in a fundamentalist Christian church, forbidden to attend dances or movies, Ryun had grown into a young man so bound by duty to meet others' expectations that each sigh of disappointment from the world after each race in which he failed to rebreak the world record had *crushed* him. "And then," he said, "in May of 1972, I accepted Jesus Christ as my savior, and for the first time in my life I had the feeling that God loved me because of *me*, not because of my accomplishments. I felt elated. At the Olympic trials I felt so light that I threw up my arms ten yards before the finish and had to throw them up again! Then I went to Toronto, and on a track that was like asphalt, with the closest runner eighteen seconds behind me, I ran a 3:52 mile — the third-fastest mile ever. A new dimension inside of me was being tapped. For the first time I was relaxed. Everything was right. And then, in the prelim in Munich, I was tripped, and the official [on the appeals committee] who could've reinstated me for the final refused to, and that was it. I had to retire from amateur running then to work and raise my family."

Ryun needed years to overcome his bitterness, to forgive the official; he knew that he had done so only when the man's image flashed up on the big screen as Ryun sat in the stands during the 1984 Olympics, and he felt . . . nothing. "I was released," he said.

"Now he runs to spread the word of Christ," said Anne. "He has found a peace that he never felt when he was breaking world records."

ELLIOTT: When I wanted to quit in training, I used to visualize a competitor on my shoulder. And I'd think, I'd rather die than let this person beat me.

IBBOTSON: I used to picture a tall shandy. That's beer and lemonade, in case you don't know.

SNELL: I used to picture handicapped people, people with crutches and wheelchairs, and ask myself, What right do you have to complain about this pain?

JAZY: I would picture Gordon Pirie after Vladimir Kuts had destroyed him in the 10,000 meters of the 1956 Olympics and tell myself to keep going so that would never happen to me.

BAYI: I'd keep saying to myself, Break the wall. . . . There is no wall. . . . The wall is in your mind.

WALKER: A little ways before the turnoff to the road I lived on, there was a sign that said 1,500 METERS. It was a three-lane highway, and each time I drove it, I'd pull into the middle lane with about 800 meters left and start passing everyone. Then with 400 to go, I'd pull to the outside lane and beat the crap out of my car. That's the image I kept using. Me pulling out in that car and then flying past everyone.

"Milers!"

"Just a minute! Got to sign all these for Derek," chirped Cram, scribbling madly.

"And vice versa!" panted Ibbotson, signing a batch for Cram. "Where's Snell? Oh, if I could only get Stevie to sign . . . I mean Peter."

"Milers, *please!*"

"Filbert, sign these."

"Herb, could you . . ."

"That's it. Good on ya, mate."

"All for charity!"

"*Milers!*" wailed the organizer of the affair, Tony Ward. In just over an hour, 730 people in formal attire would begin entering the Great Room at the Grosvenor House for the gala dinner, and Ward needed to brief the record holders on the evening's schedule of events. But now the autograph seeking had become a raging fever. Now all the milers had stacks of the commemorative dinner programs to exchange and sign.

Ibbotson had spent the previous evening with a straight-edge and twelve pieces of paper, etching fourteen rectangles on each page, with each record holder's name and time inside a rectangle to be autographed. "One complete set for each of my children, my grandchildren, my mother-in-law, father-in-law . . ."

Ward threw up his arms. "My god," he said, "they're like schoolchildren!"

Coe, finally freed from his duties as a second-year member of the British Parliament, had joined the group — nobody had his signature yet! With the look in his eyes of a startled deer, he sagged into a chair as his brothers in the club fell upon him, and then he caught the infection too. Sydney Wooderson of England, the world's oldest living mile-record holder (4:06.4 in 1937), three months shy of 80, walked ever so slowly into the room, bringing the milers' ranks to fourteen. "I just can't believe how old I am," Wooderson said, shaking his head. "I just can't believe it." Elliott and Ryun went off to a quiet corner to discuss God.

Finally, after the clan had posed for the official photograph and laid plans for regathering later in the night to cross-sign personal copies of the photo as well, they plunged into the cocktail-sipping crowd. John Walker sighed. "Just watch what's going to happen," he said. "Seven hundred and thirty sons of bitches trying to get our autographs."

Yes, it was that, but mostly it was 730 people laughing, cheering, *glowing*. The big screen showed old footage of the milers breaking and rebreaking the record, one after the other, somehow building in the Great Room a cumulative power, a feeling that there was nothing *not* possible for humanity as long as it kept producing individuals like the fourteen being honored. "Everywhere I looked all night," said Coe, "all I saw were people wearing broad grins. It was like a huge family coming together. It was the greatest sports gathering I have ever been to."

Everyone hushed when it was Bannister's turn to speak. "Old men, they say, forget," said Sir Roger. "It's true we forget the pain and the fatigue and lashing yourself to try harder next time and next, illness and injury, real and perhaps sometimes imagined, the castigations of the press and coaches — all these fade away, because memory is kind. We remember the good times, the sun on our backs, running through the beauty of the countryside, running thousands and thousands of miles. We remember laughter and friends. For us, no matter what life may bring, whatever subsequent shadows there may be, no one can strip us of these memories."

In chronological order of their achievements, each to a standing ovation, the record holders walked to the stage and shook the hands of those who had preceded them, who had pushed them to discover something wondrous in themselves. Fourteen men who had split off from the road, gone off on solitary missions, now part of a team.

"Total kinship," said Elliott. "That's what I felt up there."

"The greatest night of my life," said Morceli.

"These men could show today's athletes where sports fit into a round life," said Cram.

"The bond among us," summed up Coe, "is that which Lady Macbeth describes as a sickness: ambition, the pursuit of excellence. But you had this feeling that these were men very much at peace with themselves. That each of us realized that what we had done was neither greater nor lesser than what had come before us or after us, that we were all part of a human progression."

They rose together for one last ovation beneath the lights, in the brilliance of the shade.

J. A. ADANDE

A Furor Follows in Deion's Steps

FROM THE WASHINGTON POST

IT USED TO BE the end zone was just that. A place on the football field that marked the culmination of a successful play or drive, resulting in six points.

Now, however, it's where the action begins, a 10-by-53-yard stage for signature high-stepping dances; an arms-wide appeal to the crowd for applause; and, finally, the removal of the helmet and, for some, the ultimate bow.

It could be called the Deionization of sports, in reference to the prototype, Deion Sanders — the highly successful and flamboyant cornerback for the San Francisco 49ers, the two-sport star whose unique, controversial way of drawing attention to himself also distinguishes him when he plays outfield for the Cincinnati Reds.

Instead of being celebrated for succeeding in two professional sports, Sanders is vilified in some circles, largely because of the self-celebration that accompanies many of his touchdowns. A defensive back and kick returner, Sanders isn't content to merely run into the end zone; his scores are more of a Broadway production. There's an exaggerated, elongated stride, his right hand rising to the side of his helmet as he sashays down the field. Once in the end zone, as if that didn't foster enough consternation in opponents, Sanders punctuates the effort with a dance step that's part soft shoe and part Irish jig.

Though Sanders is not the first to take his act to the end zone, he is the star of that stage to the newest generation of football fans. To some, the end zone dances, the chest thumping and the trash talking are an entertaining part of the game, a harmless form of self-expression. If fans don't complain about players kneeling in the end zone and praying after scoring, what's the big deal about what Deion and his followers do?

But to many fans, showboating and taunting on the athletic field are symbols of declining sportsmanship and, to some extent, a breakdown in society's morals, a nightly portrait of the "me" generation in cleats.

Either way, many college and high school athletes throughout the country have seen it — each Sunday on television and on nightly highlight shows — and seized it for themselves, to the displeasure of many traditional coaches, fans and commentators. To many people, sports is a bastion of order in society, of tradition and rules.

And for some, it's not just a coincidence that the rise in this high-profile styling — in football, basketball and baseball — has coincided with the greater numbers and higher profile of African-Americans in these three team sports. Nor is it a surprise that some of the negative reaction to Sanders is as loud as past railings against, to name a few, flamboyant former heavyweight champion Muhammad Ali, baseball Hall of Famer Reggie Jackson and basketball great Wilt Chamberlain, as well as new Washington Bullet Chris Webber and his "Fab Five" teammates when they were playing basketball at the University of Michigan.

Nelson George, whose book *Elevating the Game* examined how African-Americans transformed the game of basketball, said, "It's the showmanship, it's in your face, it's [expletive] you . . . it's all of that. It's a black male thing that comes right out of the street, schoolyard ball, intimidation. It comes from the same root.

"All of this is stuff that's been in basketball for a while. It's just getting into football."

When Sanders faced the Atlanta Falcons last month and made his sideline-prancing, end-zone-dancing return to his self-proclaimed "house" — the Georgia Dome, where he played football for the Falcons last year — Harold Lusk was watching. Six days later, Lusk, a defensive back at Utah, still had Sanders on his mind as he prepared to face Colorado State in a game matching the two best teams in the Western Athletic Conference.

"Before the game, I said if I do get an interception and get a touchdown, I'm going to do a Deion," Lusk said. "That's what really motivated me."

Sure enough, Lusk intercepted a pass and returned it 100 yards for the game-clinching touchdown, high-stepping the last 10 yards into the end zone. When they showed the highlights on ESPN, the announcer couldn't help but note the similarity to Sanders.

"That's my idol," Lusk said.

"We're seeing more and more of it all the time," said Billy Nunnally, the commissioner of Northern Virginia high school football officials. "We've even had it down at the junior varsity level a couple of times this season already."

So who's setting the standard?

"They all get it from the pros," Florida State coach Bobby Bowden said.

More specifically, from Sanders.

"I like his style," Auburn safety Brian Robinson said. "That guy is very confident. As long as he gets it done, no matter what he does, you can't help but applaud him. He adds some flair to the game. He's having fun."

The Down Side

But ABC television commentator Dick Vermeil, a former coach for the Philadelphia Eagles and UCLA, is a frequent critic of such on-field behavior. "I don't think it's good," he said. "Football is the ultimate team sport. I think any kind of a show of exuberance should be a collective thing rather than an individual thing. The problem I have is nowadays kids have it programmed."

Sanders doesn't claim to be an innovator or even the reason for this resurgence in dancing among younger players.

"They've always been doing that," Sanders said. "That's where I got that stuff from, man. When I was in pee-wee football, I used to see Billy 'White Shoes' Johnson. . . . I can show you tapes when I was six, seven years old and I was high-stepping, strutting, doing that type of stuff. That's not new to me. I got that from older generations, and that's what kids do now."

Johnson might have been the best on-field dancer ever to wear cleats when he performed for the Houston Oilers and Falcons in the 1970s and 1980s, and Elmo Wright was doing end-zone dances while playing wide receiver for the Kansas City Chiefs in the early 1970s. Lynn Swann, the graceful Pittsburgh Steeler in their Super Bowl years of the late '70s, used to celebrate his touchdowns with hand-slapping routines with fellow wide receiver John Stallworth. But they seem like basic square-dance moves compared to the elaborate displays Swann sees in his job as a sideline reporter for ABC-TV.

"The most John and I ever did, we'd just give each other high-fives," Swann said. "That's it. There wasn't so much a celebration as much as a group of wide receivers saying, 'We're getting it done.' I don't think it's bad if someone scores a touchdown and they're exuberant and they celebrate, especially if it's spontaneous. But the choreographed celebrations that some guys are doing, I personally don't care for it."

Swann's outbursts of emotion were more of a shared event. Today, some players have literally run out of the arms of teammates to bask alone in the limelight.

"I don't like it," said Bowden, who coached Sanders at Florida State. "As soon as a kid makes a play, he jumps out by himself where the camera gets him. Then that helmet comes off. Then he wiggles or whatever." Added Vermeil, "I think the coaches ignored it. All of a sudden it caught up with them. Now they've recognized that it's getting out of hand."

What the Rules Say

There is a thin line between showing off and showing up an opponent, one that the game's rulemakers have struggled to define and enforce with consistency at all levels of competition. In 1984, after the growing number of dances, dunking of footballs over the cross-bars of goalposts, and group high-fives popularized by the Washington Redskins' "Fun Bunch," the National Football League enacted rules restricting the celebrations, making them punishable by a 15-yard penalty. But the blander brand of football led to critics calling the NFL the No Fun League. In 1991, Commissioner Paul Tagliabue reworked the rule, keeping the ban on direct taunting but telling the officials not to judge how much celebrating was too much. That opened a door for players such as Sanders to high-step through.

Defenders of this posturing said it was just the African-American's flamboyant nature, an aspect of the black aesthetic. To Temple University basketball coach John Chaney, who is black, it is "just bad manners."

Once, when he was a guest on a radio talk show, "some black lady called in and said she thought it was ethnic, that it was a part of our culture," Chaney said. "I said, 'Ma'am, no one has a license — black or white — on bad manners.' Here was a grown woman, a black woman, who thought that it was right for black youngsters to taunt others."

"Each era dictates its own style," Nelson George said. "But the brothers [black males] have always used sports as a form of self-expression."

Swann discounts the racial aspect. "I don't see it as being strictly an African-American thing," he said. "I think it's a sports thing."

Not every black athlete is compelled to show the world his feelings. For every Deion there is a Jerry Rice, Sanders's 49ers teammate, the perennial All-Pro wide receiver who has responded in the same low-key manner after nearly every one of his NFL-record 136 touchdowns. And if any major college player has a reason to boast this season it would be Rashaan Salaam, the Colorado running back and Heisman Trophy Award candidate who is the nation's leader in rushing and scoring. But Salaam disdains that behavior. "I don't like to do it," he said. "It distracts me from my game."

Certainly African-Americans are not the only ones who showboat. Take Brice Doman, a white wide receiver at Brigham Young University. Doman and his former roommate, Rich Israelson, are devotees of Sega Genesis video games and love to play John Madden's signature football game. In that game, players on the screen celebrate touchdowns by raising one hand, placing the other hand on their waist, shaking their hips, switching hands, and then doing it again.

Doman said recently that Israelson told him, "On your first touchdown, you've got to do the Sega dance."

"I told him I would," Doman said.

So after Doman caught a touchdown pass against Texas El Paso on October 22 to tie the score at 14, up went the hands and back and forth went the hips — life imitating video game imitating life.

Except for one difference. "They gave us a 15-yard penalty," BYU coach LaVell Edwards said. "We were already in a tight game. That wasn't very smart."

In football, if there is one group of players that is associated with the new, brash style, it's from the state of Florida. The football-rich state produces enough talent to stock three top 10 Division I-A in-state college programs (Florida, Florida State, and Miami) and still provide key players for schools such as Notre Dame and Michigan. A style built up in high school rivalries and summer games at local parks has made its mark on the way the colleges play football.

Miami linebacker Ray Lewis said, "Florida football is about showboating, hard hitting, talking trash, playing the best athletes against the best athletes."

The Hurricanes became notorious for their antics, spotlighted in their 46–3 rout of Texas in the 1991 Cotton Bowl, in which they were penalized sixteen times for 202 yards.

"It got pretty rowdy," said David Parry, the Big Ten Conference's supervisor of officials. "That seemed to really send a message to the rulemakers."

"The thing I don't like is all this chest-bumping," Edwards said. "It almost becomes a game of one-upmanship."

Nearly a decade after the NFL's initial "No Fun" rules went into effect, the National Collegiate Athletic Association enacted excessive celebration rules. The NCAA has been enforcing taunting and baiting rules for basketball since 1992 — some think as a direct result of the Fab Five. Officials said it was to prevent verbal exchanges from escalating into fights — and will make the new rules a major emphasis this season.

The National Federation of High School Sports has given referees explicit instructions to penalize taunting and excessive celebration.

The NCAA Presidents Commission formed a committee that held a two-day meeting in Boston last month and met with representatives from the four major professional sports. The members also heard a presentation from Dan Beebe, the commissioner of the Ohio Valley Conference.

That league has taken what might be college sports' boldest stance yet on behavior, composing a three-page statement on conduct in all sports and addressing the decorum of players, coaches, officials, administrators, cheerleaders, and fans. The new orders went into effect this school year, and game officials are under orders to follow the guidelines closely and enforce them without giving warnings.

The results, according to Beebe, are a greater number of unsportsmanlike conduct calls but fewer altercations. "What we've noticed is the fact that the players are getting up and walking away from stuff," Beebe said.

Some coaches allow the show to go on because it's what the players want — and it helps in the recruiting of some players. "When I played high school, our coach didn't permit all that jawing and stuff," Miami defensive lineman Warren Sapp said. Miami coach Dennis Erickson is "just like one of the guys. He's straightforward. He says, 'I don't mind you having fun, but know where to take it. Don't get that stupid penalty.' . . . He knows it's a game of enthusiasm."

Which is why Georgetown basketball coach John Thompson thinks the games are becoming overregulated. "We don't need to lose sight of the fact that it's recreation," Thompson said. "If a kid can't celebrate on the court and can't enjoy himself, he ought not to play and we ought not to call it recreation.

"The most hypocritical thing about college athletics and pro athletics is they lead in with hype and promos having trash talking, and then they are ready to fine people and [call technical fouls] on people and put them out of the game."

As BYU's Doman said: "I think you're getting a little bit too heavily regulated when you can't celebrate after scoring a touchdown."

One more thing about Doman: "I'm a huge Deion Sanders fan."

DAVE ANDERSON

Omaha Beach Has a Golf Course Now

FROM THE NEW YORK TIMES

ON A SHORT PIER in Port-en-Bessin, France, on a soft summer afternoon, rock music was thumping in a cabaret. Voices sang and laughed. The beach itself was empty and silent.

Above the craggy cliffs of Normandy, beyond the sixth green of the sea nine at the Omaha Beach Golf Club, gray steps dropped into what seemed to be a narrow ditch in the grass and wild flowers. Suddenly that ditch expanded into an abandoned Nazi bunker, its concrete cool and clammy, with the same spooky view of the English Channel that it had fifty years ago tomorrow when D-Day dawned.

But to some, Omaha Beach is a golf course now.

Every year thousands of duffers, including many returning American veterans, play the three nines of the hilly farmland course that opened in 1986. This week a European PGA event, the D-Day Seniors Open, will be staged there. Touring pros will be putting on the sixth green near that abandoned concrete bunker above the sand that stretches across the Normandy beach where the Allies landed on June 6, 1944.

"The officers and men of the 1st U.S. Infantry Division," proclaims the "1" memorial on the slope above the tidal pools in the sand at the western end of Omaha Beach, "who were killed in this period (6 June 1944–24 July 1944) while fighting for the liberty of the world."

In small worn and weathered white lettering, the names of the dead, from Acosta to Zukowski, are listed on the marble memorial. In several neat grassy cemeteries nearby, long rows of white crosses and Jewish stars mourn the total of 117,153 soldiers buried there: 39,187 members of the Allied forces (including 13,796 Americans) and 77,966 Germans.

In 1944, the St. Louis Browns would win their only American League pennant but lose a trolley-car World Series to the Cardinals. The Giants would lose pro football's championship game to the Green Bay Packers, 14–7. Maurice Richard had led the Montreal Canadiens to the Stanley Cup in April but the National Basketball Association had yet to be formed.

Of all the American athletes in service who were known then or in later years, not many were involved in the D-Day invasion.

Ben Schwartzwalder, soon to be the Syracuse football coach but then a major in the 82nd Airborne Division, parachuted into France several miles away from his target. For a week, he and his troops hid from the Nazis before being reunited with the Allied forces.

"I never thought I'd see you alive," the division commander, Major General Matthew B. Ridgway, would tell Schwartzwalder later.

In a 36-foot L.C.S.S. rocket boat a few hundred yards off Omaha Beach, a 19-year-old navy seaman first class, Lawrence Berra, known only to his St. Louis pals as Yogi, peered at the Nazi bunkers and searched the sky for Nazi planes. The year before, he had batted .253 with seven homers in the Class B Piedmont League for the Norfolk (Virginia) Tars of the Yankee farm system.

"We went out from England the day before," he recalled, "but they called it off. Bad weather. June 6 we had to go. The tide was about to change."

In the navy, L.C.S.S. stood for Landing Craft, Support Small, but its five sailors and their commanding officer, Ensign Holmes, had another name for it.

"To us it was Landing Craft, Suicide Squad," Berra said. "We went in before the army. We fired our rockets, a five-inch shell. Then the army hit the beach. The water was rough. When the shooting started, it looked like Fourth of July fireworks. I can still hear Ensign Holmes yelling, 'Get your head in.'"

While dead bodies floated in the water nearby, Berra and his shipmates had been ordered to shoot at any planes below the clouds.

"We shot down one plane we thought was German, but it was one of ours," he remembered. "The pilot lived. After he got fished out of the water, he really cussed us out."

Three weeks later, a transport took Berra to Italy, southern France, and Africa before he returned to New London, Connecticut.

"I told 'em I didn't volunteer for submarine duty," he said, remembering his Connecticut posting with a laugh. "They wanted me to play baseball there."

Also offshore on D-Day was Lew Jenkins, the skinny puncher who had won the world lightweight championship in 1940 by knocking out Lou Ambers in the third round at Madison Square Garden. He retained the title with a second-round knockout of Pete Lello before losing it to Sammy Angott in a 15-round decision less than two weeks after Pearl Harbor.

Jenkins, whose life story Hollywood has somehow ignored, would earn a Silver Star as a legendary army sergeant in Korea, but on D-Day he was aboard a Coast Guard ship ferrying British troops to Normandy.

"When they told us we were takin' the British in, my heart wasn't in it," he told Bill Heinz, then a *New York Sun* war correspondent. "You know where my heart was? My heart was with the First Division here. I wanted to be with them I knew. Then I saw the Limeys get killed, and then I liked them, too."

Those British soldiers died in the sand not far from that abandoned concrete Nazi bunker perched in the cliffs overlooking the English Channel beyond the sixth green of the sea nine at the Omaha Beach Golf Club.

Not far from the rock music thumping now in a cabaret on a short pier in Port-en-Bessin on a soft summer afternoon. Not far from the voices singing and laughing. Not far from the beach that was empty and silent.

TOM JUNOD

Montana Fading Out

FROM GQ

I HEARD THAT Joe Montana was traveling to Brunei at the behest of the royal family, and I had an awful dream. I dreamed that Joe stood alone on desert sands in his helmet and shoulder pads and jersey, surrounded, at great distance, by oil barons in their Mercedeses and Rolls-Royces. And one by one, the barons got out of their cars, trudged up to Joe and demanded "Do me like you did Dwight Clark." And Joe couldn't say no, because the barons were paying extravagantly for his time, and so again and again, until day passed into night and the only lights were the headlamps of luxury automobiles, Joe was compelled to roll right, the way he did in his first NFC championship game against the Dallas Cowboys, and lob a high, lumpy spiral to leaping oilmen . . . who, encumbered by their robes and lack of experience, dropped every pass and became humiliated and wound up abandoning Joe to the winds that scour the desert clean at night.

Never mind that I had no idea where the hell Brunei was and that the next morning, when I looked at a map, I saw that it's in the South Pacific, on the island of Borneo, and what I dreamed was desert is in fact occupied by rain forest. The dream spooked me. It carried the weight of omen, and when I finally met Joe, I asked him what he'd done there. He had gone with Herschel Walker, he said. He had stayed at the sultan's palace. He had played a lot of golf and had made a lot of money. He had been paid to throw the football to the sultan's nephew and to teach the nephew's children how to play the American game. The nephew had purchased equipment for the occasion, and he wanted Joe to suit up. *Suit up?* Well, sure —

Joe was a football player, and so here, in the oil-rich Islamic sultan-
ate of Brunei, Abode of Peace . . . here, across oceans, time zones,
languages, religions, cultures . . . what was waiting for him was shoulder pads and gleaming black helmets . . . football stuff. C'mon, Joe
— suit up! But Joe told the sultan's nephew that by the terms of his
contract with the Kansas City Chiefs he was forbidden to wear the
uniform of another team, any other team — it was a fib, but it
worked — and so Joe and Herschel played in shorts and T-shirts,
while members of Brunei's royal family, augmented by the strong-
men of the state security force, ran around in the brand-new helmets and shoulder pads.

I was frightened by the force of premonition. Yes, I know I should
have been pleased for Joe; after all, not everyone can make a killing
teaching monarchs how to throw a spiral. Still, the idea of Joe, Joe
Montana, in a role of lucrative servitude . . . especially after that
dream — well, it was unseemly. It was grotesque. It was the Mick
drying out at Betty Ford, Ted Williams hawking his wares on QVC,
Joe Willie hoofing in a dinner theater, Joe Louis squeezing hands at
Caesars, Joe DiMaggio shilling for Mr. Coffee. As a young man, I
could never watch a Mr. Coffee commercial without feeling a pang
of misery; I had never seen the Yankee Clipper play, but I imagined
that he must have been great *then*, because he sure wasn't great *now*
— he looked bereft, like a defrocked priest: Joyless Joe DiMaggio. I
did not feel sorry for him, however, as much as I felt for those who
had loved him, who had adored him and had believed that his
ineffable and defining greatness would somehow last forever.

Now it was time to feel sorry, in a strange way, for myself. You see,
I'd had another dream about Joe — *our* Joe, *my* Joe — and his journey to Brunei, and this was the dream I had invested with my own
hope and belief. I had dreamed that Joe had gone to Brunei on a
mission of dire importance; that the sultan had summoned him
personally, not for instruction or diversion but rather for survival,
to quell an insurrection of infidels. I dreamed that he did not fail,
because Joe, well, he *never* fails; that what Joe did on the football
field, he would keep on doing, outside of football, outside of sport,
forever; that he would just keep *playing*, in ever greater and more
important arenas . . . diplomacy, espionage, politics, art, literature,
music, whatever . . . and ride the whole supercool super-clutch mys-
tic mojo of his own greatness — which, after all, is partially *our*
greatness — into history. . . .

I felt sorry for myself, of course, because once I'd met Joe Montana I realized that, as the cost and condition of his greatness, he had purged his brain of grandiose and debilitating dreams and that the only dreams he had left were dreams of refuge — from history, yes, and also from us.

To explain what I mean about the costs and conditions of Joe's greatness, I would like to tell two stories about him, both of which happen to concern Tim Barnett's ears. The first is about what makes Joe legendary and the second is about what makes him — efficiently, impressively, triumphantly, magically — limited. That both stories have an aural leitmotiv just goes to show how, in Joe's case, what is legendary and what is limited are intertwined and, in the end, indistinguishable.

Tim Barnett is a wide receiver for the Kansas City Chiefs. He has unusual ears. While unremarkable in size, they are whorled and flared, distinctly shell-like, and they are joined to his head at an angle that makes them look like afterthoughts. Once Joe became a Chief, he made it immediately clear that they amused him. He called Barnett "the Doberman," and Barnett, in truth, found some comfort in Joe's mockery. Joe had joined the Chiefs from the San Francisco 49ers, where he had won four Super Bowls and had worked with the finest cadre of pass-catchers in football, and Barnett was frankly afraid that Joe would turn up his nose at what the Chiefs offered in the way of wideouts. Now, here was Joe Montana, who was the greatest quarterback ever, calling Tim Barnett "the Doberman," and here was Tim Barnett — who was, well, Tim Barnett — calling Joe "Pinocchio," on account of his prodigious beak. On his very first day in Kansas City, Joe Montana had, in Barnett's mind, become a full-fledged member of the Chiefs.

The first of our Joe Montana stories takes Tim Barnett's ears to San Diego, where, toward the end of last season, the Chiefs were playing the Chargers in a game crucial to Kansas City's playoff hopes. The Chiefs were behind by a field goal late in the game and had to score a touchdown to win. Now, as everyone, including Tim Barnett, knows, dire situations are Joe Montana's métier, and adversity is to Joe what spinach is to Popeye; still, a touchdown is a touchdown, and, as Barnett says, "when you're behind, it distracts you." It is rather like a twelfth man has sneaked into the huddle, a gloomy, twitchy, pessimistic character who, as the quarterback calls the play, shakes his head and frowns and says "That'll never work."

Well, in San Diego on that day, the twelfth man had taken his place in the huddle and the Chiefs were looking at him and he was making faces and Joe . . . well, it was like Joe didn't *see* him, or if he did see him, he didn't let on. The San Diego crowd was whooping it up, flexing its din muscles, and Joe said to his teammates "Don't worry about the clock, don't listen to the crowd, and let's have some fun." Then he looked at Barnett and said "Sorry, Tim — I guess with those ears you *have* to listen to the crowd. I guess with those ears you can hear the *press box*. What are they saying up there?" The twelfth man, of course, was not amused; he slunk out of the huddle, took his seat on the bench and watched the Chiefs win the game.

The second Joe story takes place in a middle school in Kansas City, where Barnett's ears, in theory, should have had little relevance. Joe was there — along with Barnett and backup quarterbacks Steve Bono, Matt Blundin and Alex Van Pelt — as a favor to the Chiefs' offensive coordinator, Paul Hackett, or, rather, to Hackett's son Nate, a seventh grader. As part of a fund-raiser, Nate had auctioned off an opportunity to eat lunch with Joe Montana and the Chiefs. The five kids who had come up with winning bids now sat in a little clubroom with their proud teachers, and when Joe entered, what they saw was this: a handsome man with broad shoulders, skinny calves, tanned skin, suspiciously blond hair, a slightly frayed hairline, a broad white grin, an extremely large nose, two sled-dog blue eyes centered in webs of white squint lines, a long, shiny, meat-colored scar across his right elbow and untied sneakers. The kids were not jocks; they were, for the most part, slouchy, brainy and quiet, and Joe took a seat next to a blonde girl who seemed to be the shyest of them all. For about two minutes, he spoke quietly to her, plying her with his smile; then he noticed Barnett across the table and said to the little girl, loudly, "Have you ever seen ears like those? Doesn't he look like a Doberman?" The little girl smiled but did not say anything. Joe folded his own ears forward. "Anybody have a knife?" he asked. "You can sharpen it on his ears."

Now, for a long time, I thought of Joe Montana as a "thinking man's quarterback," a "cerebral athlete" whose game — a greedy, hungry, gobbling thing, based miraculously on patience, restraint, even passivity — was an expression of some kind of Zen mastery.

Naturally, when I first heard the story of the huddle in San Diego, I believed that Joe had made fun of Barnett's ears for calculated effect, to relax his team. I no longer think so. I have seen Joe and Tim Barnett together several times, and Joe has never *failed* to make fun of Barnett's ears. I am convinced that he cracked the joke in San Diego simply to get a laugh, just as I am convinced that — at the beginning of the last-minute 92-yard drive that beat the Cincinnati Bengals in the 1989 Super Bowl — he pointed out John Candy in the stands simply because he had *spotted* John Candy and wanted to share his find with his teammates. He is innocent of calculation. He is free of ulterior motive. He is unburdened by history. His Zen is not Eastern but, rather, western Pennsylvanian. His Zen is the Zen not of the brainy but of the blessed.

"He isn't complicated," says Bill Walsh, the coach who presided over Joe's rise to professional glory. "People look for another agenda — it really isn't there. He just loves football. He loves to play the game. He plays with a smile on his face."

He plays with a smile on his face because in football he has found the magical alembic by which to turn the lead of his limitations into the gold of his legend. He loves football not because it frees him to create but because it constrains him to react, and he is very good at reacting. "A lot of people," he says, "try to do more than they're able to, than they are capable of. I don't." I once asked him if, during those famous moments of crunch time and crisis, when his team is behind and the clock is running, he tries especially hard to complete his first pass, because then he knows that the defense starts thinking, Oh, no, here comes Joe. . . . And Joe answered that no, he tries to complete his first pass because it's always better to complete a pass than *not* to complete a pass. He feels the same way about the second pass, and the third. He is a simple man who plays a simple game, and "his simplicity," in the words of 49ers president Carmen Policy, "is his genius."

"He is able to operate on a simplistic level and come to decisions that others would think of as very complex," says Policy, who ought to know, because, in the most painful event in the history of his franchise, he traded Joe to the Chiefs, and admits that he was outwitted in the process. "It's like dealing with a person who walks into a crowded party and works the room and has everybody loving him. And you say 'How do you do that?' But it's nothing you can train for, not a muscle you can develop. . . . It's not physiological. It's probably not even psychological. It's probably spiritual."

I have my own theory about Joe, of course. I have come to the conclusion that, at the moment of conception, Joe was spared the tiny whirring gear of doubt and introspection that at once hobbles, vexes and enriches our lives; I have come to believe that his mindset is a matter of circuitry, biology, evolution and destiny, and that when, at the end of this season, Joe Montana retires from football, he will become a fugitive from the very game — the very purpose — for which he was created.

What, you haven't heard? He's retiring, after this, his sixteenth season in the NFL. Walking away at age 38. This is it, folks — the last campaign, the grand finale, the final episode of the Joe Show. No more perfection in desperation, no more final-second thievery, no more long passes when logic dictates that he should throw short, no more short passes when it's clear he absolutely *must* throw long, no more soft little flares that settle into a receiver's hands at the precise moment he is ready to run forever . . . no more Joe. Oh, sure, people have been talking about Joe retiring for *years;* now, however, *Joe* is talking about it, to his wife, Jennifer, to his parents, to his agent and friends, to other retired athletes, such as Roger Staubach and Reggie Jackson. . . . No, he won't come right out and say it, because he's always resented the sporting press's counsel in the matter of retirement, but he makes it clear that he wants to get out before he *has* to get out, before his last game turns out to be like last season's playoff in Buffalo, when the Bills clanged his head against the frozen turf and he sat on the sideline with a coat over his shoulders and nothing in his eyes, looking so pale, so *puny.*

"Oh, he has to," says Bill Walsh when asked about Joe's retirement. "You lose some of your quickness; you don't move and avoid people as well as you once did, and you start taking punishment."

Of course, Walsh is justified in his concern, because, as even Joe admits, Montana has taken some shots over the years . . . there have been a few injuries . . . well, a lot of injuries . . . indeed, enough traumatized tissue to warrant surgical invasion of Joe's body on a scale more often endured by medical-school cadavers.

"I thought after Buffalo that would be it, but he wasn't ready," says Joe's mother, Theresa Montana. "But I hope this is his last year, for his sake. He needs the rest." Yes, that's it, the kind of thing a mother says, and knows: that more than anything else, her son is tired. How long has he been playing football? For as long as Joe has been at his life, he has been at his game; his mother remembers him wearing out his grandfather, playing catch with him all day long, at age two. "He liked it," she says. "You and I walk down the street; Joe picks up a ball and starts playing just like you and I walk down the street."

He was born to play and raised to compete. He was an only child, and when his parents discovered within their son some great, hulking jones to win at whatever game he played, they did whatever was necessary to feed it. To give Joe a taste of pressure, his father, Joe Sr., exposed him to the best competition possible when Joe was seven or eight, driving the boy all over the state of Pennsylvania to play in basketball tournaments. To make sure that Joe had the whitest pants on his football team, his mother didn't just wash them, she *cleansed* them. "One day Joe came home and said 'Mom, I don't know how you do it but my pants are whiter than anyone else's.' I took him down to the basement and showed him the old-fashioned washboard. I said, 'This is how you do it. First soak 'em in cold water with a little bit of Tide. Then rub 'em. Then throw the water away and soak 'em in bleach and *hot* water. Then rub 'em again. *Then* throw them in the washer.' I didn't have the new kind of washing machine, either — I had the old-fashioned wringer when I was doing his clothes."

No wonder he's tired. Metaphorically, at least, he has been wearing the whitest pants on his team for virtually his entire life. In the little leagues . . . in high school . . . at Notre Dame . . . with San Francisco and now in Kansas City . . . he has always had this blinding *glow;* he has always been the great Joe Montana, and now, well, as his mother says, he needs a rest. The thing is, I don't think he's tired of wearing the whitest pants on the team; in fact, I think he *likes* wearing the whitest pants on the team. He's just tired of everyone else getting them dirty.

It's like some freaking bad dream. Joe doesn't want to wiggle, but he winds up wiggling anyway. He tries to tell the others that he doesn't want to wiggle, but they are too tall, or too beautiful, and they can't hear him. So he wiggles. He is onstage, with Brooks Robinson and Joe Willie Namath and Veronica Webb and Danny Manning and Miss U.S.A. and Dikembe Mutombo, in the basket-

ball arena of the University of Arkansas, at a rally of Wal-Mart
stockholders. The air smells vaguely of meat, and the stockholders
are in full throat, demanding that the athletes and models do what
they do, every morning, if they work in a Wal-Mart store: the Wal-
Mart cheer. Joe is fourth in line; Joe is the hyphen, and the hyphen
must wiggle. *W! A! L!* Now it is Joe's turn, so he drops into a kind of
crouch and shakes his fanny as though he's performing an ethnic
dance back in western Pennsylvania. The crowd roars its approval
— *Joe!* — and later a goodly number of women approach and say,
winkingly, "Nice wiggle, Joe."

In a limousine, he goes from the university's new basketball arena to
its old one, where Hanes — a Wal-Mart vendor and one of the
companies that pay Joe to license his name — has provided him a
table at which he is to sign autographs. In anticipation of his arrival,
a line has formed, a line that hums with the sound of America, that
hums with appreciation of Joe.

"Is this the Joe line?"

"This is the Joe line."

"Joe!"

"Me and him — like *this!*"

Then a wife: "You guys have the patience to stand on line for an
autograph but you don't have the patience to stand on line with us
when we're shopping?"

"Hey — it's *Joe.*"

"This man is *God.*"

Then Joe comes in, and the wife fans herself. "Oh, is he a cutie.
Oh, is he *cute.*"

Joe is wearing a sharp olive-colored suit and his eyes are blue and
steely. He is chewing a piece of gum, hard. He sits down at the table
and begins signing black-and-white photos of himself. He smiles as
he moves his pen across the photographs, but the smile is pickled
and guarded, one per customer, and as he chews his gum, his jaw
muscles grab his cheek like a claw.

The line moves. People ask Joe to sign jackets, footballs and
pennants, but he politely declines, because he can sign only licensed paraphernalia. People try to take pictures. "No pictures!"
snaps a Hanes representative. A man asks Joe to sign two photographs. "Just one," Joe says. "One?" the man says. "One," Joe says
firmly. His eyes have a hunted look, and a vague air of resentment

has settled over the line. A man complains that Joe wouldn't sign his Canadian flag, and his wife says, "He's not friendly at all. He looks miserable."

As a matter of fact, he is. Joe knows that nobody at an autograph signing is getting what he wants. He knows that what the people want is a *moment* with Joe Montana, some little frisson of commonality, some indication that he *sees* them, and he knows that he has no moments to give. He is always gracious and always polite; he tries, however, to save his moments for his wife and four children. Quite often, his fans try to have some kind of moment with him when he is trying to have a moment with his children, and the result is a camera or a video camera thrust into the face of one of his little boys or girls, and Joe's miserable realization that his children have a better time in public places when Daddy stays home.

He would like to stay home, forever. He has never understood the intensity of public adulation, the sheer *need*. As a child, he never even had posters of athletes in his room, because he didn't want to watch or worship them, he wanted to *be* them; as an adult, he has always considered football merely a "fun job," and he really would have preferred playing it in empty stadiums, just him and the guys. In truth, the game he loves is already receding into the past, and his future is here, signing photographs of an old smile, among people who call him God and yet resent him for his distance, making money by learning how to wiggle.

The plane rises slowly into the sky. I pray, because I am afraid of flying. Joe smiles, as is his habit. Joe has a dazzling smile, a theme he plays with variations. I assume, at first, that this is his interview smile — helpful, hopeful and eager-to-please, even in the face of impatience and befuddlement. I am asking him what he's going to do after he retires. Broadcasting? No, he is a positive person and can't imagine being paid to criticize his fellow ballplayers. Coaching? "Successful coaches tend to be players who can be satisfied succeeding through someone else. I'm too competitive for that. I can't stand not being in there." Politics? "Politics are too political." Books? "I started working on a book once, with a writer who probably would have done an excellent job — but it was so much time and effort." Business? "I'm not really a businessman, not yet. I feel like I don't know enough about the business world to make my own decisions."

No, what Joe dreams of is, in fact, what's making him smile:

flight. He dreams of taking Jennifer and the children, with their
billowing blond hair, into his own airplane and then into the sky,
away from the people who want him, who want *them*. . . . He dreams
of coming down, behind gates, behind fences, on a landing strip all
his own, on a ranch all his own, and riding horses out to the grapes
he grows, for the wine he makes, for the restaurant he runs, for the
friends he has chosen, for the world he has created, all his own.

This is, of course, a rich man's dream, and Joe is, of course, a rich
man. He is already taking flying lessons, searching for land in the
Napa Valley and talking to winemakers about starting his own label,
though "nothing too serious." He collects wine and is said to have
discerning judgment. Joe has a "sensitive side," Jennifer Montana
says, and she hopes, paradoxically, that the public will begin to see
it, and appreciate it, once her husband gets out of football and
regains his privacy. A lot of people have high hopes for Joe's retirement. His father hopes that he will compete on the senior golf tour.
Bill Walsh hopes that he will coach. Roger Staubach hopes that he
will go into business. I just hope that he doesn't turn into Joe
DiMaggio, and so I ask him what he thinks people will be saying
about him ten years from now, what he *wants* people to say about
him ten years from now. We are flying. We are drinking wine. Joe
is smiling.

"Oh, I don't know," he says. "How about 'Where is he?'"

I am listening to Joe talk about his trip to Brunei and wondering
where greatness goes. Joe is in the Chiefs locker room with some of
his teammates, and he is taking practice swings with an imaginary
golf club and speaking about his host, the sultan's nephew, whom
he calls Akeem. "Akeem didn't have to do shit," Joe says apprecia-
tively. "When we played golf, he held out his foot and his valet tied
his shoes. When he was ready to tee off, his valet put the ball on the
tee. He didn't have to do *shit*."

Where does greatness go? I have been following Joe to come up
with some kind of answer. I have been following Joe to determine if
greatness is, like a bus ticket, transferable, from *his* world, the world
of football and holy innocence, to our world, the world of unholy
complication . . . if it is indestructible, like matter, subject only to
transformation, rather than extinction . . . or if it is as perishable as
a perfect tomato, strictly of its moment, of *our* moment, and then
gone. Now, however, I am thinking that Joe is trying to tell me

something: that greatness goes wherever it wants to go; that it goes to Brunei, if the money is right; that it doesn't have to do shit. Then Joe's teammates leave, and I ask Joe a question of great concern. I am very superstitious, and the day is Friday the thirteenth. Severe thunderstorms are galloping in from the western plains, and I am scheduled to fly out of Kansas City at the same time they are scheduled to arrive. I ask Joe if, under the same conditions, he would get on the plane.

He smiles and looks me directly in the eye. He does not answer yes or no but instead leans forward, as though telling me a secret, and says, "Friday the thirteenth? Thunderstorms? That just makes it *better*, doesn't it?"

I get on the plane two hours later. Like Tim Barnett in San Diego and, for all I know, the sultan's nephew in Brunei, I have had my Joe Montana Moment. The plane rises quickly, easily; behind me, to the west, there is an insurrection of thunderheads, glowering like infidels. To the east, though, where I'm headed, the skies have been cleansed of all dark dreams, and greatness follows me home.

ROBIN FINN

The Second Time Around for Jennifer Capriati

FROM THE NEW YORK TIMES

THE DESERT SUN is on the rise and already packing a punch only a lizard could love, and it would be ninety-nine degrees in the shade if there were any, so it's small wonder that the hot acres of outdoor hard courts at the Mission Hills tennis complex are deserted, all except for one.

On its simmering surface, a teenager with a rakish purple glaze in her ponytail and a hard-working wad of green gum in her mouth is whacking tennis balls across the net as fast as her male sparring partner can deliver them. The tear in her graffiti-print shorts is self-inflicted — tennis shorts as fashion victim — but the tears under her eyes are not tears of unhappiness from feeling victimized by everyone within staring distance. This is just plain sweat after a rigorous practice session.

"That's too good, champ," her adult opponent says as she burns a double-barreled backhand beyond his ample reach. His casual compliment brings the ghost of a smile to her face.

What's right with this picture?

The teenager happens to be that infamous tennis and twelfth-grade dropout, Jennifer Capriati, lately an alumnus of Florida's police blotter, the school of hard knocks, and two strange stints in rehabilitative facilities, where addiction and psychosis were daily subjects on the blackboards.

Six weeks ago, she and her family relocated to this recreational mecca in the California desert, prospecting for a new start after a bad time. Last week, Capriati broke her yearlong vow of silence regarding the public's need to know her private ups and downs.

From courtside at her morning practice; from the white leather driver's seat of the 1991 Volkswagen Cabriolet she purchased in Palm Springs, California; over Thai-style pizza minus its "fattening" cheese and peanuts; and romping on the sofa with the five-month-old puppy who has turned out to be her surest antidote to alienation, she waxed cautiously optimistic after a year of waning internally.

The torment, as she refers to it, is over. She hasn't solved her problems, but she has elected to survive them.

It's little surprise that the book on Capriati's bedside table is Robert Heinlein's *Stranger in a Strange Land*. She has been living her own science-fiction saga ever since fame, fortune and fear of failure descended with a boom at thirteen and she discovered, too early, that all that glitters is not gold.

"I was always expected to be at the top, and if I didn't win, to me that meant I was a loser," she said last week. "The way I felt about myself had to do with how I played, and if I played terrible I'd say, yes, I can handle it, but really I couldn't; I felt like no one liked me as a person. I felt like my parents and everybody else thought that tennis was the way to make it in life, they thought it was good, but I thought no one knew or wanted to know the person who was behind my tennis life."

When Capriati couldn't make peace between the girl in the mirror and the player who had been assigned a starring role as "the next Chris Evert," she tried to rid herself of the latter identity. Being a teenager, it seemed only logical to go to extremes to do it.

"I was depressed and sad and lonely and guilty," she said of her dismay at being the player everybody knew but a person nobody understood.

"I felt I'd give up all the material things to be with someone who would love me for me," said Capriati, who did give up her marketability and credibility in the course of the six-month walk on the wild side that landed her here on the rebound.

Yes, the Betty Ford Clinic is just around the corner. But no, Capriati isn't going there for therapy after a year of entropy that began with a destabilizing loss at the 1993 U.S. Open and culminated in her arrest in May on a marijuana charge following her own version of the lost weekend.

Instead, she's back on the tennis court, the not-so-innocuous launching pad that made her a celebrity at thirteen, broke her at seventeen, but now seems an integral ally as she picks up the pieces of a life that had, in her prematurely jaundiced vision, turned pointless, friendless, and hopeless.

Over the Edge of a Precipice

"I was pretty close to being not in existence," said Capriati, speaking at length, albeit uneasily, about the most difficult year of her life. After all, everybody else, from the teenaged acquaintances with whom she was arrested to several players and former players with whom she'd traded little more than nods, has already passed judgment.

Pantera and Jane's Addiction may still be the bands of choice on her stereo system, but regarding Jennifer's addiction, she has her own opinion to share.

"I'm not an addict to drugs, but you could say I'm an addict to my own pain. Or I was," she said, fidgeting with the toe ring that's replaced her nose and navel rings. "I had this sarcasm about everything. My spirit was just, like, dark."

Capriati's opening-round loss to Leila Meskhi at last year's Open pushed her over the edge of a precipice and into a self-destructive limbo. The self she wanted to destroy? Jennifer Capriati, tennis phenom and international celebrity.

"I burned out — I'll say it," Capriati announces with a grimace that shows she's fully aware of the chorus of "I told you so's" the revelation will inspire in the armchair psychologists and cynics who have waited for her to take a fall ever since she turned pro, and multimillionaire, as a toothy, giggly thirteen-year-old.

In 1993, less than four years after the Women's Tennis Council bent its age eligibility rules to allow this box office smash early entry to their novelty-starved circuit, Capriati left it and purposely left no word when or if she would be back.

She will be, but it will probably happen later rather than sooner.

Had a groin strain not intervened, Capriati would definitely be in Zurich next week at the European Indoors. But to return to the circuit the same way she left it, in pain, seems unwise: Capriati hopes to play every aspect of the game more wisely her second time around.

"I don't regret anything that happened in my career, except that maybe fourteen is too young to handle everything emotionally," she said. "But I know I don't want to leave tennis the way I did, crying and crawling away."

Turning Her Back on the Tennis World

Capriati, who had residual nightmares after losing her 1991 Open semifinal to Monica Seles, cried incessantly after losing her 1993 first-rounder.

"I started out O.K., but at the end of the match I couldn't wait to get off the court. Totally, mentally, I just lost it," she recalls, "and obviously it goes deeper than that one match. I really was not happy with myself, my tennis, my life, my parents, my coaches, my friends. . . . I spent a week in bed in darkness after that, just hating everything. When I looked in my mirror, I actually saw this distorted image: I was so ugly and so fat, I just wanted to kill myself, really."

So she proceeded to kill her public self. She turned her back on tennis and all it entailed. She withdrew from her family, first emotionally, then physically, and moved into her own apartment last November. "I thought the best thing for me was to be in total isolation; I didn't want anyone to know anything about me," Capriati said.

Her anonymity was short-lived once she was cited for shoplifting on December 10.

"I forgot I had the ring on, and by the time I remembered, it was too late," said Capriati, who routinely arrived for tennis matches without the right clothes, rackets, or contact lenses, and just last week walked out of a restaurant without her car keys.

Though Capriati was a juvenile at the time, her celebrity status seemed to outweigh her legal right to confidentiality; her case wound up being dismissed, but not before a worldwide blitz from the news media, most of which presumed her guilty, sent her even deeper into her shell.

"I thought, 'Am I that big that they have to make such a big deal out of this?'" she said. "And I see now that once you're considered a celebrity, you kind of have no rights to privacy. After that I kind of forgot about everything and everyone except for my brother; all I cared about was having my music and partying with friends."

For several months she refused to touch a racket, but last winter, even after the party circuit had become her only circuit, she realized she was bored and started hitting balls on the sly.

"It wasn't like I wanted to go back to it yet," said Capriati, who didn't want her parents to get any ideas about a springtime comeback, "but when I thought about the slams, I always thought, 'I'll be there again.'"

But then came another setback. Her parents, worried about her mental state, plucked her from her apartment and signed her into the Manors, a private psychiatric facility in Tarpon Springs, Florida, for a two-week evaluation in February. Capriati emerged resentful, and when she turned eighteen in March, she left her family's Saddlebrook home for Boca Raton, a move across Florida that initially received her parents' blessing.

"I was trying to get better, get happier, but I felt like people were watching me at Saddlebrook," said Capriati, whose paranoia was not unfounded. More than once she was ambushed by tabloid photographers hiding in the bushes and stalking her high school in suburban Tampa, Florida. In Boca Raton, she moved in with friends who attended the local university, and her father found her a tutor for her schoolwork.

Again, she started playing tennis recreationally and remembered that she "loved it, loved the game. But I was so out of shape I couldn't really hit for more than an hour, so I wasn't ready yet to ask my dad to find me a hitting partner."

'I'm Playing Because It's Inside Me'

Capriati's arrest occurred on May 16 inside a seedy Coral Gables motel room where she was bankrolling a party attended by an assortment of teenaged revellers she later described as "acquaintances, not real friends."

What they had in common was a complete lack of interest in Capriati, the tennis player; her generosity with her car and wallet was enough to award her a high ranking in their pecking order.

What the police, who made two felony arrests and released two others without charging them, found in Capriati's backpack was just enough marijuana to charge her with misdemeanor possession and to snap a mug shot that turned up on TV screens around the globe. Her sponsors dumped her, she went into a 28-day treatment program at Mount Sinai Medical Center in Miami Beach, and learned another lesson.

Despite reports that her name is now worth mud, the vestibule of the Capriatis' townhouse is brimming with boxes of clothing and equipment from companies like Nike, Head, and Reebok, all of whom appear to have some interest in outfitting her comeback. Wild cards are available at whatever event she deems to enter. Her father, Stefano, is happily ensconced on the practice court. Tennis seems ready to welcome Capriati back, and she seems ready to attempt a return, albeit on slightly different terms.

"It's just a game to me now; I'm playing because it's inside me. I have this desire to play and a talent to play, and I don't want to waste my talent," she said. "I don't care about being number one, but I'm ready and willing to give a battle, and that's what sports is all about. Who cares about endorsements and all that stuff? Just give me a racket. There's no ending to my story yet."

Whatever Happened to Ronnie Littleton?

FROM TEXAS MONTHLY

"I don't know if Ronnie will talk to you," one of his former Coyote teammates told me. "He's different these days."
"Different? In what way?"
There was a pause. "Well, I think you'll understand when you see him."

IN THE AUTUMN of 1969, when I was in the seventh grade in the North Texas city of Wichita Falls, I used to get on my bicycle at the end of the school day and race to the Wichita Falls High School practice field to watch Ronnie Littleton, one of the five black players on the varsity football team. It was the first year of forced busing in Wichita Falls, which had a population of 96,265, 11 percent of which was black. The school administration had shut down the black high school on the east side of town and sent the black students to one of three high schools on my side of town. School integration brought the same tensions to Wichita Falls that had afflicted most Texas cities that were integrating during the civil rights movement. There were heated speeches before the school board, and some parents tried to organize an all-white private school. Hysterical rumors ran rampant through my neighborhood about what the black students had in store for us. One was that they all carried switchblades and would stab us in the bathrooms. "They hate us because we're white," I remember one of the parents in our neighborhood telling me and my friends. "They think we've ruined their lives. And now they're going to try to ruin ours."

But in December — twenty-five years ago this month — those five black players helped lead the Wichita Falls Coyotes to the state football championship in a victory that one local sports writer likened to the stunning World Series win that same year by the underdog New York Mets. In the process, that championship season produced a new local hero for many white kids like myself — a mouthy, street-smart black teenager named Ronnie Littleton, the very type of person we had been warned against by our parents. To those of us who spent Saturday nights watching *My Three Sons* and *Green Acres,* Littleton was simply exotic. In the late sixties, no player from the conservative Texas high school powerhouses dared to do what Littleton did on the football field. Bored with the black football shoes issued to all Coyotes, he wrapped white tape around his. He wore half a dozen red and white wristbands on his arms. On the sidelines, when he took off his helmet, his Afro, the biggest at school, would mushroom straight up like an atomic bomb explosion. Each time he scored a touchdown, he performed a wild gyrating dance in the end zone, causing some parents to look away in embarrassment as if they had seen a sex act. Opposing coaches designed their game plans purely to stop him — and still he slipped around them, taunting would-be tacklers by holding the ball loosely in one hand. Playing almost every down of a game on both offense and defense, Littleton was one of the last great all-around players in Texas's high school ranks. In 1971, his senior year, he single-handedly led an average Coyote team back to the state championship game.

Today flashy athletes are so common in sports that we hardly notice them. But after all this time, I still cannot shake the memories of those years that Ronnie Littleton spent on the white side of town. It was not just his ability to move on a football field that amazed me. It was his brassy charm and unbridled confidence, his ability to move through life in such free-spirited fashion. In many ways Littleton affected me more than anyone else I had known in my youth. This past fall, I decided to return to Wichita Falls and see him again.

"He's got an unlisted phone number," said a former Coyote quarterback.

"Is he still that famous around town?"

"Oh, man, nothing like that," the old quarterback chuckled.

"So why the unlisted number?"

"I don't think he wants people calling him up to remind him what his life used to be like."

When I was growing up, Wichita Falls was so segregated that the only black people I ever spoke to were maids. Blacks rarely came to our side of town, and I was afraid to venture into the East Side, which literally was across the railroad tracks, in the bottomland. I lived in the country club subdivision, parts of which rivaled the finest streets in Dallas's Highland Park or Houston's River Oaks. Because of the area's vast oil fields that lay under the treeless plains, some extraordinarily wealthy people made their homes in Wichita Falls. A small frame home on the East Side — the kind Ronnie Littleton grew up in, for example — was smaller than the garages of the Country Club mansions.

For sheltered kids like me, the East Side was a place of deep mystery. I heard stories about prostitutes and bootleggers who stood along Flood Street peddling their wares. I was told that if whites ever drove through the East Side at night, they would be snatched out of their cars by black men and robbed. Although I didn't consider myself prejudiced in the slightest, the fact was that my knowledge of Wichita Falls' blacks was gleaned mostly from the local folklore passed around my part of town. About the only time I ever read about black people in our local newspaper was when I came across a story — always placed toward the bottom of the sports page — about the East Side's high school football team, the Booker T. Washington Leopards. My friends and I had always wanted to see the Leopards play — they had won the all-black school state football championship in 1965 and barely lost in the finals the next year — but a trip to a Booker T. game was deemed too dangerous by our parents. The adults I knew who did attend would joke about the old uniforms the black players had to wear, the silly pitchouts and reverses in the offensive game plans, and the quarterbacks who would drop back and let fly with wild 60-yard bombs. They reported that throughout the game, the black fans would stomp on the wooden bleachers and do rhythmic chants like, "Ooh! Oongowah! We got the power!" I remember one friend's father saying after he got back from a game, "It's like being in Africa." When I once asked why the Wichita Falls Coyotes never played Booker T., I was told the Booker T. players illegally stuck golf-shoe spikes in their football shoes so that they could puncture their opponents' stomachs when they stepped on them.

In 1967, when Booker T. was finally allowed to enter a white football district (a 3A district, one division lower than the 4A Coyotes), it turned out that the only controversy regarding Booker T. involved the white referees. Against all-white Brownwood High, a perennial football power in the sixties coached by the legendary Gordon Wood, Booker T. had two touchdowns nullified by penalties. Finally, after a Booker T. player ran back a kickoff untouched, all four officials reluctantly signaled a touchdown. "But their county sheriff, who was at the game, suddenly walked out on the field and called the officials over," recalled Ervin Garnett, then the Booker T. football coach. "He pointed to the sidelines and said our runner had stepped out of bounds on the 35-yard line. So the officials called that one back too." Booker T. lost to Brownwood, 21–14.

Garnett was convinced that his Leopards, given an even playing field, would eventually prove to be a better team than those from the white high schools. But in the late sixties, Wichita Falls' white school administrators realized that if they did not come up with an integration plan soon, a federal judge would come up with one for them — one that could possibly force white students to be bused to the East Side. So in due haste they decided to shut down Booker T. at the start of the 1969 school year and send its seven hundred black students to the white high schools. The Booker T. faculty and staff were shuffled to other Wichita Falls schools; Garnett, the great football coach, was named principal at a junior high school.

It was a devastating time for black parents, who said the busing plan was no different from what the slaves went through when they were shipped against their will to America. We don't have much, black parents said, but at least we should have our own school to nurture our kids, guide them, and give them black teachers and coaches who could serve as role models.

"At Booker T., the black kids knew the whole community was watching after them," said Garnett. "Even the marginal students were put in positions of responsibility to showcase their talents and give them confidence. One of my great fears was that those kids would be lost at a white school. They would be looking at mostly white teachers who were happy to pass them with a C and get them out of their classrooms."

But to the football coaches of the white high schools, integration was a godsend. They couldn't wait to get their hands on some of that East Side talent. Just imagine how far the Coyotes could go, the

Wichita High coaches said, if they only had that young teenage son of Faye Littleton's, the sweet waitress who worked at the whites-only Wichita Club on top of the First Wichita Bank building. (She had raised him alone; Ronnie first met his father when he turned sixteen.) Rumor had it that Ronnie was so skilled that he could run the 40-yard dash backward as fast as he could run it forward. The kid had even installed a makeshift weight room in his mother's garage. Everyone said he was destined for professional football.

According to local lore, when the East Side was originally divided up for school busing, Littleton's home had been placed in the Rider High School district, the archrival of the Coyotes. But a former Wichita Falls High School coach who had become athletic director for the school system just happened to get the boundaries redrawn to land the Littletons' street just inside the Coyotes' territory. Although Ronnie Littleton had no way of knowing it, he was already part of a plan to take Wichita Falls High School to the state championship.

> "When he came back to Wichita Falls, I'd see him driving up and down the highway, his music cranked up loud," said a former teammate. "I'd wave at him."
> "Did he ever stop?"
> "Well, he'd pretend not to notice you."

In 1969 boys my age who followed the Coyotes had one and only one hero: a handsome, stocky running back named Joey Aboussie. With a running start, he would lower his head and steamroll linebackers flat onto their backs. ABC broadcaster Chris Schenkel was so impressed with Aboussie that he later pronounced him the best high school player in the country. Off the field, Aboussie was the all-American teenager — an honor student in school, a persuasive speaker at Fellowship of Christian Athletes banquets, a polite star who always took the time to sign autographs or throw us his chin strap at the end of games.

"Are you boys going to grow up to become Coyotes someday?" Aboussie would ask us. "Oh, yes, sir, Joey," we'd all reply. If someone had told me that another running back — and a black one at that — was about to take Aboussie's place as my idol, I would have told him that he just didn't understand football in Wichita Falls.

For years the Coyotes had been made up of toughened white

boys, the sons of oilmen or oil-field workers who had been taught that football was meant to be played ferociously. On cement-hard practice fields, unsmiling coaches shouting, "Hit! Hit! Hit!" made the Coyotes go from one tackling drill to another. "Put the hurt on him!" the coaches would yell, blowing their whistles. Coyotes were not allowed to speak to coaches unless spoken to, and they were certainly not allowed to spike the ball and dance when they scored a touchdown. The Coyotes were so well disciplined and so brutal that other teams dreaded playing them. In the late fifties and early sixties the Coyotes went to the state championship game four straight times.

In those days Wichita Falls High School was the only white high school in town. In the sixties its stockpile of talent was diluted as the city grew and other white high schools opened. By 1969, even with Aboussie, the Coyotes were expected only to win their district championship and then get beaten in the playoffs. Nor did it seem that integration was going to help. Many of the former Booker T. stars were so angry about the closing of their own school that they hadn't even tried out for the Coyotes. Others had quit in disgust a few days into practice because, they said, they weren't being given a chance to make the starting squad. The quarterback from the Booker T. team, Lulanger Washington, who was considered a major college talent with his powerful arm, and wide receiver Eddie Bagby were relegated to the bench because, the coaches said, their pass-oriented style didn't fit into the Coyotes' run-oriented wishbone offense.

But in a move that could be likened to Branch Rickey's signing Jackie Robinson to the Brooklyn Dodgers, the cigarette-smoking, burr-headed coach of the Coyotes, Donnell Crosslin, put another black player, Lawrence Williams, at quarterback. The speedy Williams's runs around the end were the perfect complement to Joey Aboussie's inside blasts. Williams was a confident, thoughtful young man who never raised his voice or lost his cool. Still, installing him at quarterback was a huge gamble for Crosslin. At the time, there were no black quarterbacks starting for big white schools anywhere in the state, and there were plenty of Coyote fans who would have preferred a white quarterback, even if it meant another average season. But Crosslin told me years later, "My job was to go with the best player for the position, and that was that."

Crosslin also named James Reed, a quiet black teenager, his middle linebacker, the central figure for the defense. Reed stood by his locker, sullen and glowering, saying little to the white players. Just before the August two-a-day practices, Reed's father had been shot to death on an East Side street. No one was sure whether Reed would even want to play that season. But when he stepped onto the practice field, he turned into the epitome of the Coyote player — a vicious hitter who seemed to channel his anger into one punishing tackle after another.

Then there was Ronnie Littleton. Because Crosslin rarely played sophomores, everyone assumed that Littleton would spend the 1969 season doing mop-up work late in the second half of games. During one of those early practices, leaning against the practice field fence with a pack of other boys my age, I got to watch him run with the ball. Littleton started toward one hole in the line and then, with a little shake of his hips, slid toward another hole. He took a few more steps, made an impossible whirling move, and slipped like a wet bar of soap through the rest of the defense.

But that was not the part that amazed me. As Littleton trotted back to the huddle, he held the ball above his head and squealed, "*Ooh, that feels good!*" The white players looked at one another: Coyotes weren't supposed to talk like that. He was a football player, not Flip Wilson. On the next play, I watched my hero Aboussie plunge into the line with his rock-'em-sock-'em body. Then, up came Littleton again, moving faster than anyone else on the field, flicking right, flicking left, running so deftly that his shoulder pads didn't even rattle. "*Ooh, uh-huh!*" Littleton shouted. The coaches just bit their lips. As Crosslin told me, "I knew that I was going to have to loosen up our typical disciplinary attitudes so the black players could feel more welcome."

But he could not possibly have known that with the arrival of Ronnie Littleton, the Coyotes would never be the same. At the end of practice, some other boys and I hustled to the locker room door to get a good look at Littleton's frizzed-out Afro. We waited in silence as he approached, unsure of what to expect. I remembered someone had told me that the reason blacks grew big Afros was so they could hide their switchblades in them. Then Littleton turned and gave us a huge grin.

"It's the little honky brothers!" he said, giving each of us a soul shake — the first time anyone had shaken our hands like that. No one knew what to say. This cocky, muscled teenager was not like the older black men we knew who worked in our yards and spoke in soft voices. Finally, one boy asked him for his autograph. "Say, little honks, you know us black boys don't know how to spell," Littleton said, looking as serious as he could. Then, with a loud high-pitched laugh, he grabbed the sheet of paper and wrote his name.

From the day he arrived on "The Hill" (the phrase blacks used for the white part of town), Littleton became a one-man demonstration of black style. He wore flyaway shirts unbuttoned down to his chest and two-toned pants made of red leather in the front and black leather in the back. He was the first to wear sunglasses inside the high school ("My shades," he called them), and he wore silky see-through socks as a fashion statement. For his school picture, he wore a white tie with a black shirt. "I will never forget changing clothes in the locker room at one of our first practices," said Craig Womble, a Dallas businessman who played on the 1969 team. "Here were all the white boys putting on our white Jockey briefs. And all of a sudden, up jumps Ronnie onto a locker room bench, wearing a red silk undershirt and matching red silk boxers that went down to his knees. He starts singing while he's combing his Afro with one of those big cake-cutter combs. Finally someone says, 'What in the hell are you doing?' And Littleton says, 'Baby, I'm stylin' and profilin'.'"

In the hallways Littleton was always holding out his hand and giving someone "five" (which to white people was still a perplexing form of physical greeting). When he'd see a pretty girl, black or white, he'd say, "*Ooh*, baby, you butter my popcorn!" He used certain phrases — "getting some trim," for example, when referring to sex — that whites had never heard before. While my friends and I cussed through abbreviations — we said things like, "Hey, that's B.S." or "I'm getting PO'd" — Littleton made profanity sound like a glorious language. "Hello, you old poop-butt, jive-ass, booty head," I once heard him say to another black friend as a cheerful greeting.

Back in my neighborhood, the word was that these "loud and boisterous blacks" were ruining things at the high school. It was true that some black students were so upset about the closing of Booker T. that they sat in the back of the classrooms refusing to study, telling teachers their lessons were full of "*boool*-shit." Others walked through the hallways and said, "*Ooh*, smells bad in here. Smells like a whitey." Though the whites were mostly intimidated by the black students, they had their own ways of making the black students feel unwanted. During a Black History Week assembly in the auditorium, for example, some students shouted, "What about White History Week?" As tensions increased, many citizens, black and white, were convinced that integration would never succeed. Then the Coyotes started winning football games.

> "I heard he was arrested for carrying a weapon," said a former running back.
> "He had a gun?"
> "The way I heard it, a state trooper had pulled Ronnie over and told him to get out of the car. Ronnie started leaning down like he was going for something under the front seat, but then he came back up."
> "What was under there?"
> "A .357 magnum. The trooper was about to shoot him, but then he took his finger off the trigger. He recognized Ronnie's face."

In their first game, the newly integrated Coyotes squeaked by Lubbock Coronado, 10–3. But then they demolished Amarillo, 54–0, and in their third game, against state-ranked Sherman, the victorious Coyotes made 19 first downs and scored 41 points in the first half alone. Wichitans began pouring into the Coyotes' stadium to watch this collection of rich boys from the Country Club subdivision, gruff linemen from the city's blue-collar neighborhoods, and the five East Side blacks. Ted Buss, the sports writer for the local paper, nicknamed Lawrence Williams "Mr. Outside" and Joey Aboussie "Mr. Inside" because they were such a powerful one-two combination. But for me, the best moment in a game came when Ronnie Littleton scored a touchdown. He'd raise the ball high above his head and make back-and-forth movements with his pelvis while running in place. Then he'd spike the ball behind his back. I cheered for him like a lunatic. The irrepressible Buss nicknamed the dance the Littleton Limbo.

For a few hours on those fall Friday nights, two cultures came together. In the Coyotes' locker room, after Crosslin had given his standard halftime speech ("Men, you can do what you want to do — if you want to do it bad enough"), one of the black players would start a chant: "Gotta get rollin', rollin', rollin'." As the coaches cast sideways glances at one another, the rest of the Coyotes picked up the chant. Meanwhile, we whites in the stands would be singing our

dirge of a school song ("Hail to our colors. Hail to our school. We'll
back you forever. That is our rule"). Bored black fans would wait for
the song to end and then initiate a chant of their own: "Whup . . .
up . . . side . . . the . . . head. Say, whup 'em upside the head." Before
long, our whole side of the stadium had joined in.

Although Aboussie remained the mainstay of the Coyotes, even
he would later admit that integration made the 1969 team great.
After four victories in the playoffs, the Coyotes made it to the state
championship game against heavily favored San Antonio Lee. In
the first quarter Aboussie scored two quick touchdowns, then the
Coyotes fell behind late in the game, 20–14. With only minutes left
in the game, Lawrence Williams headed left with the ball on a
critical fourth-down play, and finding nothing there, went back to
the right and ran 62 yards for the game-tying touchdown. Then
Aboussie scored another touchdown to give the Coyotes a 28–20 win.

Although the Coyotes were picked to win the state title again the
next year, they were upset by Odessa Permian in a playoff game.
Five white Coyotes from the 1969 championship team, including
Aboussie, were signed by Darrell Royal to play for the University of
Texas. Lawrence Williams, who thought Royal was too racist to start
a black quarterback, went to Texas Tech, where ironically he became a wide receiver (Williams made the All Southwest Conference
team at that position anyway). James Reed accepted a scholarship
to a small Oklahoma college. Backup wide receiver Eddie Bagby,
who did not get a college scholarship, moved to California and
never returned to Wichita Falls. Also quickly dropping out of sight
after graduation was the embittered backup quarterback Lulanger
Washington, who believed he would have received a college scholarship if he had been able to stay at Booker T. and display his
passing skills.

In 1971 the only player left from the 1969 team was Littleton. By
then, he was the most famous high school football player in Texas.
Crosslin had created an offense that ensured Littleton would have
his hands on the ball on almost every play. Littleton spent most of
the game at quarterback, but he sometimes moved to tailback to
take better advantage of his running skills and to catch passes. He
also played his usual cornerback position on defense and returned
all kicks and punts. As quarterback, Littleton would saunter up to
the line of scrimmage, look over the defense, take the snap, and

then start scrambling around the field for what seemed like minutes until he found an opening. Against Highland Park High School, he caught a kickoff on his own 12-yard line and stood there patiently until the kickoff team got close to him. Suddenly, as tacklers charged in, he zigged one way, zagged another, and then jitterbugged down the field for an 88-yard touchdown.

The more flamboyant that Littleton acted with his lengthy touchdown dances, the more the other teams hated him. They dove at his knees. They tackled him after he had run out of bounds. To the Coyotes' mostly white opponents, he was an uppity black. But to us in Wichita Falls, he was our own Muhammad Ali. Unfazed by the whites around him and unaffected by any racist attitude, Littleton loved to celebrate his blackness, to poke fun at whites, and even to poke fun at himself. He occasionally walked up and down the sidelines at practice with an exaggerated roosterlike stride. "My brothers," he deadpanned to those white players who were giving him puzzled looks, "if you want to have soul, you got to have a glide in your stride, a dip in your hip." He started coming to school in a jacked-up blue Ford Fairlane that had an extra-large engine and Super Stock Formula One tires on the back wheels. He replaced the gas pedal with a chrome replica of a human foot, he put blue shag carpet on the dash, and he had a variety of beads and chains hanging from the rearview mirror. He joked to whites that it was his pimp-mobile. With his eight-track tape blaring out Jimi Hendrix's *Band of Gypsys,* Littleton would roar up to the school and hit his brakes about thirty feet from the parking lot, laying rubber, scattering rocks and pigeons. "Watch out, honks!" he'd yell, hopping out of the car.

As a freshman that year, I learned Littleton's class schedule just so I could stare at him in the hallways. "Hi, Ronnie," I'd say in my voice that had not yet begun to crack. "Hey, little brother," he'd occasionally reply. One day, during an interracial-understanding seminar I attended, in which black and white students sat side by side and talked about everyone being exactly the same deep down inside, I was asked by a teacher if I had any black friends. "Yes, Ronnie Littleton," I said as the black students around the room snickered. I realize today that it must have seemed absurd to them that a white kid could believe he could ever get close to their lives. The blacks might have spent seven hours a day with whites at the high school, but at the end of the day, they got on the school buses and went back to their separate world. Despite the promises made to them about integration, they already knew how difficult it would be for them to be accepted into white society. Only someone of Littleton's talent could overcome the barriers of race.

He rushed for 1,807 yards in 1971, passed for more than 400, and scored 26 touchdowns. He was named All-State on both offense and defense and was also named a high school All-American. Littleton took the Coyotes straight to the state championship game, once more against San Antonio Lee. When he was on defense, the San Antonio receivers he covered ran deep patterns on every play just to wear him out. Still, on offense, Littleton rushed for 181 yards and scored 2 touchdowns. But with two and a half minutes to play, San Antonio Lee quarterback Tommy Kramer fired a 35-yard touchdown pass just over Littleton's outstretched hands to wide receiver Richard Osborne. The Coyotes lost, 28–27 — and Littleton lay on the field and wept. We Coyotes fans wept with him. If we had only known that we had just seen him play the last great game of his career, we probably would have wept even more.

"I remember he'd watch all the pro games on television," said another former offensive back. "He'd see Tommy Kramer playing for the Vikings and Richard Osborne playing for the Eagles."

"The two guys who beat him in the state championship game?"

"Oh, yeah. And he'd see his friend Lawrence Williams, who played a few years for the Chiefs and the Browns. And Ronnie would get so upset that he would have to turn the television off."

The college coaches came from around the country. The University of Nebraska wanted him as its lead tailback. The University of Oklahoma promised him a position in its wishbone, then the most powerful offense in the nation. But in a stunning announcement, Littleton said he would be attending lowly Texas Christian University, in Fort Worth, a perennial Southwest Conference underdog with a weak offensive line. For three years the NCAA investigated the recruiting of Littleton, wanting to know why, after signing with TCU, he suddenly began driving a black Cutlass with a 455-horsepower engine. But the NCAA finally gave up, unable to disprove Littleton's story that his godmother had provided the car along with a monthly spending allowance.

Whatever the case, in the second game of his freshman year, Littleton found himself playing quarterback against mighty Notre Dame in South Bend, Indiana. Confident as ever, Littleton strutted to the line, looked over the Fighting Irish defense, got the ball, and was demolished. On each play, Notre Dame swarmed over him. One defensive lineman hit him from the blind side while his knee was planted. As the game progressed, he improvised desperately, trying to outrun the defenders around the end. And still he kept getting hit. After one vicious tackle, he felt something rip in his leg. Although he finished the game with magnificent courage, his future in football was already over.

Because of his bad knee, he rushed for only 133 yards and two touchdowns his freshman year. He reinjured the knee and then injured his other knee during his sophomore year. In the off-season he had operations, and by his junior year, he was being shot up with painkillers before most practices and games. But Littleton could no longer make those spit-on-a-griddle moves. Linebackers were able to catch up to him when he tried to run outside. The pro scouts stopped keeping files on him. By 1975, his senior year, his biography in the TCU football media guide devoted more space to his high school career than to his college years. He was seen by TCU students as much in the off-campus bars as he was on the field. When coaches learned he had broken curfew the night before the game against UT — he had been out partying with his friends — he was told not to suit up for the game.

The story of what happened to Littleton would soon become a familiar one as American sports became more integrated. It is the story of the kid from the poor black neighborhood, devoting himself to a game only to discover, too late, that the game has betrayed him. For Coach Garnett, who never got to fulfill his own dream of coaching Littleton at Booker T., the end of Littleton's career was a tragedy. "He never really had anyone to guide him about college or about how to handle his life," said Garnett. "No one even sat down and told him who he was outside of his life as an athlete. No one taught him what it meant to survive in the world if there was no football. And no one told him that he would be a star in the white world only as long as he kept being a star athlete."

Littleton left TCU and moved back to Wichita Falls — and that is where I lost track of him. He had gone back to his East Side homies,

guys who had also experienced their share of failures. Joey Aboussie, after a respectable career as a running back for the Longhorns
and a few years as a CPA in Fort Worth, had also returned to
Wichita Falls, to start an oil-drilling company with his in-laws. When
Lawrence Williams' three-year pro career was over, he came back,
moved into a neighborhood away from the East Side, and sold
cars and then worked as a retail ad salesman for the Wichita Falls
newspaper. It was Aboussie and Williams who were asked to give
speeches at the high school sports banquets or at the Coyotes' pep
rallies. But people didn't see Littleton. He had become an invisible
man — which is exactly the way he wanted it.

> "Oh, I guess I saw him a few years ago," said a former lineman, "at a
> Coyotes game."
> "A Coyotes game?"
> "I didn't have much of a conversation with him. I didn't know what
> to say."
> "Why not?"
> "He was drunk. Completely drunk."

For weeks I made calls to the AC Delco plant where Littleton worked
building oxygen sensors for GMC cars and trucks. I called his close
friends, asking if they could persuade him to talk. For a few minutes
we actually had a polite chat on the phone. (Ronnie: "Why do you
want to see me?" Me: "Because I think it's important to talk about
those days." Ronnie: "Why?" Me: "Because none of us can stop
thinking about them.")

Finally, this past September, 40-year-old Ronnie Littleton whipped
his red pickup truck with oversized tires and mag wheels into the
Ramada Inn parking lot in Wichita Falls. He got out, ran a hand
through his shoulder-length hair, adjusted his wraparound sunglasses, then headed toward the hotel with the same bowlegged
strut that I used to imitate years ago. In my years as a journalist, I
have interviewed many people, but I cannot remember ever being
as nervous as I was at that moment.

"I remember you," Littleton said, although I could tell he didn't.
We went into the hotel restaurant, where he pulled out a pack
of cigarettes and ordered coffee. He took off his sunglasses and
squinted at me. "You know, I've given away all those clippings, the
trophies, even my letter jacket," he said. "It's long, long gone." He

was wearing blue jeans and an athletic T-shirt that didn't quite hide his soft belly. "Man, I don't even know what I can tell you."

I wasn't sure what he'd want to talk about. I asked him about his wife, Bobbie, a nurse whom he married in 1981. "She's gone through some shit with me," he said, giving me a faint smile. We talked about why the most recent Coyote teams were lucky to have winning seasons. "I don't know if those kids are dedicated to winning like we were," he said. "We got up every morning wanting to win. It was our life then. We were united, black players and white players, to get to that state championship." His voice trailed off, and he sipped some coffee. Despite the dark circles under his eyes, he was still as handsome as I remembered from high school. "Go on, my man, ask me anything," he said in a quiet voice. He knew I wanted to hear as much about the downfall as I did about the glory days.

I had already picked up bits and pieces about what had happened to him. I had heard that when he came back to Wichita Falls, he began stopping by a liquor store on East Side Drive, where he'd purchase a half-pint of Jack Daniel's and a tall can of malt liquor. I had heard he would drive out to a farm-to-market road beyond the city limit signs and drink alone. I had heard about the one time he tried to prove himself as a football player again. He had joined a small semipro football team, the Wichita Falls Roughnecks, coached by James Reed, one of the five original black Coyotes. After graduating from college, Reed too had come back to Wichita Falls. (Today he lives in the Dallas suburb of Arlington, where he owns a small construction-cleanup business.) Littleton told Reed that he wanted to see if he could still run past people. But there were times when Reed didn't let Littleton play, because he showed up drunk. After one Roughnecks loss, in which Littleton wasn't allowed to play, Reed looked along the sideline and saw Littleton weeping at the end of the bench.

"So I heard you did some drinking," I said.

He took a drag on his cigarette. "Yeah," he said. "Oh, yeah."

"Actually," I said, "this happens to a lot of guys in sports whose careers are cut short."

"But it wasn't supposed to happen to me." He stubbed out his cigarette in the ashtray and lit another. "I know I was drinking to cover up the pain. But maybe I was mad at God too. Oh, yeah. Everything I had dreamed of for my life was gone."

For a long time, he said, he didn't want to talk about football. He had difficulty talking to his old teammates. He would start drinking on Sundays when he'd watch the NFL games, and he'd drink on Friday nights, about the time the Coyotes' games started. He did attend some games, but he kept noticing the way the white people gave him double takes — the same people who used to cheer him, who now could not believe that the young man they had once elevated to such prominence was hiding a flask under his coat. He hated it when someone came up to him and said, "So, hey, Ronnie, what are you doing with yourself now?"

The years passed, he said. He started drinking from his bottle of Jack Daniel's in the mornings. The police pulled him over for DWIs, and yes, he did get arrested for keeping a .357 magnum in his car. But he had no intention of slowing down. He tried crack. He let his hair grow down to his shoulders. Soon the East Side was full of stories of Littleton acting crazy and looking for a fight. "If he thought you said something to him the wrong way, he would explode," said a woman who knew him well. "You just learned to get away from him." Ronnie Littleton had gone from the beloved schoolboy football hero to the bad black dude.

In 1988, to keep from being fired after missing too many days of work, he went to the rehabilitation center at Red River Hospital in Wichita Falls. Thirty days later he was back out drinking. He went a second time, yet quickly returned to the bottle. His life spiraling downward, he could not imagine what he could do to raise himself back up. On the streets one day, he happened to run into Lulanger Washington, the backup quarterback from that 1969 team. As it turned out, after Washington graduated from high school, he was so angry at whites for closing down Booker T. and ruining his chance for success in college that he decided to get even. He bought a pistol and learned to stick people up. Wearing a nylon stocking over his face, Washington would wait for white people to come out of a downtown bank after cashing their paychecks, and he'd slip up behind them, aiming a gun at the backs of their heads. But by the early eighties, Washington had given up his life of crime and become a street preacher on the East Side. "There are so many of us over here who grew up with this suppressed anger at our positions in life," he said. "Some of us felt we had never had a chance to show what we could do, and we wanted someone to pay. What I told

Ronnie was that we have got to make the best of our lives, whatever our lives turn out to be."

Even as Washington said those words, he knew it was harder than ever for black people in Wichita Falls. The East Side had rapidly deteriorated since he and Ronnie were boys. With few higher-paying jobs available, residents found it harder to escape the undertow of poverty. Crack had arrived, and soon after came the gangs and the violence. A few years ago a police officer was assigned to walk the hallways of Wichita Falls High School to keep gang members from other schools from causing trouble. "You remember how you used to be scared of coming over to the East Side?" Washington asked me. "I'm telling you, it was a church picnic back then. Now even the black folks are scared of the East Side, all those guns and bullets. I hate to say I told you so, but a lot of life went out of the East Side when Booker T. Washington High School closed. The community lost pride in itself. The adults stopped watching over these kids, making sure they didn't fail. The streets just got too tempting."

But there are still many success stories coming out of the East Side. Some of them are the most unexpected. In September 1991, after he realized he could no longer remember the Lord's Prayer, Ronnie Littleton tried rehabilitation for a third time. "This time," he told me, "I was ready to make it work." He said he has remained sober for the past three years, even though there are moments when his body craves liquor. "It's a battle, my man, one day at a time — but I'm not giving up," Littleton said. And to my astonishment, he gave me that same cheerful grin that I first saw by the Coyotes' locker room door.

I wanted to tell Ronnie Littleton how I could still do a perfect imitation of his walk, and that a quarter of a century later, I was still using words and phrases that I had first heard him say. I wanted him to know how his jivey hilarious attitude had really changed my life. He had helped usher Wichita Falls through those first painful days of integration, and he had also taught many of us white kids to loosen up. But he waved me off. "That was a long time ago, and I'm a different person now," he said. "I've been given a second chance, and I just want to say, 'Thank you, God.'"

As we walked to the hotel door, he put on his wraparound sunglasses and suddenly said, "You know what's strange? Sometimes I think about the way my body moved back then, all the moves I'd make to get free. Oh, Lord, man, if I could just get around a little like that today." He laughed in his familiar high-pitched way, gave me an old-fashioned soul handshake, and got in his red pickup with the mag wheels and drove off. For an instant I thought I was back in high school, watching him in his pimp-mobile with the blue shag on the dash. I remembered how he'd stick his head out of the window, shout, "Good-bye, little honks," then lay rubber for his home on the East Side. In my mind, he will always be that glorious teenager, uncatchable, moving like a stunning burst of light.

TOM CALLAHAN

How Swede It Is!

FROM GOLF DIGEST

NOT FAR FROM Stockholm, a bewilderment of islands, sits another island, Lovön, where only the king of Sweden or his designated gunman are allowed to take an elk or a hare but the children are entitled to all the lingonberries and cloudberries they can find. It's the Sunday morning of a Swedish summer.

A lingonberry might in fact *be* a cloudberry. The American who has joined the hunt isn't very quick, either on his feet or the uptake. Crossing the bridge, passing the palace, he has stopped off in the forest (hoping to catch the king jogging) before proceeding the short distance to Drottningholm, where practically the entire history of Swedish golf is gathered in one clearing.

Back in the woods, three young mothers appear: Greta Garbo, Ingrid Bergman and Jenny Lind, with their husbands, all variations of Bjorn Borg and Ingemar Stenmark. The berries are pooled in a giant stone bowl and whipped with egg whites and sugar into pink clouds that fill the picnickers with laughter and the forest with replays of a triumphant World Cup just past. (In Sweden, third place can still qualify as a triumph.)

"It was a carnival," says Jesper Parnevik in Drottningholm. "Every time they played. Like Rio de Janeiro almost. Dancing in the street. Golf isn't nearly soccer here yet. I wouldn't say it's even ice hockey. But it's up to tennis at least, generally that big and growing. Every course is more than full."

Golf Abloom

In the early 1900s, fewer than 100 golfers (most of them transplanted Brits) could be found in this lightly populated, California-sized nation. By 1955, just 39 courses had been gouged out of the pines to humor some 7,000 eccentrics.

But then an ice hockey star named Sven Tumba took up the game, and overnight the golfing population doubled, and tripled, and quadrupled. Today, of the 8 million Swedes sprinkled the length of a long country, 320,000 call themselves golfers, and more than 300 clubs are straining at the seams.

Parnevik is in the Drottningholm clubhouse, a typically functional building that fits the flat course and unspectacular surroundings. Anders Forsbrand is on the practice putting green. Joakim Haeggman is at the driving range. They compose Sweden's "Big Three." The Scandinavian Masters, never won by a Scandinavian, is abloom. The field is covered with shoots of young blond stick figures with names like Johansson, Karlsson, Lanner, Hedblom, Hjertstedt, Fulke and Eriksson, overwhelming the visiting mercenaries (Ian Woosnam, Colin Montgomerie, Vijay Singh) at least in numbers.

Tumba, 62, that hockey player who stepfathered Swedish golf — and also devised the Scandinavian Masters, formerly known as the Scandinavian Enterprise Open — is abroad on the property accepting perennial congratulations for his legendary life. On skis, skates and cleats, Tumba played absolutely everything for Sweden.

When he was through with the Olympic Games, the Swedish National Soccer Team, and the U.S. National Hockey League (Boston Bruins, 1957), he brought Sam Snead, Arnold Palmer and Jack Nicklaus over for golf exhibitions, and he didn't stop there. He built the first golf course in Moscow and named it after himself; that is, after the name he had given himself when his real name, Johansson, turned out to be so common and inadequate. Tumba!

Prowling the grounds like a bear, if bears were in better shape, Tumba looks at all the Swedes as his sons and tries to forget the unsettled sadness around his natural son. Johan Tumba, a modest talent burdened with a grand name, has been banned from professional golf for three years for allegedly cheating at the European Tour Q School two years ago. Lawyers and forensic experts were called upon to examine the card in question. Nobody mentions any of this to the old bear for whom everyone on the midway calls and claps and cheers.

Strong Swedish Stomach

His current invention, or at least conviction, is that a point exists in the body, a *saika tanden,* two inches below the navel and two inches inside the trunk, a balance point, a human "Iron Byron," that "has every game in it." As he says, "Swedes have always been naturally athletic, but we play too much from the outside, not the inside. Everyone says 'Crazy Sven,' but I think, 'To hell with the hands, the swing, and everything else on the periphery of golf.' Keep the *saika tanden* still, rotate around that thing, and you'll find your physical and your mental balance."

That's where he believes Parnevik has come, and where he hopes Sweden is going. "Jesper's very strong in the stomach," Tumba says. "That's the place we're getting stronger. Not on the golf course. In the stomach."

Besides being a gastrointestinal phenomenon, Parnevik (he of the Rootie-Kazootie hat) is the current darling of the Swedish sports pages. His fair hair curls up in the front more or less the way Joe Montana's does in the back, and Jesper begins to cut that kind of figure. Since his brush with immortality at the last British Open, children have been gliding flaps-up all over Scandinavia.

Parnevik's bent brim could stand for a number of things, including the resourcefulness of a sponsor who takes the precaution of advertising both on the face of the crown and the underside of the bill, plastering all angles. Jesper's psychologist (read: guru-cum-witch doctor), Olof Skipper, considers the off-kilter lid "a triggering device."

Skipper sports one, too, and frankly it fits him better, perfectly topping off a yellow mane, Elizabethan beard and golden earring. "Jesper's inside himself all the time," Skipper says, "but then he opens up to play golf. You see? It's a key he uses to become someone else, a Pavlovian stimulus."

At which point Jesper interrupts to note with a sigh: "The first time, I was just trying to get a suntan actually. It rains here every day."

And, yet, he seems to see the putting avenues clearer this way.

The public has been able to make him out a little clearer, too. The tee he keeps jammed behind one ear, like a cornerman's Q-tip, elegantly accessorizes the Bowery Boy cap.

Young Jerry Pate once leaped into water hazards to distinguish himself from the other towheads. This may be just as silly, but it's considerably drier.

"Galleries laugh when they see me," Parnevik says. "If you can make people laugh, even if you look a little stupid doing it, isn't that a good thing?"

He only naturally would think so, being an offspring of a comedian, the nationally renowned Bo Parnevik. "He's sort of a Rich Little," the son explains, "but with full makeup and wigs and gestures. He can do Columbo better than Columbo, and he looks more like Reagan than Reagan does himself. I mean, he's closer to what you think Reagan is."

So what is the makeup of the boy in the cocked hat who grew up in the shade of show business?

His memories of childhood are situated not in the studios or drawing rooms of his father's career, but in the streams of the archipelago, where the family regularly sailed for solitude. "We had greens in the backyard and everything. I'd hit floating range balls out into the water, then row out to bring them in. I loved being in the streams."

Like many Swedish children, he made his way up and down the list of games — Ping-Pong, tennis, soccer, ice hockey — like racing through a field of bright, beguiling flowers. The youth camps that dot the sporting landscape were his preserves.

"Swedes are shy," Skipper says as he begins to tell the story. But Jesper stops him, and takes over. " 'Shy' is not the right word," he says. " 'Quiet' is better. Not many Swedes go around shouting: 'You're the man!' That's not a very Swedish thing to do.

"Strong physiques, healthy diets — those are certainly Swedish elements. You grow up feeling your body is important. At the same time, you try not to stick out. Especially if you're part of a team. You can only improve as the team improves." Quietly, he is setting the groundwork for explaining his eventual break from the pack of Swedish golfers.

"In the States," says Parnevik, who has come to know America in the course of that split, "it seems some parents have kids just to make them big athletes. In the U.S., fame is everything; if you're on TV, it's like you're a god or something."

As he describes it, the child athletes of Sweden are relatively innocent of parental pressures. "You start playing golf at age seven. It's very cheap, maybe $80 a year. Did you know? You have to demonstrate a minimum competence just to get on a course. You need a 'green card.' At the end of the summer, the ten best eight-year-olds, nine-year-olds and so on play a tournament. It's so much fun.

"Between ten and thirteen, you play fifty-four holes a day with your friends, and golf pros give you lessons for free. Then, when you're sixteen, you go on the Teen Tour. If you can make the national boys' team, you travel on your summer vacations playing tournaments. It's very structured, but it isn't like American Little League. It isn't for the parents. It's for you.

"In Sweden, golf is a sport, not an activity. It's not important to belong to the right club. It's not a lifestyle, an affectation. It's a sport."

Parnevik emerged from the process a surprisingly unstructured golfer. "My game is kind of bits and pieces, here and there," he says. "I play with whatever swing turns up in the morning. Yesterday, I cut every shot. Today, I drew everything. I reach into the bag and pull out what I find. To me, it's all a matter of feel."

Similarly, he felt his way free from "the team." Nothing against his countrymen: He roots for them all without reservation. But gradually, after he reached the European tour in 1987, Jesper began to arrange his practice rounds with non-Swedes and eventually took to staying at a different hotel. Instinctively he knew: "If I was to make it to the next level, I had to go alone. Golf is a game of self-improvement, self-management. Ultimately, you have to go your own way."

He had dipped his toe in America at Palm Beach Junior College in West Palm Beach, Florida, and would go back and forth in a number of ways for a number of years. In 1993, encouraged by finally winning in Europe (the Bell's Scottish Open, capping a £342,787 season), Parnevik returned to the U.S. with a resolve. He tied for fourth at the tour school on the strength of a 65–66 start and, by the time the British Open rolled around last July, he had already earned enough ($142,806) to breathe easily.

Tooling about Florida in a red '72 Cadillac convertible with "Va Da Ra" plates (translation: "What's Up?"), Parnevik showed neither his age, 29, nor his ulcer to the world. Sitting beside him was girlfriend Mia, a pocket Anita Ekberg whose hair, bunched to one side, outdazzles sunlight.

When the Nicklaus boys brought Jesper home, Jack took him for much younger. It wasn't until they were grouped together for the first two rounds at Turnberry that Nicklaus saw the golfer. By Friday evening, Jack was picking Rootie Kazootie to win the British Open.

Jesper Could Laugh

As almost everyone knows by now, Jesper could have won if only he had understood he was winning. Declining to look at the leader board, imagining a racket of birdsong trilling behind him, Parnevik did not realize he was two shots to the good on the last tee. Playing companion Tom Watson, who knew precisely where Parnevik stood, arched an eyebrow before Jesper struck a bold wood off the tee — perfectly.

"I had 155 left and hit a wedge — I changed from a 9-iron," Parnevik recalls. "Of course, I was just short, and the rough that last day was very dry. So I made bogey. It surprises even me that I didn't know where I stood. Most of the time I want to know."

Says Skipper, "I think you play better if you don't."

"No, it's just that on the back nine, I was so focused, I didn't think it mattered," says Jesper. " 'If I birdie every hole,' I thought, 'nobody's going to beat me anyway.' That's the way I felt. I was going to birdie in."

Everything the British Open owed Nick Price (a considerable tab) was paid back at 17 in either a 50- or a 70-foot eagle putt, depending on the zeal of the chronicler. Price then cobbled together a professional par at 18 to beat Jesper by a shot. Everyone glanced pityingly toward the crestfallen Swede in the funny hat.

"But don't you see?" Jesper says. "The way it turned out, I *did* need a birdie to win. If I would have been playing with Nick Price and we were tied, I would have gone for the pin anyway. I have a very tough time not going for the pin. In the downswing, my heart grabs the club."

In the next moment, he good-naturedly agreed to pop out of a suitcase for a hotel chain's television commercial: "Recently, I have had some trouble with numbers. So, I want to be completely sure of this one. To reserve a room, call . . ."

Jesper could laugh along with the world because he knew something the world didn't.

"I wasn't scared at the British," he says, almost whispers. "I didn't step down. I stayed strong. When I think back, there were a lot of testy putts, four or five on the front, and I holed all of them. You know, in putting, it isn't so much the break or the speed. It's who wants to win. It's pure willpower, I think. I hung in there. I could never do that before.

"Early on in Sweden, friends were way too kind. If I shot 80, they would say, 'Aw, too bad, it's O.K., have a beer.' In the U.S., no one cared, and that was very good. I was all by myself, except Mia. Without her, I would have been too lonely."

They married in August, the weekend following his greatest spree: a charging third (seven closing birdies) in defense of the Scottish Open, the second-place finish in the British Open and another runner-up spot in the Scandinavian Masters, when Vijay Singh's Sunday 64 kept Sweden winless in its own tournament for now twenty-two years.

The day after the wedding, Jesper went alone to the PGA championship while Mia stayed home to reciprocate for her maid of honor. Parnevik played like a single honeymooner at Southern Hills, but in the Oklahoma haziness he seemed to see his day coming closer.

But Anders Is the Best

When Bernhard Langer flirted with the British Open almost fifteen years ago, reporters asked the young German, just for their own information, who was the greatest German golfer who ever lived? He answered forthrightly. It was he.

Sweden is a little like that, new enough to golf to be living its heritage. Whoever was the greatest Swedish golfer who ever lived, he was playing in the Scandinavian Masters in July.

"It's Anders Forsbrand," Parnevik says quickly. "On the record, it has to be Anders. For now, it's he."

So many young blond stick figures with names like Haeggman and Johansson and Karlsson and Lanner and Hedblom and Hjerstedt and Fulke and Eriksson can glance over at Forsbrand on the practice putting green and think: "For now."

Thirty-three is young for a pioneer. Sometimes Forsbrand feels like the father of all the fair-haired boys he has tried both to help and to hold off. He likes them all but he isn't like any of them. He's slightly darker in hair color, and in other ways.

Forsbrand comes from steel and timber, a miniature Pittsburgh in the piney woods, where people are spread in thinner layers. Somehow he forgot to get in line for one of those unpushy Swedish fathers Parnevik described. Neither did Anders attend any of the idyllic summer camps. As a matter of fact, he has a sneering contempt for overgrown playground directors. Forsbrand taught himself to play golf — he was a 1-handicap at age fourteen — and has the most elegant swing in the country.

"I shot air pistols, too," he says, "on a team that won the junior championship. That was fun."

He makes that sound like his last recollection of fun.

Long before Parnevik — and to a considerably greater extent — Forsbrand was the original Swedish rebel, who went so far as to move to Marbella, Spain, for its balmier tax climate. Practically from the beginning, Anders recognized no authority. *He* was the authority.

Sweden's junior golf program with its comprehensive recruiting committees, regimented training camps and myriad competitions was founded on the communal slogan that "one plus one equals more than two" and yet with the expressed individual goal of turning out "the best player in the world" by 1996.

Only recently, according to the coach of the Swedish National Team, Kjell Enhager, has that ambition been downsized to the production of "players and coaches who reach their potential as human beings through the game of golf."

Far from the Swedish ideal, Forsbrand can be a Vesuvius of temper. He admires Jose Maria Olazabal's ability to curse at close range, but has never been able to adjust his own volume control. What Joe Mary mutters in Spanish can't be made out at a meter's distance; what Anders blurts in English can't be mistaken at fifteen. His personal record for lava and loathing was set at Paris this year when it took Forsbrand 93 strokes to negotiate 17 holes, and only two splashes at 18 saved him from dripping over 100. He ran out of balls.

"He's our brooding Hamlet," says Claes Lind of the Swedish press corps, "but he has a good heart. He always has time for the young Swedes."

Forsbrand has won seven times on the European tour, by far the most of any Swede, and has also directed his countrymen to World Cup and Dunhill Cup triumphs. Anders has had his moments in America, tossing a stately 66 at Augusta National in 1993. But a defining instant has eluded him. Unnoticed in Parnevik's backwash, Forsbrand tied for fourth at Turnberry. He is beginning to feel a little passé.

"It's hard to be the one who goes first," Forsbrand says softly, "when there's no one else to look up to. It's nice to be looked up to yourself, to be respected for what you've done. But there's a pressure to that, too."

Young as he still is, Forsbrand has lived a lot more than the others. For one thing, he has been divorced. Returning to Spain to a "Dear Anders" note from his Norwegian wife, a former flight attendant, he drank coffee for two weeks, nothing else, staring at the ceiling and smoking cigarettes. Looking at the new wave, he sometimes wonders if any of them has ever wept. Forsbrand has found another love but he's still staring at the ceiling a little.

"I've been thinking of America, of trying it," he says, "maybe just for a year. You can't drop in there five or six or seven times a year and expect to break through. You have to move everything you have to the other side of the ocean. You have to leave home."

He sounds nearly ready.

Handsome Haeggman

"This should be Forsbrand's time, just like it should be Payne Stewart's time," says Joakim Haeggman, who is 25 and has a lot of time. "You start off in your early twenties saying to yourself: 'I'm going to be number one in the world someday.' Not next year, or two years from now, but someday. You really believe it. But I think it's hard for golfers getting on to thirty-five to keep believing it. When they start losing that feeling, if they don't do something fast, they're lost."

He is quick to add: "Don't get me wrong. If Anders does nothing else, he already has done so much. And every one of us owes him. Our chance is better because of him. I just wish he were winning his majors now. It's time."

Haeggman, the first and only Ryder Cup Swede, is a brutally handsome ex-swimmer who still smells faintly of chlorine. Chatty and outgoing, he is sort of the male Helen Alfredsson. "When Jesper was coming down the stretch in the British," he says, "I was drinking in a lounge in Copenhagen, jumping up and down, making the usual fool of myself."

He is quiet (and slow) only on the course and the water.

"I'm not really a golfer, I'm a fly fisherman," he says reverently. "It's hard for people to understand, but it's a way of life. Winning a golf tournament is nice, but a salmon on a fly rod is the best thing in the world."

Sometimes, and Colin Montgomerie will not be surprised to hear this, Haeggman's mind can wander on the green. Lining up a putt, searching out the grain and the ripple, he sees streams converging.

"You put the fly out on the one current and it meets the other. Then slowly, you're waiting for it to happen, waiting for it to happen, when — bang! — the ball goes in the hole."

In his hotel room between rounds, Haeggman ties his flies and only occasionally reflects on that promise to his young self to be number one in the world. "Some Swede will get there," he says. "Jesper, myself, Per-Ulrik Johansson. He's just underneath, and deserves some luck. Peter Hedblom, Pierre Fulke, Mathias Gronberg, Gabriel Hjerstedt. Give them another two, three, four years."

Both the women and men of Sweden are proliferating on American college golf teams. According to Anna Brandstrom of the Sweden Golf Federation, more than a dozen of each are in circulation at the moment, and U.S. schools have been calling and clamoring for more.

In collegiate and Swedish golf, conformity is the virtue and "team" is the byword. Still, it is instructive to remember that two of the "Big Three" diverted from the Swedish team in their ways. And Haeggman is still fishing.

Anyway, only at a squint are the blonds of Drottningholm completely alike. Something distinguishes them all. Fulke is the master of the wedge; Eriksson shows the grit that won the Challenge Tour (their Nike) in '93; Hjerstedt, whose family moved to Queensland when he was ten, has given a Swedish disposition an Australian accent; Johansson appears to have profited from his collegiate association with Phil Mickelson. ("Call me Peaches," Per-Ulrik says. "That's what they called me at Arizona State." "He's kidding you," says Mickelson. "We called him Fruit Bowl.")

Parnevik figures: "If Sweden is looking for a golfing Borg, it won't find him. The same players are in the quarters of all the tennis tournaments. But, of course, golf isn't that way.

"In America, even the nongolf fan probably notices who won the Masters. Not here. Someday, I think."

All over the country, children riding their bicycles through hay fields are pulling golf trolleys behind them. That's the final postcard of Sweden, the one that stays with you. Golf is getting ready to storm all right. Pink clouds are gathering.

MICHAEL WILBON

Winning Isn't Color-Coded

FROM THE WASHINGTON POST

I'M ROOTING FOR Duke. Always do. This makes me a member of a small, tiny, wee little group: black people who root for Duke.

If you don't believe me, go ahead and conduct your own little poll. Ask ten black people who they're rooting for in the Final Four and nine of them will give you the same answer: "Anybody but Duke." For the most part, people talk around the real issue and honest feelings stay in the closet.

Occasionally, I'll ask somebody black — could be a relative, a close friend, an ex-player — why he roots against Duke.

"Because they play too rough."

So did Georgetown, but you rooted for the Hoyas.

"Because they get every call from the officials."

So did Michael Jordan, but you rooted for him.

Finally, after you play this little game for five minutes or so, those real feelings slip out: "Because Duke is too . . . too . . . white."

When Johnny Dawkins and Tommy Amaker were the stars of the team, Duke was too white. When Danny Ferry and Christian Laettner were stars in succession, Duke was intolerably white. And now, with Grant Hill leading the Blue Devils to yet another Final Four, Duke is still too white. All three of those generalizations are too prejudiced, too biased, too intolerable to be passed off as just silly. Last I checked, three of those five players are black.

Some people root for some teams for the strangest reasons: because the uniforms look nice, because the team colors are cool, because they like the style of play or so-and-so's nephew went there for two semesters. I don't care who people root for, but it's more instructive to find whom they root *against*. There are people in this country who are going to root against Georgetown simply and only because John Thompson and the vast majority of his players are black. There are fewer and fewer such sentiments about the Hoyas every year, but they're still out there and I've got the mail to prove it.

It's the same thing for Duke, just another race of people carrying different baggage. Duke has become the Boston Celtics of the college ranks, the basketball villain to too many black people. That thinking would be wrong even if Duke had an all-white team. But it's wrong and stupid because Duke's teams are never all white, never predominantly white. The irony — as I point out to blacks whenever they trash the Celtics without knowing they were the first NBA team to draft a black player, play an all-black team and hire a black coach — is that both the Celtics and Duke have provided black men with opportunities denied blacks by other organizations and colleges. And some of those other colleges we as black people root for.

Almost without exception, black kids who play basketball at Duke go to class, get their degrees on time and become contributing citizens. We won't root for them, but we'll root for, say, N.C. State, whose graduation rates for black players have been abysmal at times. What exactly qualifies an N.C. State to be "black" enough but Duke not to be? What are the criteria for being "too white"? One white starter? Two?

Is Grant Hill somehow not as black as, say, Scotty Thurman of Arkansas? How "white" can Duke be if its best player, Grant Hill, is the son of one of the most prominent African-American scholars/athletes/businessmen/entrepreneurs in the country? If Jeff Capel is "too white" that might come as a surprise to his father, the head basketball coach at historically black North Carolina A & T. You mean Gene Banks, Billy King, David Henderson, Kevin Strickland and Doug McNeely (Mike Krzyzewski's first recruit) don't count? And it can't possibly relate to playing for a black coach because a lot of those "too white" Boston Celtics teams played for Bill Russell and Tom Sanders and K. C. Jones. Tell kids these days that John Thompson played for the Celtics and that he once studied under Red Auerbach and they want to fight you.

On the back of certain models of Nike shoes are two statements: "Live Together" appears on one shoe. "Play Together" appears on the other. Nobody embodies these mottos more than Coach K's Duke teams. Nobody's teams shatter more stereotypes. He can have a tempestuous, leaping player such as Christian Laettner who is white, and a steady, thinking-man's playmaker in Tommy Amaker who is black, now a Duke assistant and one of the bright young coaching minds in the country.

The black players I've talked to about this issue over a period of years are perplexed. The most insightful thoughts I've heard on the topic have come from Laettner, who told me two years ago: "This is all about perception. I don't know if people resent us as much as they resent the way the team is portrayed by a lot of people in the media, this goody-two-shoes team that thinks it's better than other people. I never bought into it. I think the anger's just misdirected."

Hopefully, Laettner was right. If so, boo the TV announcer, boo the newspaper columnist who tells you Duke is good and UNLV is evil and that the Blue Devils are angelic and operate on higher moral ground. That kind of stereotyping builds resentment.

For the segment of the black community that feels so frustrated over generations of exclusion and therefore so proprietary about one of the few arenas black folks tend to rule, maybe it's time to transfer that passion from basketball to math and science. Many look at Duke and don't see the color balance they want. I look at Duke and see basketball, season after season, at its best at the college level. And if Duke continues to play into the spring often enough, maybe the people who waste their time rooting for Duke to lose will grow so frustrated they'll get the point.

RICK REILLY

Look Out for the Bull!

FROM SPORTS ILLUSTRATED

CALLER? CALLER? Can you turn down your radio?

Good. Now, can you hang up that phone?

Good. Now, *I've* got something to say. I quit. I can't go on. I've had to fill four hours of airtime a day, five days a week, talking about sports. This station fills twenty-four hours a day, seven days a week, talking about sports. We have beaten every issue into hotel-ashtray sand, yet we will talk about this stuff again next week. If one more person asks me if I think Tonya Harding did it, I am going to get his address, drive calmly to his house and remove his larynx with a ball retriever.

Don't you see? It is all bullspit. I don't know any more than you. I have the newspaper in front of me, same as you. A lot of the people in my line of work were second-string punt-coverage guys and country and western disc jockeys. Most of us can't get credentialed to the International Darts Festival. You ask me, "Do you think Tonya Harding did it?" And, just once, I would like to say, "I don't have a clue. I'm not within a toll call of a clue on that. I've never spoken to Tonya Harding or even overhauled a transmission with her. You might as well ask me if I know any really great lunch spots in Gdansk." But just the same, I give you thirteen minutes of prattle. Hey, I've got four hours to fill here.

The truth is, America is getting a B.S. degree in sports, and the b.s. part is spilling in through your car radio and out from under your big-screen TV. A nation that was once full of doers is now a nation full of dialers.

Three years ago there were a fistful of all-sports radio stations in the U.S. Now there are seventy-eight. There were only a few sports-roundtable TV shows. Now nearly every big city has one. ESPN has, what, seventeen? It has gotten this sick: You can even participate in a live call-in sports show while you are on an airplane.

And the passengers on the left side of the cabin will notice the Grand Can — I'm on the air? The Phillies suck!

"We have become a land of B.S. and sound bites," says CBS basketball analyst Billy Packer. "It's all diarrhea of the mouth."

This sports talk is doing bad things. Take three sports-writer friends of mine. Ordinarily you could spray WD-40 on their appetizers and they wouldn't arch an eyebrow. Yet whenever they appeared on a roundtable segment of ESPN's *NFL Prime Monday* last fall, they all became Morton Downey Jr., yelling, sneering and calling people names. What matters is not the most-considered opinion. What matters is the loudest opinion. Or, better yet, the last opinion before the beer ad.

On the Information Superhighway the only sure way to keep winding up as roadkill is to be the loudest, the dirtiest or the meanest. It's the New McCarthyism. The Everybody Here in the Studio Is Cool and Everybody Else Is a Jerk school of broadcasting.

"It has distorted all of the things that we should be getting out of sports," says Penn State football coach Joe Paterno. "Nobody ever wins a game anymore; somebody else blew it."

And it doesn't matter who gets ripped, as long as *somebody* gets ripped. A talk-show-host friend of mine calls me up every once in a while and says, "Give me something to rip him with today."

"Something to rip *who* with?"

"Whoever."

Do you really think you're getting inside stuff from guys like us? Four years ago in Tuscaloosa, Alabama, some radio talk-show hosts crawled all over Alabama football coach Bill Curry, insisting that Auburn had whipped his butt in recruiting. Before long, discontented Alabama alumni, further incensed by what they were hearing on the radio, finally got Curry fired. Three years later those players recruited by Curry helped win the national championship.

In many cases the stations with sports talk shows also own the rights to broadcast the games of local teams, which means the stations could lose big bucks if Joe Talkshowhost makes Charlie Generalmanager angry. At one Los Angeles radio station this memo was distributed to on-air talent: "A reminder to be 'friendly' to our local teams, especially our flagships. There should be no bad-mouthing of these teams and if a caller or guest instigates such talk . . . our talk-show hosts . . . should carefully change the subject or move on to something else."

But forget the hosts for a minute. Have you ever met any of the callers? Most of these guys spend their days holding down couch springs. Kentucky basketball coach Rick Pitino says they're "basically frustrated at home, can't get a date, don't do well at their jobs and are basically at the nadir of their lives." In other words, if things got any worse for them, they would host their own shows.

"I've got a new policy," Packer says. "When I'm on a show and I get asked about a player I haven't seen yet, I just say, 'Sorry, I really don't have the background to answer that question.'"

Sounds like a movement. Now I have to get all the other hosts and all their guests and all the callers to agree. Then I would really be doing something to clean up the air.

PETER ANDREWS

No Pain, No Game

FROM GOLF DIGEST

GOLF IS A MISTAKE. You must understand this elemental fact if you are ever going to come to terms with it. By rights, golf should have remained a solitary Scottish occupation like tossing the caber, which is something only a Scot would be fool enough to do. Golf is not really a game at all, but a perverse obsession designed to inflict pain on its practitioners that has somehow slipped past the borders of its national origin and is now played by people who do not realize the true essence of the endeavor.

When people blithely say golf is a Scottish invention, they do not realize the terrible implications of that statement.

Let me explain it to you. Since I am three-quarters Scot, I can say this about my people. You can't.

Ask the average American to imagine a full-blooded Scot and he will probably conjure a vaguely comic figure, fairly close with the shilling and given to whistling "Roaming in the Gloaming." Pressed to deeper sociological insights, he may talk about a prickly sense of self-possession and a stern religious strain that sorts well with the rigors of golf. Fair enough as far as it goes, but to describe a Scot in those paltry terms is to describe Genghis Khan as an agrarian reformer and horseman.

To know the game, you must first truly know the Scot. For openers, the Scot is bred from the most ferocious warrior class in history. Two items will demonstrate. When the Roman legions first came ashore after defeating the Gauls and every other tribe in the known world, they took one look at the Scots, said, "Oh my God, who are these people?" and promptly threw up a wall across the length of the island in hopes they would go away. This was the military equivalent of playing for the tie. Later, when the English felt it was their turn to rule the world, they may have been mildly contemptuous of the Welsh and the Irish, but the Scots scared them witless. An English army would no more venture unattended into the highlands than in America the Sisters of Mercy would mount a foraging party in Apache country. Scotland was eventually subdued by dint of English organization and Scottish treachery. You could always find a Scot who was as eager to disembowel his neighbor as he was to fight the common enemy.

Let us go on to the other essentials of life, food and drink. The Scot's signature dish, the one he serves on feast days to important guests, is the haggis, which is the single-most loathsome comestible ever devised. Basically, you take a sheep's stomach, stuff it with oatmeal and chopped junk culled from the insides of other sheep, and boil it. Cooking times and proportions are immaterial.

I grant you Scotch whiskey is an adornment on the altar of civilization, of which any race may be proud. However, the Scottish contribution is not as grand as you might think. Do you know how they discovered whiskey? I am not making this up. It is taken from a history book given to me by one of Scotland's leading distillers. Sometime during the Middle Ages, the Irish developed whiskey as a liniment for livestock but the Scots started taking the stuff internally. Before anyone could tell them of their error, it had become the Scottish beverage of choice. Real Scots, of course, don't drink the blended whiskey we do. They prefer single malts and the king of those to my thinking is Laphroaig, which tastes rather like iodine.

Now do you begin to grasp the nettle? If you take a warlike people who rendered two of the greatest armies in the history of the world bandy-legged with fear and whose national cuisine looks like the residue of a dreadful traffic accident, which is washed down with a drink that tastes as if it would be useful in the treatment of trench foot, what kind of game do you think they would come up with? Quoits?

They invented a hellish game full of pain and anguish. Just the sort of entertainment Macbeth might engage in while arranging to have Macduff's wife and babies put to the sword.

Ever since the invention of golf, players have tried to civilize the dreadful game. The elaborate Rules of Golf are simply window dressing to cover over the essential bestial nature of the sport. They can be likened to the laws of chivalry in a jousting tournament in which the participants made a great show of courtesy when, in fact, the whole purpose of the festivities was to take a long wooden pole and try to stave in one another's chest cavities.

The Scots in their genius, if such be the word, supplanted physical danger with mental anguish, but the absorption of pain remains central to the game. People who spend generation after generation running around the countryside in woolen kilts without underwear get to like pain. Malevolent winds, pelting rain and erring shots that bring heartbreak and despair are all part of the fun to Scots. If you took their passion for pain and moved it indoors among non-consenting adults, you would be talking about the very real possibility of jail time.

Many of us try to keep the game but take the pain out of it. This seems logical. You can enjoy boating without going to a sailor's bar and getting tattooed in the back room. To play golf without pain, however, is like going to a house of bondage and asking to be whipped with damp Kleenex. You are missing the intended effect. You might as well play lacrosse for kisses. You would have a gentler, sweeter game, but it would not be lacrosse.

But still we try because we don't have the starch of the ancient Scottish masters. We hope we can make the game pleasant when it was never intended to be so. We take mulligans because it makes for a nicer start to the game when the point is to show that it is quite useless to play at all. We give ourselves putts and thus are denied the exquisite joy of watching a friend choke on something inside the two-foot range for money he can't afford. We take carts to speed the way when the game was designed to keep us swathed in inclemency for the longest time possible.

We may want to quit but we cannot, no matter how dreadfully we are playing. If we were a boxer so inept, blessed sleep would knit up the raveled sleeve of our incompetence. A baseball manager would take us out and send us to a refreshing shower. But in golf we play on and on until we drink the last full measure of humiliation.

Everything conspires against us. The Rules of Golf are supposed to bring order to the chaos of golf, but they frequently read like the printed agenda for a carnival of dunces and make a mockery of sport. I am convinced the stricture against fixing spike marks, which is the dumbest regulation since the old English prohibition against "marriage with deceased wife's sister," is kept on the books only to frustrate and harass us. It is a lingering fear among rules-makers that there just might be a golfer out there somewhere who is actually enjoying himself. And that thought gives them the willies.

No. There's nothing for it. If the game must be played at all, it has to be played in pain as the Scots intended. Golf is an iodine game. Like children with a mangled toe, we plead for Mercurochrome because it doesn't hurt so much. But our parents always went for the iodine bottle. They said the stinging was good for us. It showed they were getting out the poisons.

I didn't know I had any poisons in me, and I always assumed my mother was lying to me for reasons of her own. Maybe she was just preparing me to play golf when I grew up.

Thanks a lot, Mom.

GARY CARTWRIGHT

Vain Glory

FROM TEXAS MONTHLY

WHEN I VISITED the Dallas Cowboys' Valley Ranch complex in mid-February, a month after the Cowboys had won their second consecutive Super Bowl, I should have guessed what was up, but the obvious somehow escaped me. Jerry Jones was in one of his "peak-on-peak" modes, a phrase that the effervescent Cowboys owner had coined to describe his determination to take "America's greatest sports franchise to the next level." He was fairly bouncing off the walls, juggling a dozen decisions at once, that trademark grin frozen to his lips and his hungry eyes glistening like those of a cat locked in canary heaven. He had just come from a meeting in which he browbeat the sales representatives from several jewelry manufacturers while inspecting designs for a second Super Bowl ring. This turned out to be an omen: A year ago Jimmy Johnson had taken credit for designing the ring, but on this day Jimmy was nowhere to be seen. Now Jerry was scurrying to an allotted ninety-minute interview, after which he had to rush off on a personal errand before catching a plane for Mexico City to arrange a preseason game with the Houston Oilers. Peak-on-peak was the beginnings of a master plan bubbling in the back of Jerry's brain, not yet fully articulated but almost certain to be noteworthy, if not revolutionary.

"I just read a poll that revealed that the Dallas Cowboys are the favorite sports franchise of seventeen percent of the people in this country, which means that we've surpassed the New York Yankees!" Jones gushed as I followed him along a corridor. "Sure, we could sit back and smell the roses. But I've never worked harder in my life. We're fueled by my own energy and enthusiasm." Jerry recalled for

me the celebrated salary negotiations with running back Emmitt
Smith — Emmitt had held out for two league games, both of which
the Cowboys lost — and made the astonishing revelation that the
real holdout wasn't Emmitt but Jerry.

"By structuring the contract the way I did, I saved the Cowboys
one million dollars for each year that Emmitt plays," Jerry beamed.
"That means that under the salary cap, we have an extra million
dollars to pay a Nate Newton or a Daryl Johnston who does the
blocking that makes Emmitt the great ball carrier that he is." As
Jerry rambled on, talking so fast that his words became jumbled,
using the pronouns "we" and "I" interchangeably to refer to himself, a
larger question kept nudging me: What the hell is going on here?

Five weeks later — when Jerry gave Jimmy the hook — I got my
answer. Shedding Johnson was part of what he meant by taking it to
a new level. Sure, there would be a firestorm of protest, no doubt
worse than the protests sparked by the firing of Tom Landry in
1989, but Jones knew that the Cowboys would ride it out. Jones had
predicted more than a year ago that when the salary cap became
effective in 1994, the league would be playing with a new deck, and
he had made his plans accordingly. Everyone knew that Jimmy
Johnson was relentless and ruthless, but so was Jerry. His conclusion that Jimmy was expendable showed a Machiavellian cunning
that took the sports world by surprise.

The blinding speed with which Jones changed coaches during
that incredible three-day drama in March knocked the wind out of
everyone, friends and foes alike. "I've been writing sports for twenty-
eight years, and I thought I had seen everything," said Randy Galloway, the *Dallas Morning News'* sports columnist and a frequent Jerry-
basher. "But that scene at Valley Ranch was history unfolding before
your eyes, the sports equivalent of the Waco compound. People in
sports will be talking about this fifty or a hundred years from now."
Jones wasn't just replacing a coach, he was issuing a manifesto.
Jerry Jones *is* the Dallas Cowboys. He had said that before, but
nobody believed him. And incredibly, by day four, the man on the
street was speculating not how far the Cowboys would fall without
Johnson but how far they would go with his successor, Barry Switzer.
Troy Aikman, who had played briefly for Switzer at Oklahoma before transferring to UCLA, went before the media and described
the new Cowboys coach as "the best motivator" he had ever played
for. Jimmy *who?*

"Everyone is saying that I've put my neck on the chopping block, that if we don't go back to the Super Bowl, then I'll get the blame," Jerry told me when I interviewed him again on April 26, the day after the National Football League draft. "It's true that I've made myself an easy target. But if Jimmy had returned for another season, with everyone knowing of the problems between us, and if we had failed to go back to the Super Bowl, I would be targeted anyway."

"Jimmy would have made sure of that," I joked, hoping Jerry would take the bait. When things had gone badly for the team in past seasons, Jimmy had been the first to point a finger at Jerry.

Jerry's smile got a little wider, then he said, "If you're asking will it take more of an effort to return to the Super Bowl without Jimmy, the answer is yes. But that may be just the thing that causes it to happen."

Unlike baseball's New York Yankees owner George Steinbrenner, who is not above telephoning his manager during a game and ordering him to change pitchers, Jerry Jones has proven over and over that he is nobody's fool. Only in an enterprise as narcissistic as professional football could a man be accused of "meddling" in his own business. Jones told us that he was a meddler back in 1989, when he bought the franchise. He wasn't trying to be cute when he said that he was going to handle everything from socks to jocks. He meant jocks like Jimmy Johnson too.

"People who think that it's meddling when I involve myself in the football aspects of this business aren't looking at the real world," Jones told me. "Decisions about what happens on the field — between the white lines — are made by the coaches. I never second-guess those decisions. Then there is an area just outside the white lines, but one that is still perceived as football by media and fans. In this area I rely on our coaches and scouts. They make recommendations. I blend them in with the overall picture and decide what direction we will go. Thirdly, there is the financial area, which includes salaries and negotiations, the acquiring of players either through trades or draft decisions — injury risks, character, other things. These skills are not unique to football. Until 1989, neither Jimmy nor I had ever made a trade or a draft pick. But if I hadn't been a pretty good trader, I wouldn't have had the money to buy the Cowboys in the first place. Having said all that, if someone still wants to call it meddling, screw 'em."

*

The Dallas media, and the fans who live by the wisdom of those media, have subjected Jerry Jones to a curious double standard. Jimmy Johnson's monstrous ego was greatly admired by the media and credited as the secret of his success, but the same trait in Jerry was ridiculed and regarded as detrimental to the team. This is partly Jones's fault, but it can also be attributed to Jimmy's skill in choreographing his own image — usually at Jerry's expense. Jimmy always left the impression that Jerry was just along to carry the money. Unaccustomed to being in the spotlight, Jones came across in the beginning as clumsy and bungling. The media pictured him as an Arkansas hillbilly who probably peed off the front porch and ate goober peas with a knife. Or, alternatively, as a womanizer and cretin who used his fortune to buy acceptance. Jerry's reputation as a nocturnal carouser with a taste for strong drink and an eye for pretty women was not altogether undeserved, but the rumors that circulated in 1989 that his marriage was on the rocks were just that — rumors. Jerry has been married to his wife, Gene, a former Miss Arkansas, since 1963, when they were students at the University of Arkansas, and he is devoted to his three children, two of whom work for the Cowboys. Once the Cowboys started winning, Jerry's hillbilly studmuffin image vanished, but it reappeared as though by magic the week that Jimmy Johnson was dismissed. "It's no coincidence that all those rumors of family problems popped up again when the thing with Jimmy happened," Jerry said, his voice more ironic than bitter. Jerry-bashing was back in style, at least for the moment.

Jimmy had always promoted his own image as a larger-than-life anti-hero, a maverick to be feared and respected, a gambler who would risk it all on one turn of pitch and toss. The media gobbled it up. Jimmy took all the credit for the landmark Herschel Walker trade, but what really sealed that deal was Jerry's willingness to pay Walker $1 million to leave Dallas. Jerry ponied up another million to get Charles Haley and yet another million for Bernie Kosar, two reasons why Jimmy was able to win a first and then a second Super Bowl. Jimmy was up-front about his flaws and vices: He had no friends, except a small clique of trusted assistant coaches, nor did he need any; he had no interests outside of football; and though he had a wife while playing and coaching college football — because that was the convenient and socially acceptable thing to do — he divorced her when he reached the pros. Why couldn't Jerry be more like Jimmy?

Almost from the beginning of the Jaybirds' tenure in Dallas, Jimmy dropped hints that his boss was a lightweight, a whiner, and a pest. Jimmy let it be known to a *Dallas Morning News* sports writer that Jones had come to him after the 1990 season and told him, "I want it to be Jerry and Jimmy . . . not just Jimmy." In private and public conversations, Jimmy claimed that he — not Jerry — made all the football decisions. Jerry made the same claim about himself, though less adroitly. Jimmy and Jerry both courted the media shamelessly, but with different degrees of success. A perfect example of the double standard was a remark Jones made before the playoff game against Detroit in 1991. As an injured Aikman fretted that he was being shoved aside by fill-in Steve Beuerlein, Jones took it upon himself to tell *Fort Worth Star-Telegram* beat writer Mike Fisher what Johnson should have already made clear — that Aikman's career in Dallas was safe and secure. When Johnson read Jones's remark in the *Star-Telegram*, he was outraged. "Who is running the football team?" he roared. "Is Jerry the coach or am I the coach? To hell with it! If I'm not running things, maybe I should take my whole staff and we'll move to Tampa Bay!"

More enthusiastic than articulate — especially when he has consumed a few beverages — Jerry isn't always able to get his message across. In interviews, Jerry has led people to believe that he seriously thinks that he could coach the Cowboys. That's not what he means — not exactly. He keeps trying to tell people that the opportunity to coach has passed him by, that "when they put me in my grave, my coaching record will be zero-zero." But as he starts and stops and changes directions in mid-sentence — droning on about his motivation and his famous people skills — what one remembers is Jerry's celebrated pronouncement in *Vanity Fair:* "I could coach the shit out of this team!" His meaning is fairly simple: Had he decided back in the sixties to be a football coach instead of a multimillionaire, he would have been a damn good one, just as he has been damn good at everything he has ever tried.

Jones did not misspeak, however, the night of that famous barroom incident following the NFL owners meeting in Orlando, Florida, when he told a group of sports writers that he intended to fire Johnson and hire Switzer. It wasn't the whiskey talking in Orlando:

Jerry knew exactly what he was saying, though on sober reflection he probably would have picked a better time to say it. But Jerry had been thinking about firing Jimmy for at least two months, since Johnson had remarked to the media — on the eve of the NFC title game with the New York Giants, no less — that, yeah, sure, he would be interested in a job with the new expansion franchise in Jacksonville, Florida. Jimmy was contractually committed to the Cowboys through the 1998 season, so it was obvious to everyone in football that he was just jerking Jerry's chain again. Jerry had done some needling himself, but this was different. "What Jimmy said about being interested in another job, that was part of it," Jerry told me. "But the other part, and this took me a little by surprise, was that I realized that it didn't bother me. I could see by then that the Jimmy-Jerry issue wasn't going to go away. The careless way we were handling our relationship, the way we were using the media to jab at each other, was taking its toll."

What the writers in Orlando didn't realize until later was that Jones had endured what would be his final insult from Johnson earlier that same evening. At a party for NFL executives, Jerry had approached a table where Jimmy and some of his former coaches and staff were having a private conversation. Jerry should have known better than to butt in: He had fired two of the people at the table. "As luck would have it, we were telling Jerry Jones stories when he walked up," recalled Bob Ackles, who was the player-personnel director for the Cowboys before Jones canned him and is now the assistant general manager of the Arizona Cardinals. "We had just gotten to the one about the ESPN cameras on draft day of '92." According to Jimmy, when the cameras turned in their direction, he had orders to pretend to be consulting with Jerry on which player to select. Jones probably didn't hear them tell the story, but the cool reception that he received — particularly from Jimmy — set off the events that followed. Within a week Jimmy was history.

The one dig that Jerry Jones cannot tolerate is the insinuation that he used his fortune to buy his way into an exclusive club to which he had no place and no right. Randy Galloway in particular loves to push that button, as does fellow *Dallas Morning News* sports columnist Frank Luksa, both of whom have covered the Cowboys since the early sixties (and are old friends of mine). Over the years they have portrayed Jones as a buffoon, a hypocrite, a liar, and worst of all, a football wannabe. "More than anything," Galloway has written, Jerry "wants to be known as a 'football guy.'" This is the unkindest cut of all, like saying that while money can buy property, it can't buy class. One cannot help but hear the echo of Jimmy Johnson in these sentiments.

The criticism is unfair but not altogether untrue. Jerry Jones does want to be a football guy. "I bought the Cowboys not for financial gain but basically because I'm a frustrated coach," Jones told me. In his most formative years, between the ages of 10 and 22, the two most important things in Jerry Jones's life were football and the family business. Jerry was a plugger-style fullback in high school — "that tough-assed Jones kid," a coach on an all-star team called him — and later a guard and co-captain (and teammate of Jimmy Johnson's) on the University of Arkansas' national championship team in 1964.

Jerry grew up in an apartment over the family grocery store in the rough-and-tumble Rose City (a.k.a. Dogtown) section of North Little Rock. The store was the center of family life. "When Jerry was just a little boy," his mother, Arminta Jones, told me, "we dressed him in a black suit and bow tie, and he stood by the front door, saying, 'Can I help you find something, ma'am?'" Pat Jones remembered that his son worked and played football with equal ferocity. "I always told him there was nothing he couldn't do if he wanted to do it," he said. The store was open every night until midnight, and as a teenager, Jerry sometimes stayed up all night helping restock the shelves. "We're not much for sleeping," Pat Jones added.

Switzer, as assistant coach at Arkansas in the sixties, recalled Jerry Jones as "a try-hard guy . . . exactly as you see him today . . . a total extrovert, a promoter, a salesman who could look you in the eye and talk right through you." Jones and Johnson both played for some of the finest coaches in America, including Switzer, Frank Broyles, Jim MacKenzie, Doug Dickie, Hayden Fry, and Johnny Majors. Jones told me, "The things I was exposed to and learned playing football were more fundamental to my makeup than all the things I have been exposed to or learned since that time. I am fundamentally sound in my business and my philosophy because of what I learned playing football."

By the time Jerry had graduated from college, Pat Jones was in the insurance business and owned five companies. Jerry worked for one of the companies while he was in college, and after his graduation in 1965, he took over as executive vice president of his father's flagship company, Modern Security Life Insurance. But Jerry still had football on his mind. A year later, at age 22, he almost bought the San Diego Chargers of the American Football League. He had the necessary financing — $5.8 million — but backed out at the last minute because the debt seemed so staggering. This turned out to be a costly mistake. A year later, when the AFL merged with the NFL, the Chargers franchise sold for $11 million.

By the mid-seventies, Jerry was a major player in oil and gas, banking, real estate, and various other businesses, a millionaire many times over and a behind-the-scenes power in Arkansas politics. He kept a low profile until the eighties, when the now infamous Arkla gas deal brought him both controversy and millions of bucks. In 1982 Jerry bought a half interest in some gas leases from Arkla, a utility then headed by an old friend, Sheffield Nelson. The contract obligated the utility to buy almost all the gas that Jones's company produced — at $3 per thousand cubic feet, far above the market rates, which in the glut of the mid-eighties dropped as low as sixteen cents. A lawsuit filed on behalf of the ratepayers by Fayetteville attorney Tom Mars charged that Jones and Nelson had cooked up a sweetheart deal. As part of a settlement, Arkla ended up refunding $13.7 million to ratepayers. The Arkla scandal became a bitter campaign issue in the 1990 Arkansas gubernatorial race, in which Sheffield Nelson lost to Bill Clinton. Jones eventually sold his interest for a profit that *Forbes* estimated at $140 million — the same amount that he paid for the Cowboys. Jones scoffs at the suggestion that he bought the team with his Arkla profits.

"That $140 million figure isn't close to being accurate," he told me. "The profit I made on Arkla wouldn't have paid for Troy Aikman's contract, and I'm talking about the first one [for $11 million], not the $50 million he signed last year." Tom Mars, who was Jerry's bitter enemy during the lawsuit, is now a Cowboys fan and a Jones admirer. "We never claimed that Jones had done anything illegal or inappropriate," Mars said. "He was legally and morally obligated to look out for Jerry Jones, not the ratepayers. In hindsight, I concede that he made a very shrewd business deal."

In the five years that he has owned the franchise, Jones has recovered all but $25 million of his initial investment. Moreover, the Cowboys now are worth an estimated $190 million, making it the most valuable franchise in sports. When Jerry bought the team, only six of the 118 luxury suites at Texas Stadium were leased. Jones has expanded the number of suites to 368, and most of them are taken through the year 2008, at prices of up to $2 million. Local advertising revenue now totals $15 million to $20 million a year, about ten times what it was when he bought the team. The Cowboys have sold out every home game since the season opener of 1990.

Jones has not just remade the Cowboys, he has become one of the most influential owners in the NFL, the leader of a clique of younger executives who are reshaping league policy. "Jerry Jones has brought a different mindset to the league, in that he is not afraid to operate his team as a business," said Lamar Hunt, the Dallas oilman who owns the Kansas City Chiefs and was one of the founders of the AFL.

"His hands-on approach is unique, different from that of any other owner I know of. We need more of that and less of the owners who never come around or take an interest in their teams. I can name you several owners who haven't been to a league meeting in years." One of the revolutionary ideas that Jones has championed is the salary cap, which the owners got as a tradeoff for free agency with the NFL Players Association. Though the $34.6 million cap kicked in only this year, it's already apparent that the players got snookered. A few players are going to become very rich, at the expense of the vast majority.

Jones's bottom-line philosophy probably has made more enemies than friends. He faces several lawsuits from fans, disgruntled by a variety of complaints, ranging from insufficient parking for the handicapped to the loss of seats by longtime season-ticket holders, who had to make way for the additional luxury suites. But the move that has established Jones as one of the most ruthless and dispassionate owners in sports was the lawsuit that he filed in January to recover money that sixteen former Cowboys had received for permanent disabilities from workers' compensation settlements. In some cases, the funds were designated for future surgeries. For example, former receiver Mike Renfro received a settlement of $22,000 to be used for a plastic right knee joint and a new left shoulder. What makes this lawsuit seem particularly cold-blooded is that fifteen of the sixteen played before Jones owned the team: He never paid a penny of their salaries or insurance premiums. More-over, the players that Jones picked on were, first of all, low-salaried journeymen — Hall of Famers Randy White and Tony Dorsett could have been included in the suit but were not — and second, players who were experiencing acute financial problems. When two of the former Cowboys were discovered to have filed for bankruptcy, Jones's lawyers asked for injunctions to prevent settlement funds from being used to pay for "the necessities of life," contending that Jerry Jones would otherwise suffer "irreparable injury."

This is a highly complicated lawsuit, reflecting changes in insur-ance regulations and the Cowboys' future obligations in perma-nent disability cases. Jones said that the purpose of the lawsuit isn't to prevent former players from receiving new shoulders and knees but to establish a precedent. "In the future, these funds will have to come out of the salary cap," he told me. Dallas attorney Steve Carlin, one of the lawyers representing the former players, sees it in a harsher light. "The money here is the value of Mike Renfro's knee and shoulder. Jones is saying that he owns these players, or at least he owns parts of their bodies."

Saying that Jerry Jones is not a football guy makes as much sense as saying Tex Schramm was not a football guy. Neither of these Cow-boys general managers was especially conversant with the X's and O's, but each had a pair of Lombardi Trophies on the shelf — and Jerry collected his in just five years. Jones isn't destroying the Cow-boys, he's making them leaner and more fit to survive the rigors of the future. More than any other owner, Jones anticipated the salary cap. In the past year the Cowboys have re-signed Troy Aikman, Emmitt Smith, and Daryl Johnston to the largest contracts ever paid to their respective positions. Eight of Dallas's eleven Pro Bowl players have been retained — the only exceptions being linebacker Ken Norton and safety Thomas Everett, who were deemed expend-able, and center Mark Stepnoski, who hasn't yet signed his 1994 contract but probably will remain in Dallas. The Cowboys have lost some players to free agency but so have the other twenty-seven teams. "Don't look at what we lost," Jones said. "Look at what we kept." And look at what the Cowboys got. Barry Switzer, who won three national championships at Oklahoma, was at least as good of a college coach as Jimmy Johnson, who won one at Miami — probably even better. There is no reason to think he won't do as well in the pros. The Cowboys retain the same system, the same assistant coaches, and essentially the same group of players. And don't forget the owner and general manager. Jerry Jones counts too. As the world is quickly learning.

Behind the Icy Glare

FROM THE SPORTING NEWS

IN THE MOVIE *A Bronx Tale,* a young boy asks the local Mafia Don if he would rather be feared or loved. "Feared," the Don says. "Fear lasts longer than love."

Mike Keenan smiles. "Feared and loved?" he says, thinking. "I'd rather be respected." Then he adds quickly, "By my players, I mean. I'd rather be loved by my family."

Keenan has spent most of his adult life trying to reconcile these two often opposing forces in his life. He still is. Players and family. They are a lot on his mind these days as coach of the St. Louis Blues. He left the New York Rangers in a contract dispute almost immediately after leading them to their first Stanley Cup in fifty-three years. The dispute has yet to be resolved. Now he has moved into an empty apartment in St. Louis — an expanse of white carpet littered with a few cardboard boxes, a pair of sneakers, a lamp, an empty book shelf, a Stanley Cup cap, a view of St. Louis from the sixteenth floor, the bits and pieces of a coach's life — while he waits out his divorce from his wife of twenty-two years.

"Are you married?" he says. It's the first question he asks men. "Oh, divorced! Was it painful? Isn't it painful? Very, very painful." He looks down at his white carpet, defeated, a boyish-looking man who will turn 45 October 21. Pink skin; pale, unblinking, blue eyes; thinning hair slicked straight back; a sparse, reddish, brush-cut mustache that makes him resemble a London Bobby, or a British soldier in the Bengal Lancers. He seems a mild-mannered, youthful-looking man in constant pain. He's been a hockey coach for all but one of the last fifteen years.

"We moved fifteen times," he says. "It took a toll. My wife had six miscarriages. [They have one daughter, Gayla, fifteen.] One year I was [away] for two hundred days. And when I was there, well . . ." He shrugs. "A hockey coach never has a day off. I prepare myself to have the least bad hair days of any coach. I was on a fast track. To reach an elite level you have to be abnormal. Can you imagine living with that? Two hundred days gone and when he's here, he's like this! My wife couldn't comprehend it. I can't blame her. She'd put up with a lot. So she asked me to give up hockey." He looks up with those pale, blue eyes. "I couldn't give up hockey. It's my life." He sighs again, expressing that defeat known to men whose work is their life in a way some women cannot understand. "So we separated," he says. "Now I cry a lot."

Crying is not an emotion people in hockey associate with Mike Keenan. Even his sister says she never saw him cry as a child. When one of his young players, Pelle Lindbergh, was killed in a car accident, Keenan says, "I did not shed one tear. I couldn't cry. I don't know why." A Philadelphia reporter, who saw Keenan at the hospital where Lindbergh died, said, "Even then, [Keenan] had on his game face."

Tears are not what people expect from a man who has called himself "macho," "stoic," "driven," "without fear" and whom others have called "Iron Mike," "a goon coach" and "the Devil." He drove his players so relentlessly at Philadelphia (1984–85 through 1987–88) that one player told the media that most of the team "hoped he'd get fired." His players at Chicago (1988–89 through 1991–92) said, "You can only whip a horse so long before it eventually quits on you." One player told his wife that if he had to play for Keenan one more season, "I'd be in a mental hospital by next Christmas." Even the Rangers' front office, for whom he won a Stanley Cup, described him in its lawsuit (for leaving the club) as "a faithless employee" who "betrayed" the team and its fans. (Keenan was suspended for sixty days for breaking his contract. He was reinstated last Saturday.) That lawsuit further pointed out that Keenan was fired in Philadelphia for being brutal to his players, and he was fired in Chicago for being confrontational to the team's front office. Former Madison Square Garden president Bob Gutkowski said, "Mike has baggage wherever he goes."

A Philadelphia player said that Mike Keenan was "a tough man to work for," and he meant even in practice. Keenan has been known to make his players practice hours on the ice, without a puck, until they're exhausted. If they displease him, his temper explodes. He's thrown his hockey stick twenty rows into the stands, broken it over the net in a fury. Before practice, and after, and before games, and after, he holds endless team meetings to prepare his team mentally. "Psychological preparation makes all the difference," he says. "Everybody has talent. Coaching hockey is not just a matter of X's and O's on the ice. It's understanding all aspects of a player's being."

What Keenan calls "psychological preparation" others might call tyrannical behavior. One of his psychological ploys was to take a disrespectful player's belongings out of the team's locker room and throw them into their minor league locker room. When one player refused to take part in a pregame warm-up because he knew he wouldn't dress for the game, and it embarrassed him, Keenan stuck his face very close to the offending player's and said in a soft, level voice, "How much money do you make to play hockey?" The player said, "$750,000." Keenan said, "You tell me you're not going in the warm-up and you make $750,000! Get in the warm-up!" When a goalie he had benched refused to answer his question during a game, Keenan grabbed him by his uniform jersey and screamed at him in full view of thousands of fans. When a timekeeper cheated his team out of precious seconds, Keenan ran across the ice to attack him. "I saw myself strangling him," Keenan says. "But I didn't. I stormed into the locker room and tore the bathroom stalls down." Even after games, Keenan's temper didn't seem to subside. He once threw a star player out of the team hotel in an argument. "I guess I scarred enough people," Keenan says.

Keenan's reputation is so well documented throughout this country and Canada that sometimes people close to him use it to their advantage. When his daughter, Gayla, started dating recently, she had some trouble with a boy. "You don't want me to tell my father," she told that boy. "Don't you know who my father is? He's crazy."

Keenan's absence from his daughter is one of the reasons he cries a lot these days. She's the most important person in his life, he says. That's why he took the job in St. Louis, only five hours by car from her home in Chicago where she lives with her mother. One of Keenan's most vivid memories is of the day he left that house, alone, to drive to New York to take over the Rangers job. His wife refused to go with him, and it was the beginning of their separation.

"I rented a U-Haul," he says. "My belongings took up only a little corner of it. My wife was playing the piano in the living room when I drove off; I began to cry as I left that house. Then, I cried outside of Toronto, where I grew up. When I reached Rochester, where I coached in the minors, I cried again. I cried all the way to New York and my new house in Greenwich, Connecticut." Keenan cried a lot, alone in that big, empty country house during his season with the Rangers. Sometimes, he couldn't bear to return to it, so he slept on the sofa in his office at the team's Rye Playland practice rink. He felt comforted by the color photos of a Stanley Cup on the wall, by the NHL standings on a bulletin board, by all the statistics and records posted in the players' locker room.

During the 1993–94 season, Keenan was declared "a new man" by his players. They were somewhat shocked by his transformation. He began to call certain players "sensitive individuals" who wear their "heart on their sleeves." During meetings, he talked to them about the importance of family in their lives. "Family has to be the highest priority," said the man who had always put hockey above family. "When football or hockey is over, family will still be there."

Keenan began to talk like a social worker or an amateur psychologist, one of those "feel-good" people who eventually write books with titles like *I'm OK, You're OK*. He said his separation from his family had taught him that, as a coach, he had "to show compassion" toward his players. He had to "create a climate of sensitivity in which individual players can bond with each other more quickly. . . . [He was beginning to sound like one of those macho-sensitive Iron John–types, crying and hugging one another in a wilderness.] People have to feel good about themselves before they can feel good about one another."

The Rangers' team psychologist, Dr. Cal Botterill, said, "Mike has really evolved." His players began to refer to him as "composed" and "patient," two words his players at Chicago and Philadelphia would find difficult to use to describe "Iron Mike." The height of Keenan's newfound sensitivity came in his speech to the Rangers before their final Stanley Cup game, when they beat Vancouver. Mark Messier, the Rangers' captain, described that speech as "the

most powerful, most intense, most emotional speech" he had ever
heard in sixteen years in hockey.

Keenan is dressed for dinner. His Pat Riley mode. (Riley is his idol.)
Slicked-back hair. Double-breasted, navy, pinstriped suit, silk tie. He
stands in his deserted St. Louis apartment and says, "The speech? I
just told them they owed nothing to anyone. Me. The city. Nobody.
They had done everything I'd asked of them, and they should be
proud of themselves no matter the outcome of the last game. I told
them to just play hard and enjoy themselves. Yeah, my eyes got a
little red. They saw an exposed side of me. You know, I wouldn't
have been able to come up with that speech if it wasn't for my
daughter. She was staying with me at the time. Two days before the
final game, she said, 'Dad, do me a favor. Promise me you'll spend
the next two days thinking only of hockey. You owe it to yourself.
You've spent your whole life to get to this point. I don't want you to
worry about me or Mom or the divorce.'" Keenan stops talking a
moment.

After his team beat Vancouver, the first person Keenan looked
for was his daughter. "I took her to Europe after that," Keenan says.
"Monaco, the Italian Riviera. Then I told her, 'Let's see some guy
top that.'" He laughs, just as the phone rings. It is the woman he's
been dating since his separation. Dating is something he still is not
comfortable with, he says.

He describes the woman he is dating as "an adult. I could never
understand older guys who dated young women. What do you talk
to them about? A friend of mine, fifty-five, married a girl twenty-
six." Keenan's friend is a nurse from Maine. She's a fine athlete,
basketball and skiing, and Keenan is quick to mention her height.
"Five-eleven," he says. "I asked her if she liked short, fat, bald guys."
(Keenan is pudgy, not fat.) She knew nothing of his hockey fame
when she met him for their first date in Florida. While they waited
for a cab, people driving by shouted out his name. "Who are you?"
she said. "Somebody?" (Keenan likes to be recognized, as he often
is already in St. Louis by bellmen, cabbies, waiters, passersby on the
street. He says hello to everyone, even if they don't recognize him.
It's a habit of a small-town Canadian, or maybe it's a desire to give
strangers a chance to recognize him.)

When Keenan gets off the phone he is smiling, like a teen-ager new to the mysteries of women. "She's a lot like me," he says, meaning she, too, has a temper. "We've had some real Pier Sixes. She told me, 'I hope you don't scare off easily.'"

Keenan describes his relationship with his soon-to-be former wife, Rita, as even now "wonderful, very close, loving." They grew up together in the farm town of Whitby, outside of Toronto. Rita's family were farmers (Keenan's father worked at the Ford plant). Her father, a Czech Jew, and her mother, a survivor of Auschwitz, were the only Jews in Whitby. It was a close, protective family. "Rita wasn't a risk-taker," Keenan says. "She always saw the glass as half-empty, know what I mean?" Keenan, even as a boy, was a "risk-taker," driven toward goals he set for himself. He describes himself then as "an Irishman trying to fight my way out of a bad situation." He means his family life, which was the polar opposite of Rita's. One of his two sisters says, "It was no Ozzie and Harriet." (Another brother died of pneumonia at the age of one.) The family was very poor. Keenan's father drank. "There were fireworks," Keenan says of his parents, who divorced when he was very young. And heartache. Keenan had to watch a beloved grandmother die slowly and painfully of multiple sclerosis when he was a boy. And discipline. Keenan went to parochial schools, where nuns strapped his knuckles for talking in class. "She'd ask who was talking," he says. "I'd always say, 'Me.' After a while she'd say, 'That's enough. At least you're honest,' and not strap me anymore." Keenan was an altar boy for eight years, serving at the 6 A.M. Mass every morning. And he worked. Loading Coca-Cola trucks as a teen. Cutting lawns. As a welder. On construction. Until finally at seventeen, he escaped on a hockey scholarship to St. Lawrence University in Canton, New York. "I had to get the hell out of that environment," he says.

St. Lawrence, during the late sixties of the Vietnam War, was a school for wealthy students. Keenan, one of a group of Canadian hockey players there, arrived with only his hockey jacket on his back and little money. When girls hinted at dates, he had to tell them, "Only if you pay." He and his fellow Canadians spent most of their time hanging around with returned Vietnam veterans in their dorm rooms. The vets drank beer and had women in their rooms, which was against school policy. One night, a dean came in on a vets party and told them there was no drinking or women allowed in the rooms. One vet pointed to his leg, shot off at the knee in Vietnam, and said, "I got my leg shot off for you, and you want to tell me I can't drink?" Another time, Keenan introduced a drunken vet to the dean. The vet grabbed the dean in a headlock and said, "Have a beer, Dean." Keenan said, "No, no, he is *the* dean."

"I remember sleeping in rooms with those vets," he says, "and waking up to their screaming nightmares."

Keenan earned pocket change as a bartender, waiter and with a rock 'n' roll band called Nicky and the Nice Guys. They played soft rock, called bubble-gum music, with songs such as "Peanut Butter." (The band is still performing today, with only one original member remaining.)

He graduated in 1972, got married to Rita, and went with her to grad school at the University of Toronto. After he earned a degree in physical education, he became a high school teacher in Toronto. "I taught sex ed, too," he says.

It was there, in high school, that Keenan began to use his temper in sports. A big student was bullying the other students. So one day Keenan got him on the lacrosse field and ran over him. "I hurt him," he says. "Then I told him, 'Don't abuse these children again.' He became my best friend."

Finally, in 1979, Keenan told his wife he wanted to try coaching hockey. She didn't understand what he meant at first, until he told her he had gotten a job as coach of the Peterborough Petes, a team of sixteen- and seventeen-year-olds. "How far do you have to drive to get home?" she said. "You don't get it," he said. "Peterborough is our new home." Rita never did reconcile herself to her husband's coaching, Keenan says. She would periodically ask him, "When are you going to get a real job?" But that was his real job, the only job he ever wanted, and it led him, at 34, to his first NHL job, in Philadelphia. He led the Flyers to the Stanley Cup finals twice, and then he led the Chicago Blackhawks to the finals once, before winning the Cup with the Rangers last season. Rita called him after the final game. She said she was pleased for him, and then added, "Thank God I'm no longer a part of that. What if you had lost?"

Keenan leaves his apartment for dinner. He stands, waiting for the elevator, and says, "That was the essence of our problem." He shakes his head, remembering something, and smiles. "You know, I was a hard-ass coach even in the minors. I made my team leave on a bus Christmas night for a game two days away in another town. Two days! I acted like it was the most important game in the world. I wouldn't let my guys drink. When I stopped the bus because I smelled cigarette smoke, all these liquor bottles rolled to the front of the bus. I had a tantrum. Now, of course, that would never happen. You know, there are things in your life you wish you'd done a different way. But all that matters is that you learn from your mistakes."

The elevator arrives. The door opens, and Keenan gets in alongside a white-haired woman in her late seventies. She is all made up and dressed in a pretty pink and white silk dress. Keenan smiles at her and says, "You look beautiful tonight." The woman looks at him. She was once beautiful, and she knows it. She also knows that now most people see her only as an old woman. "Thank you," she says. Keenan adds, "Watch out I don't follow you." She says, levelly, "No one's followed me in years."

The Italian waiters at Gian-Peppe's Restaurant in "The Hill" section of St. Louis are wearing tuxedos with frilly shirts. They hover around Keenan at his table as if he were the Mafia Don out of *A Bronx Tale.*

"I used to hang around with seven Italian brothers when I was a kid," he says. "I was the only Irish kid. If they got a beating from their mother, I got a beating from her, too." He laughs, and drains his beer. Keenan asks a waiter to bring him a phone. He has to call his daughter, who will visit him tomorrow, and he's worried that she might not have gotten the airplane ticket he sent her.

"It causes me great pain to be away from her," he says as the waiter returns with the phone. "I'm proud of my accomplishments, but maybe my ambition was selfish. You pay a personal price. Loneliness. It's the only thing that scares me." He makes the call, but his daughter is not home. The other waiter returns with a beer. For a tough-guy hockey coach, Keenan talks a lot about pain and loneliness and even fear. He had a fear of failure when he took over at Philadelphia.

"I was confident," he says. "I felt ready. But there's always that fear in hockey if you're not successful you'll never coach again. I felt I had to be firm with my players and then I'd back off after a while, you know, the way a teacher does. But the players didn't think I let up as much as I should have. I like to think my relationship with players as improved. I've improved. After the separation, I learned to reflect on life. To be introspective, tolerant and understanding. It was an awakening." He picks up the phone and dials his daughter again.

Keenan has always felt that he and his famous temper have been misunderstood. He claims that he has lost control of his temper only once, when he raced across the ice to strangle that timekeeper. "I accomplished something with that, though," he says. "The NHL instituted a video review of the time after that." Keenan says most of his temper tantrums were calculated. "I lose my temper for the right reason," he says. "To make my players better. I always know what I'm doing with my temper. I think about it for months."

He points, as an example, to that young player whose belongings he threw into the minor league locker room. He did it, he says, to teach him respect, because the player had gone over Keenan's head to complain to the front office about the way Keenan was treating him. "Maybe I should have had a talk with him first," Keenan says. "I should have slept on my temper. Now I know that my temper is only a tool."

Sometimes fans and players alike misunderstand Keenan's temper. For example, he has a reputation for yanking goalies quickly in a game, sometimes changing goalies two and three times a night. Some fans and players think this is his show of anger at a goalie's inadequate play. Keenan disagrees. "I love goalies," he says. "They are my best friends. But sometimes if you have a good goalie, the other players rely on him too much. Their play becomes soft. So I put in a lesser goalie to make the players play harder. But people don't get it."

Keenan says he hardly lost his temper with the Rangers last season, although he still has plenty of anger toward the Rangers' front office, especially General Manager Neil Smith. "I just had a meeting today with my lawyer over their lawsuit," he says, draining his beer. "It really pissed me off. I'd looked forward to the challenge of coming to New York. It was an energizing place. You can ride that energy. I love it. I prefer the pressure of being a favorite. It gives you a psychological edge. Other teams play scared. They fear you. Underdogs have an excuse to lose. Favorites don't."

Keenan almost didn't make it to the Rangers. He had signed a contract that season to coach the Detroit Red Wings of Mike Ilitch, the Little Caesars pizza mogul. Ilitch's family "became incensed at his hiring me," Keenan says, "because of my reputation. Ilitch waffled and breached my contract."

After Keenan signed with the Rangers, he declared that "Neil Smith is my boss," and then immediately undermined his boss by going over his head to force the Rangers to make trades Smith knew nothing about. It rankled Smith all season. Keenan says Smith got even with him by making his bonus payment late, and for less than it was supposed to be, which gave Keenan an excuse to leave the team. Smith claimed the check was only a day late. "Bull!" Keenan says. "He knew about it for forty-five days. He intentionally made it late to set up a course of action. He wanted me out because I got too much credit (for the Rangers' Cup victory). So I became the bad guy leaving. But I didn't want to leave. Neil Smith didn't want me there."

After dinner, Keenan is in a relaxed mood; he drives over to the Soulard section of St. Louis to shoot a game of pool and listen to some jazz at Molly's. The streets of Soulard are crowded with cars — Jaguars and Mercedes Benzes and a few stretch limousines. The clubs around Soulard are in old, red-brick buildings that have been restored. Keenan gets out of the car in front of Molly's and is not recognized by the bouncer at the door, who demands $2 for admittance. Keenan pays and goes inside, where a group of musicians are setting up their instruments to play. Keenan throws an arm over the shoulders of one musician and talks to him for a while. Then he goes to the telephone near the men's room and phones his daughter once again. Still, she is not home. Keenan is getting worried now. "I hope she got the ticket," he says. He orders a beer at the bar and goes upstairs to shoot pool. He and another man are partners against two grizzled-looking men who recognize Keenan, but don't make much of it.

"So you're the tough guy, Mike Keenan," says one man. Keenan just smiles, bends over the table and lines up his cue stick for the break. His fingernails around that stick are bitten down to the cuticle. They are red-rimmed, sore-looking, the fingernails of a man possessed by demons he sometimes cannot control no matter what he says. Fear. Loneliness. Guilt. Inadequacy. Things, he admits, he inherited from his hard-scrabble childhood he is trying so hard to dissipate. He's successful off the ice, at times. An amiable man. Quick to smile and laugh. But on the ice, standing with his players, he sometimes becomes another man. "My teams are aggressive," he says. "Physical. They intimidate with passion. Hell, it's an aggressive sport. Let's get it on!"

Keenan and his partner win $40 from the other two men. Keenan's partner pockets his twenty, but Keenan gives his twenty back to the men. "Come to a game with it," he says, and leaves Molly's for the ride back to his apartment late at night. "I want to get home to see if my daughter called," he says.

Driving through St. Louis's streets, Keenan gets lost. He drives through the center of the city, past the famous arch along the river, where this afternoon he was photographed for this magazine. St. Louis is a beautiful city at night, with its clean, gleaming new skyscrapers. Keenan looks at them and shouts, "I'm gonna love it here! A nice city, eh? I'll have fun here." He should. The Blues are paying him $2 million a year for five years. But it's not money that motivates him. Nor winning the Stanley Cup. "I don't need that for vindication," he says. "I coach hockey because I'm an artist. It's like a chess match. You read the situation and maximize it. To be great, you have to be creative. That's the art of it." He smiles. "Isn't life grand? I've learned to live every day to the fullest. A day at a time. I got that from my father. We've become close again after we had drifted apart. Last season I took him on a road trip before the playoffs. Six weeks later I had to tell him he had to go home. 'I need time to work!' I said." He laughs. "He's my hero, you know. He always wears this T-shirt that has written on it, 'Irishmen fight with each other because they can't find a worthy opponent.'" Keenan laughs again. His father has two tattoos, he says. One, a musical note on his back. The other, a shamrock on his thigh.

MARK KRAM

Bully Ball

FROM ESQUIRE

BUDDY RYAN SITS AT HIS DESK in the swank Arizona Cardinals'
facilities in Phoenix, rather contentedly, like a mollusk that has
found its rock. His office reminds one of a small county official,
maybe in charge of truck weights, who breaks every day for a pitcher
of beer and a pair of catfish sandwiches, then burps his way back to
his chair. There are no campaign artifacts here or call-back-the-
memory pictures from so many embattled Sundays, just a white film
screen that in the coming months will be animated by falling figures
and compel him to mutter or chuckle.

For any player who has ever been hitched up to Ryan's Way, these
are profound noises. "When he mutters," an ex-player says, "you
could be on the bus or sit down so long you wish you had a steel ass.
Unless you've got a lot of those chuckles in the bank." So much can
bring the mutter. If you are stupid or stand round out there "killing
grass," if you evaporate before a big play or are a heretic of *the Way*,
Ryan will mutter you into a hell that has more circles than the one
in Dante. But if you stay smart, have the will to commit destruction,
believe, he will chuckle you into thinking he is like some sort of Pike
Bishop in *The Wild Bunch* — dust-coated, trying to outrun civilizing,
his strange, taut laugh the signature of an unspoken idea of personal honor and duty. "You don't find that much anymore," says
Ryan, "but those kinds of horses can take you to the big game." *The
Super Bowl.* Those words do not trip out lightly; they hang on the tip
of his tongue like a chunk of concrete.

"Hell," says Ryan, "I've been there before. I've been there. Three
times." True — in a cameo role: as a defensive coach for the Joe

Namath Jets, again with the Vikings, and then with the rude, Ryan-like Chicago Bears in 1986. "Yeah, I've been there," he says absently.

Nostalgia?

"What's that? Some kind of flu? I don't live in the past, just sayin' the way it is."

In the new age of sports, a PC time when young men with the look of eagles, tech-heads with corporate patter, are sought after as head coaches, Buddy looks as if he should be propped up on the porch of memory. He doesn't fit the PC mold. Nurturing is for the goats on his farm — not players. Sensitivity is for when one of his dogs is sick. Football politesse is for career officers.

No one, it seems, is passive on the subject of Buddy. "He's danger-ous," New England coach Bill Parcells once said. "He's not afraid of consequences and doesn't care what *anyone* thinks." When Ryan's twin sons were thrown in jail after a fight in which they'd been defending him, Buddy said while getting them out: "Hell, if you fight everyone who hates me, I'll be here every day." When he took the Arizona coaching job this year, he was more specific: "There are two kinds of people — those who hate Buddy Ryan and can't beat him and those whose ring he won't kiss."

This insolence helped to get him fired from the Philadelphia Eagles in 1991. Back then, NFL punditry put a tag on his toe. For two years, Buddy fed his horses in Kentucky. Then, last year, he did what no one thought he ever would or could do — he stooped to conquer. He took over a good but dispirited Houston Oiler de-fense, whipped it into a gleaming meat grinder, the talk of the NFL, then, in a blink, with his career seemingly resuscitated, he threw a feeble right hand at the Oilers' offensive coordinator, Kevin Gil-bride. It was the meat of psychotic-fan buzz for weeks on talk radio, the old heads of the league pursed their lips and shook their heads, and a few commentators suggested Ryan should be banned for life.

"I didn't do," he says, rather placidly, "what somebody else didn't do — and better. Jim Stanley, the line coach, kicked the shit out of him before I got there. Gilbride's a nice young man, 'cept he's stupid. You can't get to the big game bein' dumb. I could've gone back to Houston. Everybody loves me in Houston."

Instead, Ryan signed with the Cardinals. The hiring, reported at the same time as Jimmy Johnson's split with Cowboys owner Jerry Jones, provoked steady speculation. Season-ticket sales in Phoenix soared to 49,000 from 24,000. "Buddy Ryan has made us a national team," says the Cards PR guy, as if he still can't believe it. He also made them a menacing favorite in the NFC. Ryan, in turn, named general manager as well as coach, finally acquired an owner, Bill Bidwill, whose reticence is magnificent.

"Bidwill saved Buddy's bacon," says one former general manager. "I guarantee you there wasn't an owner in the land who was ready to hand over a team to Buddy. He's from the ice age. But if you're really serious about winning, you can't do better. You just better have a stiff back and a good disposition."

Wherever he goes, Ryan is the filter for the kind of energy that lifts rockets, the kind that can put one in a room with a keeper. All coaches say they love that energy; they don't. Watch them over a couple of grim seasons. Their features begin to melt, the resolved jaws droop, neon eyes that once promised dim. All you see with Ryan when days are bad is indifference; raise the heat in the kitchen and he'll suck it up and ask for more. If he has any wit at all, it's that of a hog butcher, clean and sharp to the gristle of his players. "Hell, I don't have any wit," he says, "just cheap sarcasm." The voice does not fit his reputation; it is soft, wispy, as if coming from a man who finds the smallest explanation too rigorous. He is at least 60 years old — some say 63 — and looks it. The face is splotched with red marks. A Band-Aid on his cheek covers the results of a recent skin treatment. He produces a cartoon of himself. Obviously inspired by the Gilbride incident, it shows him laughingly muscling up a right hand. He then flips a football card sent to him by Jimmy Johnson. It is of Buddy when he was a young lineman at Oklahoma State; strength fairly ripples out of the little card.

"Jimmy's from Oklahoma State," he says. "I told him the other day he oughtta come to our camp, be a guest coach. I told him that oughtta tighten Cowboy asses down there. He was quiet, then said, 'What's those dates again?'"

Jimmy and Buddy as friends? The consensus was that Johnson was a paid-up member in Buddy's hell, just a level above the bottom sinner, Mike Ditka. Now, there's a magic name, might even bring Ryan out of his chair. After the Bears' Super Bowl victory, when the team carried Buddy off the field, Ditka said that never again would he allow an assistant to get so much credit. It was Ditka, sounding every bit the cosmic harmonist, who also said upon Ryan's leaving:

"There's an old coaching philosophy, to beat 'em down, beat 'em down. When you get them to a pulp, you bring them up." This was Buddy's way. "That way of coaching is finished with the Bears." A story had been going around for years, Buddy. Is it accurate? The Bears were undefeated and playing Miami. You kept begging Ditka to let linebacker Wilber Marshall cover the slot receiver. He relented, and Wilber got beat, costing the Bears the game. Ditka grabbed you by the shirt and said: "You do that again . . . I'm gonna take you outside and kick your ass."

"Never happened," Buddy mutters. "We *never* talked 'bout anything I did. Old George Halas hired me, not Mike Ditka. Besides, catch me askin' a dummy to do something. If Ditka ever came down to talk about the defense, I'd tell him to go fuck himself."

The mutter turns into a chuckle: "Kick my ass. That would be the day."

"What you have to understand about my dad," says his son Rex, "is that he's an *Okie*. Plain and simple. If Ditka ever came on like that, and I doubt it, well, I'd want to be outside that stadium." *Okie* was once a pejorative for the ghostlike masses who fled Oklahoma during the Great Depression or stayed behind and suffered, as dust storms blacked out the sky and carried away everything they owned except their hearts. Where life was much better, as in California, where the Okies sought work, they were seen as a threat, their hard edge as violence, their desperate migration as shiftlessness, their fierce dignity as isolation. It's all in *The Grapes of Wrath,* by John Steinbeck, the life that Ryan was born into in the 1930s.

Ryan says, "I'm very secure in what I do, and I guess when you're born in western Oklahoma, you have to be secure." He was raised in Frederick, a farming town with two stoplights, twelve miles from the Red River. "You don't know how poor that boy was," says J. Robey Smith, who grew up with Ryan. There was no electricity or indoor plumbing. His father, Red, was a housepainter who rode bulls in the small rodeo circuits. "He wouldn't have even a damn jacket if he didn't letter in football. I hear people say Buddy's mean. He doesn't have a mean bone in his body. He's tough. Toughest sumbitch I've ever known."

By 1951, Ryan was in Korea, in the cold and snow, still an improvement over the hysterical wind of Oklahoma. "Like livin' with a hair dryer full blast in your face," he says. He spent time in Japan first, "hardly able to wait to see if I was bulletproof, just a dumb kid, the kind that got killed quick." He went to the front on a Christmas Day. He became skilled at leading ambush patrols, a dreaded exercise for which he seldom had trouble getting volunteers. "He was just a young squirt," says Ryan's son Rob, "and they'd follow him. He doesn't talk about the war. But an old soldier once told me: 'He traded his light machine gun for one on a tank.' The tank guy said he was crazy, carryin' that big thing. Dad said he wanted to make sure that if he hit anything, it stayed down."

He got out of Korea with a case of frostbite. "The one time," he says, "I was in the meat wagon. Guys were there shot, bleeding, crying, their guts hangin' out. I felt like shit, lyin' there with a cold toe." He left the field as a master sergeant, a top kick, the backbone noncom of the old Army, known for their cunning, their verbal stiletto, and their acid disdain for bosses. Back home, he saw a makeshift boxing ring being put up by his father in the backyard among the cottonwood trees. He had seen it often before. When he was growing up, Buddy and his three brothers would fight in elimination rounds to see who would meet their father. He put on the gloves, but he didn't want to hurt his old man. Before Buddy raised his gloves, Red stepped on his foot and sucker punched him. He looked down at Buddy and said: "Just in case you forget what life's about."

After a career as a lineman at Oklahoma State, Ryan got his first coaching job at Gainesville High on the Texas border. When he left, they knew he had been there — and his memory still elicits sharp recall. Larry Sullivant got a bad cut on his hand during a scrimmage. Ryan inspected it and said, "Looks bad, it'll need doctoring." He then spit on the wound, rubbed dirt into it, and said, "That'll do you. Now get back out there." Another time, Sullivant had two teeth knocked out. Buddy stuffed cotton in his mouth, then said, "That'll hold ya." Mike Rigler remembers: "Knowing now what we know about dehydration, I guess we're all lucky to be alive." Bill Williams remembers, too: "If nobody was bleeding at the end of practice, he would line us up for one-on-one, two-on-two drills until somebody took a lick. Eventually, people would throw elbows, try to clip your lip, just so we could get off the field."

He was just as hard on his bosses. Leo Swick was a member of the school board, and Jim Campbell was the Gainesville principal. "He made an impression . . . because nobody could control him," recalls Swick. "He wasn't a fellow you'd enjoy being around. Too egocentric. He wasn't lovable." He once stood up before the students, says Campbell, and said, "I don't know who's runnin' this school, but give me two years and I'll be runnin' it." Buddy was fired after three years. Seems he spent all the athletic money on football, nothing on track or basketball. "He wasn't an all-around bad guy," says Campbell. "He just got out of hand. If he rang my doorbell today, I'd let him in. You gotta like him sometime."

Says Sullivant, whose father was in a wheelchair when he was growing up: "I loved the man. Buddy got me at a time when I didn't have any idea who I was or wanted to be. I weighed 185 pounds and stood five foot ten, and when I was interviewed for a scholarship, they showed me a picture of a 250-pound starter. I told them, 'He's a good player, but he never saw a day in his life he could whip me.' Buddy Ryan did that for me. He would knock you down, but he knew exactly how to pick you up. To me, he is a great man."

Ryan's three sons feel much the same way. Rex and Rob, the 31-year-old twins, are now assistant coaches with the Cardinals. Jim is a marketing man, sometimes for his father. Jim once told Buddy he wanted to be a sports writer. "Like being a Republican and saying you want to be a Communist," Jim says. "He didn't like it." Rex and Rob were difficult kids when living with their mother in Toronto; they were sent to live with Buddy. "He laid a curfew down," says Rob. "We were never in on time; we were in ahead of time. Why fool with dynamite?" Rex and Rob will not be spared insult as coaches. Ryan worked them to exhaustion on the Kentucky horse farm. He once said to Rex, displeased with his weight: "Good thing you didn't go [to the beach]. Somebody woulda mistaken you for a whale and harpooned your ass."

A player who is overweight can drive Ryan, well upholstered himself, to cover his eyes; fat reflects frivolity. A hamstring injury can lower him into a rage of silence; the player didn't work hard enough. "If you've got a hamstring," says Rob, "better to say you got shot in the foot." If he doesn't care about a player, he'll ignore him. Sometimes, he'll express his unhappiness with a player by feeding a lacerating remark to a beat reporter. And if he really likes you, he is confrontational. Former Bears safety Doug Plank says: "On a plane flight, he said, 'I really like you, you're really a funny guy. But you can't play safety worth a damn. . . . I tried to teach you, but I can't do it.' By the time he finished, I felt like crawling in the throw-up bag." Says Mike Singletary, one of Buddy's favorite players, "I owe Buddy a lot. But it wasn't always fun. It took two, three years before he gave me his first compliment. Then, he would take it back, say something, 'Nice play — but you're still stupid.'"

"I hired Buddy Ryan for his résumé — not his personality," says Bill Bidwill. Whatever the reason, the union is bizarre: the dirt-road autocrat and old-money Bill — a collision of class and style. Bidwill is seen as an old-guard reactionary, reclusive and emotionally inert, an owner capable of spectacular idiocy — as when he warned then-coach Joe Bugel last year that he would have to finish 9–7 to keep his job. He's been through seven coaches in seventeen years. But Bidwill is not patrician. His father, Charlie, was a bookmaker who founded the team in Chicago. He grew up in the frontier days of the NFL and, as a ball boy, was ragged every day by hardboots like Ryan. Bidwill may be viewed as being socially impotent, but he's no fool. With Ryan, he gets a full-metal jacket; no more incoming. What if, a reporter asked, Buddy starts calling him the fat man in the bow tie? "I'll just shrug," said Bidwill.

In answer to a similar question, Ryan was sensitive; he's not big on interrogatives. "Especially after a game," he says. "When the adrenaline's pumpin', I don't do it well." Anyway, the question zinged out on Buddy's relationship with Bill. "Where the hell did you come from?" he said to the reporter. "You're a pain in the ass, you know that? Why don't you go interview somebody else?" What Ryan sensed was the shadow of Norman Braman, his former boss with the Eagles, who lived part of the time in France, was never around, and, most of all, wouldn't pony up the money to get players like Wilber Marshall and Jim Lachey. "The Redskins got 'em," he says. "In our division. It made things hard." To Ryan, Braman was a dilettante. He took to calling him "that guy in France" and said that Harry Gamble, the team president, was "Braman's illegitimate son."

When Ryan took over the Eagles in 1986, he found a wretched player pool and a Woolworth franchise. In his last three years, he made the playoffs, the team's paramount feature being its "body bag" kind of defense. His offense averaged only 8.3 points a game in the playoffs, suggesting he had a genetic intolerance for the soft side of the ball.

He's not much for scrawling algebraic football equations across a blackboard or using jargon with his offensive coach. He simply says run or pass. With the Eagles, he could often be seen walking agitatedly by Randall Cunningham, an improviser of high order, muttering, "Make something happen. Do it yourself." He is much more precise with defense. He is the architect of the celebrated forty-six defense, an exciting, intricate, punishing effort to strike quarterbacks down, and players like Seth Joyner, Clyde Simmons (now with the Cardinals), and Reggie White know that Ryan got them near the big money and on the superstar track.

But results were never the problem. It was the appearance of things, the image of the Eagles: when he clashed with Braman during a strike season, Buddy siding with the players (afterward he gave "scab rings" to Braman's personnel); when he humiliated the Cowboys' Tom Landry by having Cunningham fake killing the clock in waning moments, then stand up and throw for a score (Landry blew him out unmercifully with regulars in the strike season); when he was accused by Jimmy Johnson of putting a "bounty" on kicker Luis Zendejas; when he bludgeoned the Dolphins with a superfluous score to settle another payback, causing Don Shula to say that he had come to expect that sort of thing from Ryan. "I'm glad he follows my career," Buddy said.

Most of all, Braman couldn't bear Ryan's not shaking hands with the opposing coach. The performer Elton John, who owned a soccer team, even took a shot at Buddy. The Eagles, he said, were coached by a pig on two legs. "If you can't shake hands after losing," he said, "what's the use? Buddy Ryan is an asshole." Buddy chuckles: "The game's over. How can you shake hands, kiss 'em after they knock the hell out of you? Most coaches would like to have the guts to be a Buddy Ryan. Do and say things like me. They're afraid."

After Ryan was fired, Braman's people accused him of being too loose with players, allowing them to womanize on the road and to engage in high-stakes poker on the plane. A collector of old wines and fine art, Braman couldn't stand owning kitsch, having a possession that made him wince, employing players and a coach who were crude, without sensibility or etiquette. They were all of that, yet the looseness contradicts the essence of Ryan — discipline. Here's a coach who will bop a player on the head if he sees a helmet chin strap unfastened — even if it's on the ground. Here's a guy who wants absolute decorum during the playing of the national anthem. "It made me sick in Houston last season," he says. "I want heads up, helmets in the left hand. Down in Houston, heads were down, they chewed gum, scratched their asses, all that bullshit. That's terrible." He implies that his Eagles were not elegant café sitters in Paris. "What can you say?" he says. "Image don't mean much to me. They were my boys — tough, loyal, the kind you go to war with. They and I built the Eagle franchise, so he [Braman] was able to sell it for $180 million."

Ryan has a curious relationship with players. He is close to the ones he comes to believe in, yet maintains a large degree of separation. He doesn't shout on a practice field; he just glides about and whispers, as one player put it, "seeing everything, like God." Players will play for him with the most awful injuries or defend him with passion, as they did often in Philadelphia. He is not garrulous, chirpy with clichés, or comforting when he cuts a player and says, "You better find your life's work." For a coach whose teams come out of a shotgun, he is strangely unemotional.

For Ryan, the center must always hold; it's part of being a man, the old American man he was raised to be, and the kind he knew he had to be in Korea, when he would play volleyball with friends, then see them the next day draped dead over tanks. "Dad," says his son Rob, "he's not sentimental. I've never seen his eyes water. But I think he cried once. The death of Jerome Brown like to leveled him."

Brown was a three-hundred-pound destroyer — raw, profane, one of Braman's gargoyles. Buddy never tried to rein him in as long as his big fin moved through backfields on Sundays. Buddy, chuckling, liked to call him Brains, for the kind of thinking that clanked. Jerome would sit in Buddy's office all day just to be near him. In the summer of 1992, he flipped a sports car in Florida and was killed. On the day of the funeral, Buddy went to the airport. Bad weather delayed his plane. He began to sweat, to panic, his eyes back and forth to the clock. Finally, he knew he would not make Jerome's funeral. He went into a rest room, put his fist to a door, then sat down and put his head in his hands. And for a frozen half hour, he was a long way from the ruthless man who calls players by numbers, not by their names. So very far from the man the football public sees in the same light, as a charity "roaster" once did in Philly. "I was in the hospital," he said, "and given six months to live. Buddy sent me an Eagles calendar. And he took the time out to remove the months I didn't need."

JERRY TARDE

Can Golf Survive John Daly?

FROM GOLF DIGEST

THE MIXED FEELINGS about John Daly go right back to the moment he won the PGA championship at Crooked Stick in 1991. Waiting for Daly to show up for his post-round press conference, a group of PGA of America officers were standing around the back of the media center looking as if their golf shop had just been foreclosed on. It seemed odd to us "scribes," as the club pros like to call us, because the PGA championship had finally broken its string of Jeff Slumans and Wayne Gradys with a heroic winner. Then one PGA officer made it all clear when he sidled up and said, "Daly's your kind of guy," nudging me in the ribs. "He likes his moonshine."

First, I should make it clear. I am not known for liking my moonshine. I have to admit I am a lightweight, if not in size, at least in alcohol tolerance. The application of after-shave lotion makes me tipsy.

While writers of yesteryear had a reputation for hard drinking, the beverage of choice for today's "scribe" is diet Coke, preferably caffeine-free. So the only thing this exchange with the PGA honcho proved was that he knew Daly better than he knew modern journalism.

What he knew was that Daly drank too much, partied too loudly and trashed the occasional hotel room. He concluded, as many others have, that Daly was bad for golf.

In the three turbulent years since that PGA, Daly entered a rehab center, gave up drinking, got married, divorced, became a father, got reattached, won a tour event, got suspended, signed what may be the most lucrative endorsement deal in history, and took a voluntary suspension.

More than once, he has dangerously launched balls over the heads of galleries. He's withdrawn from tournaments or purposely signed incorrect scorecards to get disqualified. He's accused fellow players of taking drugs without naming names. He's driven into players on reachable par 4s. And most recently, he's wrestled with the 62-year-old father of a fellow player whom he had driven into. None of these misdeeds is defensible (although the father deserves a share of the blame for throwing the first blow after an exchange of expletives). One might easily add it up and conclude that Daly *is* bad for golf.

It should be remembered, though, that John Daly is not the John McEnroe of golf. For one thing, he is a better guy than McEnroe. Despite his frequent lapses of judgment and taste, Daly is a giving person in a sport full of takers.

Professional golf raises a lot of money for charity and the PGA tour enjoys the credit, but it is actually the local tournament organizers who do the fundraising. Pro golfers contribute very little of their own money to charity. They'll lend their names, or put in a paid appearance, but few actually write checks. As one golf executive likes to say, "Pro golfers rate well below NBA and NFL players when it comes to charitable giving." Daly is the rare exception — and he wrote checks to charities when he barely had enough money in the bank to clear them. While a struggling pro on the Hogan Tour, he regularly made sizable contributions.

Three days before Daly's wrestling match at the World Series, a bystander near the 18th green noticed about thirty autograph seekers, twenty-five of them under the age of fifteen. One by one players came by, some ignoring the kids completely. Stars like Jose Maria Olazabal and Greg Norman rushed past without signing a single autograph. Then came Daly. He stopped, talked to the kids and signed every autograph, every one of them.

Just this month, a reader named Bradley B. Brunken wrote to tell the story of his eight-year-old daughter Mary who was saving for "a college education" by selling used golf balls at a course in Memphis. When she approached a golfer who she didn't know was John Daly, he said sure, he'd buy a few balls. He reached into his pocket for some money and handed it to her. She thanked him and offered her selection. He said, "No, I have plenty of golf balls. You keep the money because you are a pretty young girl." When he left, Mary showed the rolled-up bill to her sister Rachel. It turned out to be three bills, not one, three $100 bills. They ran to return the money to Daly, thinking he'd made a mistake. Daly said there was no mistake, autographed a new ball and handed it to them. It was only when the girls went home and showed the autograph to their mother that they learned who John Daly is.

As Daly continues to learn who Daly is, he deserves a second or fifteenth chance. He's one who is worth saving.

But harsher judgment seems more in vogue in this Year of the Ban. First, pressure was put on the AT&T Pebble Beach Pro-Am to ban Bill Murray. Then the Masters actually did ban Gary McCord. Now, by mutual agreement with the tour, Daly banned himself.

Golf always seems to be at the mercy of people who take themselves too seriously. I don't think Murray or McCord is funny, and Daly deserves a kick in the pants, but let's not take this banning business too far. Golf is strong enough to survive them all, even John Daly.

There's another misconception — that television exposure is valuable. The truth is, televised games are seldom seen by balloteers because they're covering other games, or traveling to or from. But little note is made of this.

It's a circus, friends, with three rings, clowns, and animals. Some model citizens have Heisman Trophies in their den, none more model than the year-ago winner, Charlie Ward of Florida State. Great was the furor when he wasn't drafted by an NFL team, but success in the pros isn't something the Heisman is concerned with. Jay Berwanger never played a down as a pro, nor did Dick Kazmeier, Pete Dawkins or Doc Blanchard, and some were busts, like Terry Baker, John Huarte and Gary Beban, and some found trouble with the law, like Billy Cannon, Johnny Rogers and O. J. Simpson. And so we can see that no guarantee comes with the Heisman, nor a great lot of pleasure dealing with it.

That being the case, I hereby withdraw and tender my resignation as state chairman to the Downtown Athletic Club, with thanks. I'm just sorry your good intentions got so far off the track.

ROBERT F. JONES

Wampus Cats & Oyster Toads

FROM SPORTS AFIELD

Few interesting areas of the sea do not have at least one old moss-backed monster of whatever species is most sought after, to make life more exciting for old-timers and novitiate anglers as well. Tahiti has a giant 20-foot marlin with an underjaw longer than its upperjaw; Madagascar has a sailfish fully 25 feet long. Even the Florida Keys has an ancient jewfish called the "Brunose-Wampus-Cat," with enough old hooks, lines and leaders in his mouth to open a tackle shop when the critter's finally caught — or so they say.

— George Reiger, *Profiles in Saltwater Angling*

IF YOU'VE SPENT A LOT OF TIME fishing, as I have, sooner or later you're going to catch the big one — marlin or muskellunge, tarpon or brown trout, bonefish or striped bass or bluegill . . . maybe even the Wampus Cat of a lifetime, so big that it's probably the world record.

If you're a politically correct, ecosensitive kind of guy, you'll unhook your Wampus Cat as gently as possible, make sure its gills are pumping, and release it to swim off, stunned and sullen but with little harm done.

If you're a true gentleman, you'll never utter a boastful word about this encounter, nor of the fearsome battle the great fish gave you on the lightest possible line.

And if in the future you should happen to see another angler subdue a particularly large specimen of the same kind, and hear him exult in his triumph that it must surely be the largest ever taken — anywhere — on rod and reel, you will bite your tongue and nod in smiling agreement.

Sure you will.

Men compete — it comes with the testosterone. Maybe even before that, as in "Mine's bigger than yours."

That's what records are for.

David Goodman, a flyfisherman, was brooding over a solitary supper one foggy March evening at his home on Nantucket. A ceramic tile setter — a craft he pursues to keep body and soul together between fishing excursions — Goodman had just broken up with a longtime girlfriend, and he still ached at the broken places. He was dining that night on a mess of white perch he'd caught earlier in the evening on nearby Sesachacha Pond, where he'd gone, as was his wont, to knit up with flyrod and feathers the raveled sleeve of his care. Now, as he picked at the platter of bones before him, it occurred to him that these perch were among the largest he'd ever caught on the island. Someone at his fishing club, The Nantucket Anglers, had recently posted a list of gamefish available on the island, along with the current world-record weights for them. Goodman checked the list.

He'd just eaten a couple of world records — white perch that no doubt exceeded the existing marks in at least two flyrod categories. He felt pretty good about it. But why hadn't he weighed them — and submitted them for recognition — before scoffing them down?

Well, there'd be bigger perch available tomorrow — they were thick on their spawning beds right now. But did he really want a world record? At the age of 43 David Goodman was old enough to remember the sixties, when the ego trip ranked right up there with short hair and male chauvinism as a bête noir of the Boo Decade. This was 1991, though, and his ego needed a little inflation. A modest ego trip was clearly in order. After all, it wouldn't be so gross a sin. Even if he broke a world record, David Goodman would hardly be breaking Lefty Kreh's rice bowl, much less that of the world's most obsessive billfish and tarpon angler, the redoubtable Billy Pate.

I mean, a white perch, *Morone americana* . . . No big deal.

Goodman sorted through his collection of tapered fly leaders, found a fresh one that maxed out at 10 pounds, and decided to go for it — in the 12-pound tippet class, which at that time stood at a the measly 1 pound 1 ounce. By sundown the next day, March 26, without even breaking a sweat, he owned the new world angling record for white perch taken on a flyrod: 1 pound 12 ounces.

But of Course That Wasn't Enough

"I'd always kind of wanted to hold a world record," he says now, looking back on it all, "but it's like one of those deals where you can't eat just one. Suddenly I wanted all of them, all six of the tippet records in the white perch category. When it comes to compulsion, Ahab had nothing on me."

Over the next five months — sometimes rising at an ungodly 4:30 or 5:00 A.M. to be on the water when the fish started feeding — Goodman flailed Sesachacha Pond to froth, caught white perch hand over fist, muttering to himself whenever he fell just a silly milligram short of the mark, exulting whenever one of his catches broke the record, and virtually rewrote that chunk of the book, filling the 2-, 4-, 8-, 12-, 16-, and 20-pound tippet classes. His biggest white perch, caught on July 20 on 4-pound tippet, was a whopping 2 pounds.

Was it worth it after all?

Well, during the course of his marathon assault on the record book, David Goodman found himself a new lady (this time one who shared his love of flyfishing), moved to a new address, and landed a satisfying new job as fishing columnist for Nantucket's 170-year-old *Inquirer & Mirror.* Go figger.

The International Game Fish Association, founded in 1939 and headquartered in Pompano Beach, Florida, currently maintains all-tackle catch records on 498 species. They range from the subtropical agujon (8 pounds 3 ounces) to the subarctic zander (25 pounds 2 ounces), with stops at such aquatic marvels as the Chinese seerfish, South African geelbeek, Austrian tolstolob and Swedish vimba. They include the largest fish of any species caught so far on rod and reel — Alfred Dean's 2,664-pound great white shark, taken while surfcasting near Ceduna, Australia, thirty-five years ago — and the smallest, a 1-pound grass pickerel landed at Dewart Lake in Indiana by Mike Berg in 1990. (Yes, smaller fish have been caught — I've caught plenty myself — but the IGFA requires that any fish submitted for a record weigh at least a pound.) Some of the better-known and more glamorous marks, like oilman Alfred C. Glassell Jr.'s 1,560-pound black marlin, caught back in 1953, and Dr. W. J. Cook's brook trout of 14 pounds 8 ounces, taken in 1916 on the Nipigon River in Ontario, seem unassailable, if only for their longevity.

The fiercest competition occurs in the IGFA's line-class slots, covering 328 "game" species, fresh water and salt, caught by means of conventional tackle (trolling, baitfishing, plugcasting or spinning) or by flyrod. In the conventional categories, separate records are maintained for men and women. Flyfishing, however, is democratically unisex (like those baggy chest waders de rigueur among trout anglers regardless of gender). Every year nearly seven hundred anglers apply for new records, and about half of those usually pass the IGFA's scrutiny. (Record applications must be accompanied by photographs of the fish, measurements of its length and girth, readings by an impartial weigh master from approved and accurate scales, corroborating reports by two eyewitnesses unrelated to the angler and an intact sample of the line-class leader or fly tippet used in landing the fish.) Of the 3,588 IGFA record slots available, hundreds are still vacant, mainly in the flyfishing category.

Until recently, the most prestigious records were those set for billfish — black, blue, striped and white marlin, broadbill swordfish, and Atlantic or Pacific sailfish — usually taken on heavy line up to 130-pound test. Big tuna, especially "granders" (bluefins of 1,000 pounds or more), used to make headlines in the sporting press. But tuna of all colors and dimensions are getting scarce in the waters of the world, thanks to the appetites of sushi-snarfing Japanese. Tokyo fishmongers pay hefty fortunes for fresh-caught horse mackerel, and their agents wait on our docks, cash in hand, for sportboats to come in, ready to buy any tuna for the equivalent of a year's wages.

Diehards and Maniacs

In the early years of this century, big tuna outranked even marlin or broadbills for bragging rights among gentlemen sportsmen. When Zane Grey, that indefatigable angler, joined the Catalina Tuna Club in 1914 and began catching broadbill swordfish in the waters off Avalon, old-boy members merely sniffed. Time enough for handshakes when this brash "young writer of Westerns" (he was 39 at the time) should manage to boat his first Blue Button tuna (100 pounds or better) — a feat Grey couldn't accomplish until 1919.

In 1917 a fellow club member, William C. Boschen, added injury to insult by catching a bigger broadbill than "Pearl" Grey had ever hung: a 463-pounder the Tuna Club promptly proclaimed a world record. Stung to the quick, Grey retaliated by spreading word that Boschen's hook had penetrated the big fish's heart, thus rendering the fight "unfortunately" one-sided. Boschen did not deign to reply.

Then in 1920, Grey caught the biggest broadbill of the season — 418 pounds — and went around the club boasting that his fish, though 45 pounds lighter than Boschen's, had been hooked in the lip, not the heart. He buttonholed anyone who would listen, boring them stiff with blow-by-blow details of his fight, explaining ad infinitum how he worked out on rowing machines all winter to get into shape for the big fish, even soaking his hands daily in salt water to harden them for the arduous piscatorial battles ahead. But the following summer a female Tuna Club member landed a broadbill that outweighed Grey's by eight pounds. Gleeful members took turns phoning Grey every few minutes that night to suggest that perhaps he should give up salt water and try soaking his hands in Jergen's lotion.

Grey resigned his membership and fished only with sycophants from then on — though in the 1930s he tried to line up Ernest Hemingway for a *mano a mano* fishing trip around the world on Grey's 52-foot cruiser, *The Gladiator.*

Hemingway — just reaching the apogee of his career, while Grey's was already in decline — wisely said no. If Grey, who was twenty-four years older than Hemingway, had outfished him, Hemingway knew he would never have lived it down. You can't help but wish that the trip had come off, though, both for the fish and the potential fireworks.

During the filming of *The Old Man and the Sea* in 1956, Hemingway talked producer Leland Hayward into a month's fishing on the famous marlin grounds at Cabo Blanco in Peru, hoping to come up with appropriate footage of a big blue marlin jumping for background shots of Santiago's battle. But Papa's luck ran as poorly as the Old Man's. The seas were as steep as the Andes. For 10 days, while the wind off the Desierto de Sechura blew sand into everything, Papa's crew saw not a single fin. Then it calmed and they got a few hookups. Hemingway whipped a 680-pound marlin in eight minutes flat (no mean feat for a man in his late fifties — or any man, for that matter), then let it run again to get jumping shots for the camera. But it was too small. Later he boated another of 915 pounds, but the bigger fish refused to jump. Hayward was finally forced to pay $250,000 for film of Alfred Glassell's fight with the record 1,560-pound black marlin, caught three years earlier in the same waters.

But to film the marlin alongside Santiago's skiff, Warner Brothers concocted a mechanical fish twenty feet long with a motor inside to make the tail and fins wiggle. Hemingway, who had been paid $150,000 for the rights to the book along with his services as technical adviser, dubbed the rubber marlin "The Condomatic" and swore he would never work for Hollywood again.

"No picture with a rubber fish ever made a dime," he said.

The Cabo Blanco marlin fishery collapsed in the late fifties, done in by a combination of overfishing for marlin and overnetting of the *sardinas* — baitfish — they fed on, plus (some said) a shift in the Humboldt Current that took the big fish elsewhere. The focus of billfish record action shifted to Cairns, Australia. For thirty years now, wealthy big-game and tournament anglers have been seeking The Double Grander, aka The Big Mamu or The Wampus Cat — the legendary 2,000-pound black marlin — somewhere off northeast Australia. A friend of mine, Joe Judge of Centreville, Maryland, spent three months a year (September through November) during 1973 and 1974 bouncing around off Lizard Island, in the company of such fishing nuts as Australia's Peter Goadby and actor Lee Marvin (who owned the ultimate fishing platform, a converted U.S. Navy minesweeper), in pursuit of The Double Grander. The biggest black marlin he could come up with was 1,143 pounds.

"You know he's out there," Judge says, "and he could hit you at any moment. So you have to keep alert all the time, day in, day out. One lapse, one momentary foul-up, and you might have blown the only shot you'll ever get in your lifetime." The hopes of these diehards were — and still are — fueled by reports of huge marlin well over the one-ton mark, blue as well as black, caught and processed in both the Atlantic and the Pacific by long-liners. Yet with each year the commercial fishing pressure increases, and the supply of big fish — marlin or tuna or you name it — continues to shrink. Glassell's record may well stand forever.

In recent years the focus in angling has switched to light tackle and less spectacular fish — ones that don't carry swords on their snouts. But while it lasted, there was nothing to match the quest for big tuna or billfish, either in grandeur or expense. Not to mention sheer arm-deadening, back-breaking hard work. An old-time 14/0 Vom Hofe reel, finished in German silver, weighs 13 pounds. The short, stiff greenheart or bamboo big-game rods of the 1920s and 1930s, before fiberglass or graphite came along, were as thick as broomsticks and about as limber. Just by itself, the 700 yards of Ashaway 54-thread (162-pound test) linen line that a big broadbill or marlin was likely to peel off in a single scorching run weighed more than all the trout a latter-day trout fisherman will catch in a whole season.

The pursuit of today's glamour fish — tarpon, permit and striped bass in salt water, Atlantic salmon, brown, rainbow and brook trout, as well as largemouth bass in fresh — isn't nearly as expensive as tuna and billfishing were in the Golden Age. For one thing, you don't need a big seagoing boat. Back in Depression-strapped 1934, Hemingway paid $7,500 for the *Pilar*, his black-hulled 38-foot Wheeler. Now you'd pay $10,000 to $20,000 a linear foot. An equivalent boat today — Hatteras, Rybovich, Luhrs or Bertram — could cost up to half a million or more.

By contrast, an Avon raft or Mackenzie boat for floatfishing a Western trout river like the Big Horn or the Madison might cost you $1,500 tops. Even a Hughes skiff replete with 150-horse Johnson for fishing permit or tarpon or bonefish on the Florida flats, or a Ranger bassboat "loaded" (i.e., with GPS navigation system, side-scanning fishfinder sonar, pump-fed livewell, Astroturf no-skid carpeting, single-sideband radio and a plug-in fridge to keep your brewskis chilled) would cost no more than $20,000.

Yes, small-game fishing is the poor man's sport — that's why so many writers take up the flyrod. I've been fishing for more than fifty years now, with a canepole when I was a kid growing up in Wisconsin, then graduating to a baitcasting rod for muskies and a flyrod for bass, trout, salmon and the saltwater species. Along the way I've managed to catch five world-record fish — or at least they would have been if I'd chosen to submit them.

Two of the fish were respectable — a 125-pound sail taken off the Bat Islands in northwest Costa Rica on 20-pound flyrod tippet in 1991, the first year that the IGFA slot was open, and this year a decent pink salmon on the same outfit while I was fishing for 30- to 40-pound chinooks in British Columbia.

But if the IGFA had a category for ugly, three more of my record-size fish would have made the book in that slot as well. I'm proudest of them. I was throwing deerhair poppers for largemouths into Lake Champlain not long ago when the world's biggest rock bass smacked the bug. The rock bass, for those unfamiliar with it, has a mouth like the late Totie Fields's and the colors of a recovering burn victim, with maybe a little psoriasis thrown in for texture. Its dorsal fin is a fright wig with spikes. This guy — or probably gal, since the biggest fish of most species are female — weighted well over a pound, closer to two. I shook her off when I had her at my waders and cursed her back to her lair. Rock bass will drive you crazy by slamming your fly before the fish you really want has a chance to make up its mind.

Later that night, though, I was leafing through the IGFA's annual *World Record Game Fishes* and noticed that all the tippet slots for rock bass were vacant. I thought of going back to that spot the next day, à la David Goodman for his white perch. The notion had its appeal. Holding the world record for a really goofy-looking fish, one of angling's undesirables, would be more fun than holding a trout, say, or even a tarpon record. Then I remembered my friend George Reiger, author of such books as *Wanderer on My Native Shore* and *Profiles in Saltwater Angling*, who while trolling the Virginia coast for sharks had suddenly snagged what he took for the bottom. But no, it moved. When he finally cranked it in, it proved to be a "monstrous oyster toadfish."

As a joke, Reiger submitted the fish to the late Elwood K. Harry, longtime president of the IGFA, for a new all-tackle record. "Elwood, the sweetie, wrote back very apologetically to say there was no category for *Opsanus tau* just then," Reiger recalls, "but he hoped I wasn't too upset by this news. I wrote back and told him I was. It's shameful, I said. The oyster toad is as noble and valiant a battler as any fish in the sea. Beauty should have nothing to do with it. Now I notice that the IGFA has indeed added the oyster toad to its all-tackle list. But the spot is held by a lowly 3-pound 10-ounce specimen caught off Okracoke. Why, my toad could have et that one for breakfast — and begged for more."

Of course, ugly as she was, my rock bass could never have contended with an oyster toad for ugly. I promptly forgot about the record.

Another time, fishing from the rocks around the power station at Port Washington, Wisconsin, I landed a huge brown trout on a 4-pound flyrod tippet. This was during the fall, when the browns spawn, and it was a hen fish. She leaked roe as I unhooked her and weighed her. Never has there been an uglier brown trout, nor a more sluggish one. She was little more than 24 inches long but with the girth of a medicine ball — like a lady dwarf two months overdue with sextuplets. She weighed 18 pounds 10 ounces. Since the brown trout fly record for that tippet class was only 10 pounds 13 ounces back then, she would have been a cinch for a legitimate glamour-species mark — one that would have held to this day, when the record stands at only 12 pounds 3 ounces. But I have sympathy for the ugly, a kind of grudging respect tinged with awe — a feeling of kinship renewed each morning when I shave — so I slogged out into the surf (the water temperature was about 52 degrees Fahrenheit that late September day, and I wore no waders) beyond the breakers and held her head-on into the waves until her strength came back. Then I shooed her back out to the sand flats where she'd been digging a redd. Perhaps one of her daughters is out there in Lake Michigan right now, growing to record size. I only hope she doesn't favor her mommy for looks.

The Best I've Ever Done

But my personal best for ugly, as well as big, weird and hazardous, came nearly thirty years ago in East Africa. I was writing the post-Uhuru stuff for *Time* magazine back then, and I'd been taking a look around Kenya, Uganda and Tanzania to see how independence was faring. It wasn't faring well. Sick of cooling my heels in Nairobi, waiting for an interview with Jomo Kenyatta that never came off, drinking too many chota pegs at the Long Bar in the New Stanley, I chartered a bush plane and flew up to a lake on the Northern Frontier, where I'd heard the fishing was good.

Some lake.

Some fish.

Imagine a six-foot turbojet engine painted in camo colors —
olive drab on the top, silver on the belly — that's fallen from a
fighter bomber at full blast into a 150-mile-long trough full of bitter
green water. There's a sandstorm blowing over the trough, the
temperature is 120 in the shade, 15-foot crocodiles bask on the
banks, and wildmen called *shifta* are waiting out in the desert for
night to fall so they can shoot you full of holes with Russky bullets.

That was Lake Rudolph in 1964. It's called Lake Turkana now,
but it's not that much better, despite the politically correct name
change. The shifta are Somalis, poachers of elephant and rhino
armed with Kalashnikovs, and they feel — perhaps rightly — that
the whole northern end of Kenya belongs to them. (The colonial
powers were arbitrary when they sliced up the African pie.) The
turbojets are Nile perch (*Lates niloticus*), close relatives of the hard-
hitting Australian barramundi. They range from Egypt to Nigeria
and Benin, and clear on down into Lake Tanganyika. Recently they
were introduced into Lake Victoria, where they're said to be thriving on an abundance of tilapia. They grow to more than 200 pounds,
and larger fish, up to 500 pounds, have reportedly been netted but
have never been officially recorded.

There was a fishing camp on Rudolph at that time — perhaps
half a dozen thatch-roofed, open-sided bandas and a kitchen with
makeshift bar — run by a most happy fellow named Guy Poole, his
Kenyan wife, his children and an Italian named Tony, an ex-POW
from World War II who served as the camp mechanic. We fished
from an ancient, round-bottomed, single-screwed African Queen of
a vessel with split-cane boat rods that were even more venerable,
and rust-pitted Penn 12/0 reels spooling what looked like miles of
130-pound DuPont monofilament line.

The wind died toward sunset, and we started hooking turbojets.
The Nile perch came up from the greasy green depths, smashed
the foot-long wooden plugs we were trolling, and took off on long
screaming runs reminiscent of marlin or wahoo — 300 or 400 yards
at a whack. Our gaffer was a tall young El Molo tribesman, imagina-
tively named "Molo," who harpooned the big fish when we finally
got them alongside. He was deadly. No catch and release in East
Africa. The largest Nile perch I caught that blood-red evening —
and I pulled them until my arms went dead — weighed 187 pounds

8 ounces on Guy Poole's scale when we brought them ashore. My record would have held for twenty-seven years.

But I didn't bother to submit it. Instead we ate it for supper that evening — Guy Poole, his wife and kids, Tony, my pilot, Dick Prewitt, and a talented *Time-Life* photographer named Priya Ramrakha, who was killed by a sniper in Biafra a few years later. The whole bowlegged El Molo tribe, root and branch, joined us at the table. Only the bones remained when we'd finished.

That night, which happened to be my thirtieth birthday, I lay full-bellied under the mosquito netting in my banda while hyenas whooped me to sleep. Eighteen months later shifta fell upon the camp, tortured and killed Guy Poole and a Catholic priest who was there to fish (Poole's wife and children had gone to Nairobi for supplies), shot up the radio, generator and three of the trucks, and burned the camp. They disappeared into the desert in the fourth camp truck, the El Molo said later. Tony was driving with an AK pointed at his neck — once again a POW. But not for long.

They were bound for a well called Gus, the El Molo said. When they got there, they filled their water bottles, burned the truck, banged Tony on the head, and skinned him out like a catfish. They took the hide for a trophy.

That's a real fishing story. Forget the records.

JAY SEARCY

Worth More Dead Than Alive

FROM THE PHILADELPHIA INQUIRER MAGAZINE

A Matter of Breeding

IT IS A HOT SUMMER DAY IN Bridgehampton, near the eastern tip of Long Island, where 1,200 of the most talented and expensive horses in the country have been shipped to compete in one of America's largest horse shows. Beaches are crowded, hotels are full, nightclubs are buzzing. The beautiful people, many of whom summer here from around the world, are having a colossal party at the Hampton Classic.

They buy up ringside seats at $1,750 apiece and drink Evian and French champagne under gaily colored tents at tables draped with purple and white linens and adorned with fresh flowers. Before the week is out they will have spent more than $3 million, competing for $375,000 in prize money and, far more important, for prestige among their peers.

These people gather often at the big shows — West Palm Beach, Newport, the Hamptons, Devon — wearing their $750 shadbelly coats and $300 triple-knit breeches, their $50 hunt caps and $900 baby-calf dress boots, bouncing confidently in their $3,000 jumping saddles. They are mounted on gleaming, elegantly groomed horses with French-braided manes and storybook names: French Rapture, Madam X, Jiminy Cricket, Snowball.

Christopher Reeve sometimes rides among them. So does Calvin Klein's wife, Kelly. Jockey Julie Krone. Paul Newman's daughter Clea. Randy Quaid's wife and Joan Lunden's daughter. The children of Peter Jennings and Tom Wolfe.

This is the top of the line, the magnificently glamorous world of the horse show. This is where America's Olympic equestrians are molded. This is as close as this country ever will come to having a sport of royalty.

And this would seem to be the most unlikely environment in the world to spawn a niggardly, brutal insurance-fraud scam. But it did, and the scam went virtually undetected for two, three, perhaps four decades.

Not that many of the elegant globetrotters of the horse-show set didn't suspect something was going on. You would hear through the grapevine, they say now, that there was a suspicious fire somewhere in the Midwest, a barn torched, expensive horses burned alive for insurance money. You would hear rumors of a horse mafia that corrupted trainers, stole horses, threatened or maimed anyone who dared to talk. You would hear of people switching cheap horses for expensive ones, bilking rich widows, inflating the price of horses, then insuring them and killing them. You'd hear of horses suffocated by Ping-Pong balls stuffed up their nostrils. Injected with putrid slop-bucket water. Electrocuted, smothered, bludgeoned.

But you never knew anybody who *did* any of these things.

Until this year.

On July 27, a special federal grand jury in Chicago indicted twenty-three people — veterinarians, owners, trainers, riders, and some of the richest members of the equestrian aristocracy — in a wide-ranging series of horse scams. The charges generally have dry, bureaucratic names: *mail fraud, insurance fraud, conspiracy to commit wire fraud.* But the actual deeds involved — to which most of the accused have pleaded guilty — have a far more gruesome sound. For example:

• Tim Ray, a tough, boyish eighth-grade dropout living near Chicago, was a horse assassin for hire, killing at least seventeen insured horses, mostly by electrocution, for fees ranging from $5,000 to $40,000.

• Ron Mueller, 52, a former trainer from Chicago now living in Canada, killed six horses so that their owners could collect insurance. He beat one horse over the head with a crowbar, bludgeoned another with a sledgehammer, electrocuted another and burned three alive in a van.

• Donna Hunter, owner of a suburban Chicago stable, arranged to have one horse killed in hopes that its unsuspecting owner would buy another from her with the insurance.

• Paul Valliere, a prominent trainer and riding coach from North Smithfield, Rhode Island, pleaded guilty to conspiracy to commit mail fraud and wire fraud in connection with Ray's electrocution of Roseau Platiere, a horse insured for $75,000.

• Virginia homemaker Nancy Banfield, 36, hired Ray to kill one horse so she could collect $50,000 and pay off $16,000 she owed on another.

• Chicago businessman Allen Levinson arranged to have a horse named Rainman killed so he could collect $50,000 in insurance. (On November 3, Levinson, a 51-year-old millionaire, became the first indictee to draw a prison sentence — twelve months, plus a $20,000 fine.)

As the stories unfolded, they were greeted by shock, then repulsion and anger. How could people who spend their lives with such elegant creatures kill them so coldheartedly? And why would somebody rich enough to join this glitzy world in the first place risk career and reputation — not to mention a jail term — for nothing but a little more money?

The epicenter of the horse scams was Chicago, where the history of hustling goes back to the turn of the century: Horse trains from the East were held up by gun-toting rustlers as they passed through nearby Elgin on their way west. In more recent decades, the patriarch of the area's equine underworld was Silas Jayne, a barn-burning swindler who was convicted in 1973 of paying to have his own brother killed in a feud that started over show-ring jealousy.

When strange accidents — or fatal ones — happened to horses connected to Jayne and his associates, "those at the top looked the other way," says Robyn Douglass. Douglass, a former movie actress and longtime animal lover, boarded horses in the 1970s at a stable owned by one of Jayne's associates — a man named Richard Bailey.

"Everybody else was afraid to talk" about stable scandals, Douglass says, "lest your horse be found dead." Or lest you be found dead yourself, or not found at all.

Like Helen Brach.

Helen Vorhees Brach was the widowed heiress to a $30 million candy fortune, a one-time Rita Hayworth redhead with a fondness for pink cars and helpless animals. She so doted on her pets that she once chartered a plane from the Bahamas to be at the side of a sick dog.

In the 1970s, she met Bailey. He was charming ("the poor man's Errol Flynn," Douglass calls him), and he knew his way around horses. Bailey took Brach dancing, he took her to fancy restaurants, and, according to a 28-count federal indictment, he took her to the cleaners. He sold her cheap, lame horses — some for a few thousand dollars, some for hundreds of thousands. (He scammed a dozen other wealthy women, the indictment says, in similar ways.) "Helen had two kinda scruffy horses next to mine," Douglass recalls. ". . . He [Bailey] would tell her that he had a nice horse that needed training and that if he couldn't find an interested owner soon he would have to send it to the killers. And she would say, Well, how much is it? and, Can I see it? and he would dope up this old horse to hide the pain and sell it to her. She used to come by in the evening and feed them Brach candies."

Apparently, Brach got wise. In February 1977, she told a sister-in-law she feared that Bailey was swindling her. A few days later, she disappeared.

Police searched for her for years, aided by psychics, a private detective and a $500,000 reward put up by an animal-rights group that had counted on her charity. To no avail. In 1984 she was declared legally dead, the richest woman in America ever to vanish without a trace. In accordance with her will, the bulk of her estate was used to establish a foundation to support animal-welfare causes.

But that didn't settle the matter. A few years later, after a complicated series of events — including the 1987 death of Silas Jayne, which loosened a lot of tongues around the stable set — the FBI reopened its files on Helen Brach. This summer, seventeen years after the widow's disappearance, Bailey was charged with conspiring to have her killed. He has denied any wrongdoing.

It was in the course of that investigation that federal agents wandered into a tangle of horse-world intrigue that would overheat a Dick Francis novel. At its heart they found Tim Ray, equine assassin to the upper crust, and caught him in the act of having a horse killed. Once Ray started naming names, all bets were off.

*

Of all the show-horse people in America, few are richer or have enjoyed a more promising career than George Lindemann Jr., whose father is on *Forbes* magazine's list of America's 400 wealthiest men. George Sr., 58, graduated from Penn's Wharton School and went on to make three fortunes — one in soft contact lenses, one in cable television, and one in cellular telephones. Grand total: nearly $600 million.

George Jr., now 30, grew up in Manhattan and attended the Collegiate School, an exclusive boys' school on the Upper West Side; he threw lavish teen parties at Studio 54 and learned to ride at the Clairmont Academy. Despite legs so short they hampered his style on horseback, young George became an avid show jumper.

He was an underclassman at Brown when, in 1984, his father bought him a 51-acre horse farm — Cellular Farm — between Armonk, New York, and Greenwich, Connecticut. Once he graduated, the young man devoted himself to riding. He worked hard, and, with the aid of $150-an-hour lessons, mounted on some of the best "ready-made" show horses money could buy, George Jr. made himself into a top contender on the international grand prix circuit. In the 1989 Volvo World Cup of show jumping, he placed third — the best showing of any American rider. He was named to the U.S. equestrian team but fell short of his goal of making the 1992 Olympics.

But Tim Ray talked to the FBI, and he turned Lindemann's luxurious world upside down.

In 1991, Ray told the FBI that he had been paid $35,000 to kill a champion hunter belonging to George Lindemann Jr. The horse had been insured for $250,000, and the claim was paid. Lindemann was indicted on two counts of mail fraud connected with the horse's death. He was the most prominent person named in last summer's indictments. Unlike most of the others, he did not plead guilty. He has denied any wrongdoing and contends that he is the victim of attempted extortion.

Many of Lindemann's acquaintances don't think he could possibly be guilty. A woman who knows him well — she declined to be identified — said he is known for visiting sick horses in their stalls at night, and for retiring older horses to the grazing fields. Friends say he's not an irresponsible rich kid, that he normally tries to do "the right thing." Even those who don't like him find the accusation hard to believe.

Nevertheless, after the indictments came out, Lindemann was booed when he competed in a show at the Palm Beach Polo and Country Club, where the family had been regulars for years, and was laughed at when his mount knocked down a rail. He has since competed successfully in Europe, but in August his professional riding career was effectively halted: The American Horse Shows Association suspended him and banned him from AHSA-sanctioned competition.

George Lindemann Jr. isn't talking to the press. His father dismisses the charges as nonsense. "I don't think the family needs that [insurance] money," George Sr. told *Connecticut* magazine. "I think you'll find that we donate about five times as much as that to charity each year."

"Ninety to 95 percent of show horses have a fabulous life," said George Morris, a former U.S. Olympic rider. At 56, Morris is one of America's most distinguished riding instructors and trainers, with a 55-stall, 100-acre facility in Pittstown, New Jersey. "I'd say most show horses are taken care of better than most children."

Indeed, most show horses are fed well, bathed often, checked regularly by veterinarians, X-rayed and scoped, brushed and braided, and exercised daily. Some are pampered to a fault with professional massage, magnetic therapy, chiropractic treatment, whirlpools and even acupuncture.

Unlike racehorses, who begin competing at age two and usually are retired before age ten, show horses are trained until about the age of six before entering major competition, and some perform into their twenties. The most popular disciplines are the three Olympic events: dressage (gait performance), hunter-jumper (obstacle course), and three-day eventing (combined dressage, jumping and cross-country endurance).

There's a lot of expense involved in all this, far beyond the hefty purchase price of a horse. "I charge $825 a month stable fee," says Ralph Caristo, a Long Island trainer and horse-show judge. "That's general care of the horse — hay and feed — not including vet bills, shoes or transportation." Caristo, who works about three shows a month year-round, says it costs about $1,000 each time a horse is entered in a show. Riding lessons average about $50 an hour, and most serious young riders get two or three a week.

There's very little way to win any of that money back. The grand prix circuit, the highest level of show jumping, offers a total of just over $3 million in prize money for its thirty-three events. By way of comparison, thoroughbred racing offers three times that amount in a single afternoon at the annual Breeders' Cup. The all-time leading money-winning AHSA show rider, 43-year-old Michael Matz of Collegeville, Pennsylvania, won purses worth $830,136 from 1983 to 1993. A top racing jockey like Pat Day can win more purse money than that in a weekend.

In other words, if you can afford a show horse at all, you probably can afford to lose money.

Most people can't afford a horse, or don't have time or a place for one, and millions have never even seen one up close. But horses have a special place in the hearts of Americans, who insist and assume that they are treated with a certain regard, whether they pull a tourist carriage or win the Kentucky Derby.

Horses helped build America, grew up with the country, hauled loads and worked the fields, bucked cowboys and pulled buggies, became both real and mythical heroes — Trigger, Silver, Man o'War, Secretariat, Black Beauty, Dan Patch, Cyclone. Americans broke them, trained them, raced them, traded them, stole them. But Americans don't kill horses — not that most of us know of — and don't take kindly to those who do. If one must be "put to sleep," it is hidden, the way it's done at the racetrack when a horse breaks down: Shield the suffering animal behind a big blue screen and let the vet administer a lethal injection while the folks in the stands go make another bet.

Something many Americans don't know is that about 80 percent of all thoroughbreds in the United States go to slaughter, killed for human consumption primarily in France, Belgium, Germany and Japan (Japan prefers ponies for the smaller cuts). There are nine slaughterhouses across America, and last year they killed more than 170,000 horses. Almost 50,000 others were sent to Canada for slaughter. In all, America sent more than 71 million pounds of horse meat abroad last year at a retail butcher's value of more than $99 million. The United States, with more than six million horses and seventy-five breeds, has the largest horse population in the world, with the possible exception of China, and is the world's leading supplier of horse meat. The only government requirement for horses slaughtered for human consumption is that they arrive at the plant live, standing on all four feet. The dead and the crippled are sent to rendering plants for $80 apiece, where they become pet food, fertilizer, bone meal, paint brushes and glue.

What all this means is that a horse insured for, say, $100,000 that sustains a career-ending injury, or isn't fast enough to race or athletic enough to jump, is worth 50 cents a pound (about $500) if the owner gets it to a slaughterhouse.

If it dies on the farm, it's worth $100,000 in insurance.

The temptation to owners is obvious. Why not simply put down horses that can no longer perform?

Or that merely don't perform up to expectation?

Such a horse was Charisma, a five-year-old bay gelding with a white star on his face who was found dead in his stall on a cold December morning in 1990, just hours before he was to have been taken to Florida. He had not been ill, or sore, or lame. He had appeared rambunctious, as usual, the night before.

He was bred in North Carolina, the son of thoroughbreds, but his original owners, Mr. and Mrs. Thomas J. Brennan of Charlotte, never intended to race him. They named him Kerry Lad, and they trained him for the hunter ring. "He was a nice horse, such a sweet horse," Brennan remembers. "The children used to ride him all the time. They were devastated — the whole family, we were just devastated when we learned about his death."

Brennan sold Kerry Lad when the horse was three years old — about the time the eight Brennan children began going off to college. Over the next few months, the horse was sold three more times and was renamed Charisma. He was shown in children's hunter divisions and accumulated a string of ribbons for green, or novice, competitions, including the prestigious first-year green hunter championship in Washington.

In 1989, George Lindemann Jr. bought him for $250,000. That's an unusually large sum for a show hunter, which is judged on jumping style and "way of going" and competes primarily for prestige. Even at top shows, hunters rarely win a purse larger than $200.

And so Charisma came to Cellular Farm, with its green meadows and stately pine trees and white fences, its horse showers and its extensive staff. On his stall door, his name was engraved in brass.

But Charisma didn't win prizes with Lindemann on his back; federal indictments say the horse "performed very inconsistently" for his new owner.

Tim Ray learned that Lindemann was unhappy with his purchase, and he says that in late 1990 he offered his executioner's services to Marion Hulick, manager of Lindemann's farm. According to Ray, a deal was made. Lindemann was in Europe — nowhere near Cellular Farm — when Ray flew from Chicago to Connecticut to do the deed. It was ten days before Christmas. This is how Ray describes what happened:

He got a room at the Danbury Hilton and called Hulick for instructions. She drove him around the farm in her Cadillac, showing him a side road onto the property. She walked him to the barn and showed him to Charisma's stall. The usually crusty Hulick had tears in her eyes.

"Put the dogs up tonight," Ray told her, "and turn off the barn lights."

Ray returned around 10 P.M., driving a friend's car. He parked on the side road and made his way down a dark path to the barn, using a tiny penlight to navigate.

He had brought with him the usual tool of his trade: a rig he'd made from a heavy-duty extension cord by splitting it and attaching hand-size alligator clips to the bare wires. He clamped one alligator clip to Charisma's ear, the other to the horse's anus. Then he plugged the rig into a socket.

The horse dropped dead instantly.

Any vet examining the body would have said the gelding died of colic — a commonly fatal stomach ailment. That's why Tim Ray liked electrocution; it is virtually undetectable.

Charisma was insured for his purchase price — $250,000. General Insurance Company of Trieste and Venice, a company based in Italy with branches in the United States, paid up.

Hulick, like Lindemann, has pleaded not guilty to the federal charges.

It is not a crime for owners to kill their animals in this country, whether they are lame or healthy. They may shoot them for food or for mercy or for convenience or for no good reason. It is only a crime if they are killed inhumanely (electrocution is not consid-

ered inhumane), or if an attempt is made to collect insurance
fraudulently.

So insurance fraud is what the July indictments were all about.
The swindles seem to have worked for three reasons: Claims were
scattered among several companies in various parts of the country,
so that no pattern was detected; some insurance companies were
intimidated by big-money clients; and those in the show-horse industry who knew about the practice, or should have known, did
nothing about it.

Unlike the automobile insurance industry, horse insurers have
no central data base, no clearinghouse. "Various underwriters of
horse insurance are so used to competing with each other that we
are not exchanging information on the claims side," said Richard
Vimont of Equitania Insurance Co. of Lexington, Kentucky. "I don't
know what American Livestock in Chicago is doing, and they don't
know what I'm doing." Even so, Vimont said, his small company
uncovers about one fraud case a year.

Not all insurers are so suspicious. "If there was this person who
had been insuring with me for four years," said Robert Marcocchio,
an equine insurance broker from Chicago, "and he is president of a
bank or owner of a truck company, would I think that he would take
a chance in killing a $50,000 horse and be indicted and lose his
reputation and disgrace his family name? If there's no great reason
for suspicion, you pay the claim because you don't want to insult
the owner, or think he'd be involved. I'd be a lot more suspicious if
he was living in a $15,000 home and had a broken-down car and
hadn't paid his bills in seven months."

Eric Straus, assistant executive director of the AHSA, a horseman
and former show-horse manager, said he never heard the killing
rumors and denies that leaders in the sport ignored signs of scandal. "In point of fact," he said, "when the FBI investigation began is
when it became knowledge to many, and at that point there was
immediate cooperation. Nobody ever knew about it as a practice
going on until it was brought to public light. . . .

"In terms of insurance," Straus said, "we don't keep track of who
has horses insured and who doesn't, and if there was a tragedy in a
barn burning down, we wouldn't track that either because we don't
get into that level of our individual members' private business."

Terry McVey, president of Equine Adjusters, says about 5 percent
of horse insurance claims are questionable. Tim Ray thinks fraud is

not only widespread but also universally known: He says a strange woman at a show once approached him and asked, "Do you think you could kill my horse for $10,000?"

"So I did," said Ray. "She bought another with the insurance money and came to me two months later and asked me to kill her new one — she didn't like it.

"Everybody knew what I was doing and nobody cared," he said in an interview. "It was like a game: Beat the insurance companies."

Donna Ewing, president and founder of the Hoofed Animal Humane Society, said, "I've been called many times by insurance investigators about suspicious events in the Chicago area. But it is so hard to prove because there are a lot of legitimate accidents and it is difficult to differentiate between a leg that has been broken in an accident and one that was man-caused."

It was a horse's leg broken with a crowbar that finally blew the lid off the horse-insurance scam.

The horse was a seven-year-old chestnut gelding named Street-wise, and he belonged to Donna Brown, a well-known horsewoman from Palm Beach, Florida, and Oyster Bay, New York, whose husband, Buddy, rode in the 1976 Olympics. Brown had paid $6,500 for Streetwise. She insured him for $25,000, then hired the ever-popular Tim Ray for $5,000 to kill him. (Brown, indicted in July, pleaded guilty in October. She will be sentenced in February.)

The problem was, Streetwise's insurance didn't cover death by colic — the standard explanation of electrocution. So Ray brought along a powerfully built accomplice named Harlow Arlie, and staged a "loading accident."

On a wet February night in 1991, Ray and Arlie entered a horse lot near Gainesville, Florida. Ray held Streetwise's reins while Arlie shattered the horse's right hind leg with a crowbar. The horse went down, struggled up, then got up and ran off on three legs, screaming in the darkness, his broken leg flailing.

What Ray and Arlie didn't know was that a Florida agriculture department investigator was watching from the top of a nearby horse van. He and other agents waited while a veterinarian was summoned to put down the horse, then pounced on Ray and Arlie a few miles down the road as they were leaving in Ray's pickup truck.

Streetwise's broken leg was amputated, frozen and hidden away by the FBI to serve as evidence.

Ray recalls now, "I went in there [the local sheriff's office] after the arrest thinking there's going to be a couple of rednecks and I'm going to lie my way right out the door, you know.

"About eight o'clock next morning [the FBI] shows up. Then people from the Justice Department, state police, somebody from the Secret Service was there, Florida agriculture investigators, Treasury Department. They're showing me all my bank records, showing me copies of plane tickets, copies of checks."

He says he never intended to admit to anything, and expected some help from the wealthy people who had hired him for years. But Tim Ray spent three weeks in jail without hearing a word from his erstwhile employers, and he began to talk. And talk. Federal agents called the people he implicated; by the middle of this year, the number of people questioned was in the hundreds. One confession led to another. Some, hoping to strike better sentencing deals, wired their bodies to help catch others. "It took me almost two years to come completely clean," Ray said.

The people indicted in July have been going to court in Chicago since August, pleading their cases one by one. At this writing, sixteen have pleaded guilty.

Despite the horror and the scams, the indictments represent a victory for a sport seemingly too beautiful to have a seedy side. Steven Miller, special prosecutor for the FBI, says he is going to insist that every guilty party serve some time, whether or not he or she cooperated with the government.

Why did they do it? New Jersey horseman George Morris, who is *the* trainer of America's top riders and show horses, would not comment on specific cases. But generally speaking "they do it for one of three reasons," he said. "Desperation for money, greed for more money, or ego." People involved that deeply in the horse-show world, he said, can't stand to have a horse let them down. "They just can't accept the mistake."

GEORGE VECSEY

The Survivor Won't Let
Time Slip By

FROM THE NEW YORK TIMES

NANCY KERRIGAN had already skated a gold-medal performance. The people running the figure skating championship did not even have the Ukrainian national anthem at hand, but it is a safe guess they knew exactly where "The Star-Spangled Banner" could be found. And then the hauntingly gifted young woman from Odessa began to skate.

She is different, this young woman with the circles below her eyes, this young woman with grief lines on her face. It is impossible to stop staring at her. She knows how to express herself with her hands at all times and her slender body gyrates with emotions no instructor can supply. She was in pain from a dreadful collision in practice on Thursday, but Oksana Baiul is no stranger to pain.

She began to skate and the entire audience gazed at her, and so did the nine judges, even though all nine of them had just voted Nancy Kerrigan first, up to that moment. She skated, and within the Olympic Amphitheater of Hamar, the mystery of art asserted itself over the practicality of science. She made everybody stop and think that maybe Nancy Kerrigan's by-the-numbers, totally competent performance was not quite enough.

The name of the Ukrainian national anthem, by the way, is either "The Ukraine Has Not Died" or "The Ukraine Has Not Perished," depending on the translation. There has been much death, much perishing of joy and hope, in the sixteen years of Oksana Baiul, but last night she was alone on the ice, and she skated to negate the pain of her mother's death, and her grandparents' death, and the defection of her first beloved coach, and perhaps even the political disruptions and the deprivations of her homeland.

She skated with all the intense feeling of eastern Europe, the region that raises ballerinas and figure skaters the way America raises rock stars. She is only sixteen, and the laughter and the tears come bubbling out of her, but she is also a survivor, wily enough to know that nearly four minutes of skating were not quite enough.

She had not been perfect, because genius cannot be perfect; it must live on the edge. But this is also an athletic performance, with points added for this jump, with points detracted for that omission, and Oksana Baiul was not yet satisfied.

Seeing her mother die of ovarian cancer three years ago, sleeping in the rink for a while, now living in a borrowed bed in somebody else's apartment, she has learned to make the most of every chance. Last night she still had a few seconds until the music stopped.

She was due to perform one more double axel, but instead she tossed in a triple toe, and then she did a combination of a double axel and a double toe, a very demanding performance for anybody at the end of four minutes, particularly a girl who has been run down by another skater in practice thirty-two hours earlier, particularly a girl operating on three stitches and a pain-killing injection, a girl living on nerve.

Tonya Harding, America's alleged survivor, had not been able to get on the ice with proper boots on her feet. Harding and her advisors had looked like Curly, Moe and Larry living out a hideous nightmare, but Ukraine's survivor made time stop. Then she looked to the heavens in much the same way Dan Jansen of the United States had recalled his dead sister a week earlier.

"This difficult life gave me the strength to excel," she said later. "Yes, my mother was with me at the moment of victory." And she claimed she had not thought that she was pulling out a gold-medal performance.

"Certainly not. I could not think of the gold medal after that performance. I never do. My goal is to do well and give joy to the spectators and show myself to the judges. Tonight, judging from the applause of the audience, I thought I had done that."

She did more than that. Five judges from nations with links to the vanished Soviet bloc gave her higher grades than they had given Nancy Kerrigan. The Ukrainian judge is the father of her former coach. Much will be made of that in days and years to come, but I submit that all the old political favors are long gone, and that we are left, in moments like this, with feelings.

Five judges felt the gifted young woman from Odessa had skated the best last night, and so did I. This takes nothing away from Nancy Kerrigan's grace under pressure in these last two ugly months, but the young woman from Odessa also had courage, and she had genius, besides. And then somebody located the national anthem of the Ukraine, and a gifted young woman's face showed tears and laughter, at the very same time.

JOAN RYAN

The Cold Wars:
Inside the Secret World
of Figure Skating

FROM THE SAN FRANCISCO EXAMINER MAGAZINE

I MET BILL BRAGG a few weeks before I left for the United States Figure Skating Championships in Detroit three months ago. I had gone to the ice rink at the Fashion Island Mall in San Mateo to watch skating lessons as part of research for a book I'm writing about figure skating and gymnastics. Bragg was drinking coffee at a table beside the rink watching his seven-year-old daughter, Holly, spinning and leaping under the tutelage of coach Tracy Prussack, a former national pairs skater.

Bragg, a former swimming coach, had watched Dorothy Hamill win the Olympic gold medal in 1976 and decided right then that if he had a daughter she would be a figure skater. Holly hated skating when Bragg enrolled her in lessons two years ago. For six months, she complained and he cajoled, bribing her with dollar bills for landing ten jumps in a row.

Holly slowly fell in love with the ice, and she and her father — who had custody of Holly after his divorce — spent every afternoon at the rink. When Bragg was laid off from United Airlines and could no longer afford lessons, he still scraped together $10 every day during the summer to pay to keep Holly on the ice for two daily public sessions, from noon until 10 P.M., with breaks for lunch and sometimes a bargain matinee movie. "I was going through tough times, but I got Holly to the rink every day," Bragg said.

Then Bragg lost his apartment. He and Holly moved into a shelter for six months. They lived on food stamps, unemployment checks and handouts from churches and friends. Still, Holly kept skating. "I heard complaints from parents that Holly was skating too much and they were saying, 'You don't have the money.' But I see it as she's staying out of trouble and she's always around winners," Bragg said.

In October, when they had used up their time at the shelter, Bragg moved into his car. Holly bounced from one friend's house to another. "She never lived in the car, but she came close," Bragg said. And still, Bragg got her to the rink. Prussack tried to help Holly out when she could, taking payment from Bragg when he had it.

When Holly's mother found out her ex-husband was living in his car, Bragg said, she went to court to get custody. He said his ex-wife was not supportive of Holly's skating and wouldn't take her to the rink if she regained custody. So Bragg made a decision. Rather than see his daughter give up skating, he proposed to the court mediator that neither he nor his ex-wife have custody of Holly. He proposed they hand her over to Prussack. The mediator asked Holly what she wanted. She chose skating. Holly moved in with Prussack, thirty-one, who is now Holly's legal guardian and full-time coach.

Bragg found work again at United but hasn't pulled together enough money to get an apartment. He sleeps in his car at an Interstate 92 rest stop and showers at a 24-hour Nautilus that gives United employees free trial memberships. He still goes to the rink every day to watch his daughter, though it is Prussack who takes Holly to school, holds her hand crossing the street, and tucks a blanket around her at night.

"I've seen such a difference in Holly," Bragg said. "She's such a little lady now. As parents, you've got to think, 'What's best for your child?' I'd be very selfish to keep Holly in my situation." His eyes rested on the face of his daughter, who was listening intently to Prussack's instructions down on the ice. "Even though I fear I'll lose her."

I filed my notes on Bragg into my computer and soon left for Detroit and the U.S. championships to do more research. Twice a day in the four days leading up to the competition, I watched the young women skaters practice in three groups of six or seven. Even in practice, they dolled themselves up like Estée Lauder cover girls, hair in French braids and ribbons, bodies in backless costumes of gold lamé and black Spandex. They knew they were being watched, by rival coaches and skaters, by a smattering of die-hard fans and by the judges, who were already sorting the skaters into three categories: those who looked likely to win a medal, those who were long shots and those who had no chance. The official competition might not start for a few days, but the real competition began in these practice sessions.

Only the top two finishers in Detroit would go on to the Olympics the following month in Lillehammer, Norway, and everyone in the competition knew they were fighting for second place. Nancy Kerrigan had a lock on first. One skater, Nicole Bobek, went so far as to say before the competition, "I imagine if she doesn't do well, the judges will hold her up." Kerrigan was the one true star among the women in Detroit. She had risen like a real-life Cinderella from the working-class, hockey-playing, beer-and-pretzels Kerrigan clan to American Ice Princess, a stunning young woman with $13,000 designer costumes and a smile of newly capped teeth. She was the reigning national champion. She already had an Olympic medal, a bronze in 1992. She had national endorsement contracts for Campbell's, Reebok, Seiko, Evian.

The afternoon of January 6, a day before the start of the technical, or short, program, Kerrigan owned the ice. She glided around the rink in Cobo Hall in her white lace costume with six other women in her practice session, but she might as well have been alone. She drew the eyes of everyone in the arena. When the practice session ended, Kerrigan was first off the ice, pausing to slip skate guards on her blades, then striding through the blue curtains that separated the rink from the locker room hallway. Other skaters and coaches gathered their belongings to follow her. No one had noticed a man in black slip behind the curtains before Kerrigan. Unless you've been orbiting the earth or adrift at sea the past three months, you know the rest. The man whacked Kerrigan just above the right knee, knocking her from the competition.

With the field clear of Kerrigan — who had beaten 1991 national champion Tonya Harding in their last five meetings — Harding won her second national championship, securing a place on the Olympic team. Soon afterward, Jeff Gillooly, Harding's ex-husband, confessed to hiring the hit man. Thus began a media feeding frenzy that made last year's sordid accounts of Amy Fisher and Joey

Buttafuoco look like *Masterpiece Theater.* Gillooly accused the skater of approving the plot and paying for it with training money she received from New York Yankees owner George Steinbrenner. Harding denied any wrongdoing and, because she had not been charged with any crime by the start of the Olympics, she was allowed to skate for the United States in Lillehammer.

One question dogged me as the bizarre story unfolded.

What would drive someone to risk everything in his or her life — freedom, career, reputation — for a skating title?

Was it simply money?

Even Gillooly had to know that a national championship by itself meant nothing financially, as evidenced by the fact that Harding reaped little reward from winning it in 1991. And even if the blow to her knee had kept Kerrigan out of the Olympics as well, there were still Oksana Baiul, Surya Bonaly and Chen Lu standing between Harding and any medal at Lillehammer, much less the gold. Something more drove Harding's ex-husband, and perhaps Harding, to risk so much for such an uncertain payback.

Then I thought of Bill Bragg.

He risked everything — in this case, the love of his only child — so she could have a shot at skating success. To him, skating was more than a sport. To succeed in skating was to succeed in life. It was a road to potential fame and fortune and, perhaps more important, it was a road to a respectable life, one of restaurants with cloth napkins, hotels with marble lobbies, a life where a girl from the wrong side of the tracks could be somebody.

In researching my book, I have found many people in skating driven to extremes in pursuit of the success Bragg wants for his daughter, the success Harding so desperately wants, from girls starving themselves to achieve the Peggy Fleming–thin skating body, to parents mortgaging their homes to pay the $20,000 to $30,000 yearly skating bill, to parents sending children away from home to work with a famous coach, to sabotaging a rival's equipment, to taking a child out of school so she can train eight hours a day, to giving up custody of one's own child.

So while the Kerrigan attack may be an aberration, figure skating at the highest competitive level is often a messy soup of jealousies, politics, ambitions, sacrifices and egos that can drive otherwise normal people to madness, as one skating mother put it. Skating is unlike any sport on the planet. Its unique standards and its subjective nature conspire against the simple equation of most athletic endeavors: Talent plus Hard Work equals Success. With no stopwatch, no cut-and-dried point system and no yardstick with which to decide its champions, figure skating often sees athletes and coaches resort to dangerous and sometimes unethical measures to curry favor with the powers that be, the ones who anoint the next champions.

The plot to attack Kerrigan apparently began late last year, when Harding finished fourth at the NHK Cup in Japan. The skating cards seemed stacked against her. Even though Kerrigan didn't compete at NHK, Harding, or at least Gillooly, decided that no matter how well Harding skated, Kerrigan would always stand between Harding and the shiniest medal. As long as Kerrigan was around, Kerrigan would get the commercial endorsements, the magazine covers, the starring roles in the ice shows. Harding would get nothing. Harding wasn't being paranoid. She was right. Kerrigan was the chosen. Skating is as much about politics and appearances as it is about athletics. Being the highest jumper and the fastest spinner guarantees a skater nothing. Athleticism counts — but so do beauty, grace, deportment, weight, hair, makeup, costume, music.

"Image is everything," said one skating coach. Judges regularly call the parents and coaches of a skater to suggest she wear more pink, or grow her hair back long, or see a dermatologist to clear up patches of teenage acne. One judge reportedly told one top skater to get a nose job because the girl's nose was "distracting." A skater who rebuffs a judge's suggestions risks repercussions come competition time. Skaters and coaches even invite local judges to come to the skater's rink and evaluate her program before she goes to a competition. Most skaters genuinely want the judge's input, others do it merely to stroke the ego of the judge, yes-yessing every suggestion the judge makes, then rolling their eyes when the judge leaves, changing nothing in their programs.

Some coaches, and even some parents, lobby the judges. Though Kerrigan's coach, Evy Scotvold, says he doesn't do it, he was spotted after practice one day in Lillehammer chatting and laughing with Margaret Weir, the only American on the women's judging panel. They likely were not talking about Kerrigan — she hardly needed a boost — but the appearance of a coach and a judge fraternizing just days before the most important competition of the skaters' lives couldn't have made Kerrigan's opponents sleep easier. Harding, or at least her coach, surely noticed. Parents frequently call local judges at home after a competition to ask them to explain their marks. Coaches ask other coaches, who might be particularly close to a judge, to put in a good word for their skater. Other coaches include judges on their Christmas card list. "One judge, if you told her she looked good in her jeans, she loved you," said Keith Lichtman, a pairs coach from Boston.

It's the game within the game, and Harding never learned to play. She refused to learn. Yes, she came from a family with little money or education, but she wasn't the only one from the working class. Kerrigan is as blue collar as a dime-store clerk. Nicole Bobek, too. Harding's unforgivable sin in the skating community was not that she had no class or taste but that she refused to allow anyone to give her some. She wore hideous, homemade costumes. She had a ratty ponytail, garish makeup, fake nails. She plowed through her routines like a bull, connecting one explosive jump after another with footwork about as complicated and graceful as a square dance. She had a pear-shaped body with heavy legs and beefy arms. "Hair and weight are everything in this sport," said ice dancer Susie Wynne, exaggerating only slightly.

It also didn't help that Harding was neither deferential nor sociable. When she won the national championship in 1991 by landing the first triple axel by an American woman, she snubbed the formal champions dinner afterward. She put on jeans and a sweatshirt and shot eight ball with her friends in the hotel bar. During the week of the 1992 World Championships in Oakland, she refused to eat in the skaters' dining room at the hotel, where the meals were free. Despite complaints of money problems, she ordered room service every night, which she had to pay for herself, rather than eat with the rest of the skaters, coaches and officials.

Harding refused to help her chances of winning by playing politics, yet she wanted to win more than she wanted anything in her life. She dropped out of school in tenth grade to concentrate full time on her skating, throwing all her eggs into this one precarious basket. Most elite skaters tend to live in a bubble, but Harding was particularly ignorant of the world beyond the rink and the pool tables. After the 1991 World Championships, where Harding finished second, the top skaters were invited on a European tour. Harding said she would go only if her husband could accompany her. As each skater was allowed to bring one guest, Gillooly went. Kristi Yamaguchi and Kerrigan, who finished first and third, respectively, went by themselves and roomed together. At the stop in Rome, the local skating club arranged for a special tour of the Vatican. When the team leader, an International Skating Union official from the United States, asked who wanted to go, everyone but Harding raised their hands. The team leader took Harding aside.

"You know, Tonya, this is a special tour of the Vatican; you might never get another chance to experience —"

"What," Harding asked, "is the Vatican? Some kind of religious place?"

The team leader, flabbergasted, tried to explain that it was also a place of great art, of Michelangelo's "Pietà" and the Sistine Chapel.

"Who's Michelangelo?" she asked.

As the rest of the group boarded the buses for the Vatican, Harding and Gillooly headed out to buy T-shirts.

Unlike Harding, Kerrigan allowed herself to be molded into a made-for-media princess by the expert hands of coaches Evy and Mary Scotvold. The Scotvolds performed magic with Kerrigan, considering that she has a less than scintillating personality. Her interviews came across as snippy and always, always dull. She mostly shrugs. But she looks the part. She's thin, beautiful, graceful, well groomed and polite to the judges. And, of course, on the ice, she's a dream.

"It's a packaging process, very much so," Evy Scotvold said. "You're trying to become a princess of the ice. . . . You try to make sure they know they have to behave, they have to have good manners and they have to be well dressed. They know they will be watched on and off the ice."

As for the skating itself, "The judges are all probably thirty-five to sixty-five, so you've got to give them something that they can understand," Scotvold said. "And if there's some new hip-hop kid thing from MTV, you're probably making a mistake [to use it as accompaniment to a skating program]. . . . You must not mistake who [judges] are and what their tastes are. You're trying to appeal to them, that's for sure. You're not trying to appeal to your own taste. If you don't have the right taste, learn it. But don't show them your bad taste."

It's a mistake Harding made over and over, even at the Olympics last month. The bordello-red sleeveless costume she wore for the short program was hideous, especially in contrast to Kerrigan's sophisticated black-and-white number. Harding's costume for her long program at Nationals was so awful — it gave the illusion that Harding was mostly bare-breasted — that the judges deducted points. So Harding wore a different costume in the Olympics. (Not that it made a difference. She finished eighth.)

Most concede judging is less political than a few years ago, now that school figures have been dropped from competition. Judges could rank a skater low enough in the figures portion of the competition — without fear of public reprisal since the press generally didn't cover the tedious event — that the skater would be out of medal contention before she even got to her technical program. But most everyone in figure skating agrees that allowances are — and should be — made for the top skaters.

"They're not going to keep Nancy Kerrigan off the Olympic team because she has an off night," Mary Lyn Gelderman, who coached former world champion Elaine Zayak, said before the U.S. championships. "That would be stupid. Everyone accepts that would be stupid. I would be shocked if they ever would do anything as dumb as that. That [kind of judging] will always exist. But it's not like it was before, when they could end your career if they wanted to."

Harding knew no such allowances would be made for her. She would have to make her own allowances. She had much at stake going into Nationals. She hadn't finished any competition in 1993 above third; now she had to finish in the top two in Detroit in order to qualify for the Olympic team. And she had to go to the Olympics. This was her last chance. Only an Olympic medal could reap a payback for everything she put into skating.

What a payback it could be. Agents said a gold was worth $10 million in endorsements, ice shows and appearances. Gold medalists spend the rest of their lives trading on their names. In fact, in a poll last year by the Dallas-based Sports Marketing Group, Dorothy Hamill — seventeen years after winning the gold — was named America's most beloved athlete along with gymnast Mary Lou Retton.

Figure skating is more popular now than ever before. Corporations that once sponsored tennis and golf are switching to figure skating. "Figure skating," John Bennett, a senior vice president at Visa, told *New York* magazine recently, "is the closest you can get to sex in the Olympics." Television ratings are phenomenal: An eight-month-old tape of the 1993 World Figure Skating Championships drew a larger audience last fall than a live broadcast of the Indiana-Kentucky college basketball game. The ratings for the women at the Olympics broke records. One billion people watched the women skate in Lillehammer, including more than 100 million in the States. The night of the women's technical program drew the highest ratings ever for an Olympics broadcast and the third-highest for a sporting event in the history of television. (Only the 1982 and 1983 Super Bowls did better.)

Those who shine on this stage can become icons. Figure skating champions represent an old-fashioned and, to many, a comforting feminine ideal not found in other female athletes. They are demure, beautiful, lithe, vulnerable and a bit spoiled. They're starlets in blades, with agents and fans fluttering about them.

In climbing toward this life, and knowing that talent alone might not carry them, skaters have resorted to unseemly measures to gain advantage. Tracy Prussack recalls someone stealing her skates. Another time, she returned to her car outside the rink and someone had vomited on it. At the Pacific Coast Sectionals this year, a competition that determines who moves on to Nationals, one young skater received an anonymous letter special delivery at the rink shortly before the competition, calling her names and making fun of her skating. The same skater had to switch practice rinks because the parent of a rival skater kept following her around the ice with a video camera.

"Lots of crazy things," Prussack said.

The 1989 U.S. champion Christopher Bowman once returned to the locker room to find his skate blades bent and scratched; someone apparently had beaten them against the radiator. To this day, Bowman's coach, Frank Carroll, never leaves his skaters' bags unattended. The mind games are more common than the physical sabotage. Mostly it's little things, like Surya Bonaly doing a spectacular but illegal back flip right next to Japanese competitor Midori Ito during practice for the Olympics in 1992, drawing accusations that she was trying to psyche Ito out. When they were both in their prime in the eighties, three-time national champion Jill Trenary hired the same choreographer as rival Caryn Kadavy behind her back, upsetting Kadavy. Even Kerrigan got in her digs at the Olympics: She wore the same white costume to her first Olympic practice with Harding that she was wearing the day Harding's ex-husband had her clubbed. The incidents sound petty and silly, but in the small world of skating where, as one coach said, "everything counts," paranoia is an occupational hazard.

So for Harding, who had good reason to feel the skating community was against her — mostly of her own doing, though she could never see that — it's not surprising that she might have resorted to desperate measures to try to even the playing field. Perhaps after the NHK Cup and with the Olympics looming close by, Harding and her camp panicked. All the training and sacrifice, the beatings from her mother for missing a jump, the humiliations, the battles with her weight, the money spent, the education lost — they would all come down to six minutes on the Lillehammer ice. It's a heavy burden to carry on a pair of quarter-inch-thick blades. Perhaps all this crystallized for Harding. The Olympics was her last chance to make something of her skating. In four more years, at the next Olympics, she would be too old to be a contender. This was it.

The attack, with all its bumbling and muddled objectives, was the work of desperate people. As events turned out, even if Kerrigan had not competed in the Olympics, Harding still would not have won a medal.

So what's the motivation behind attacking Kerrigan? My guess is jealousy and pathological denial. Harding still wasn't going to admit her own failures, such as not training hard enough, smoking despite her asthma, refusing to accept advice. She saw her failures only in relation to Kerrigan's success. Get Kerrigan out of the way and all would be fine.

Kerrigan represented everything Harding could never be. Nancy had beaten her at everything for two years. Everyone loved Nancy; it didn't seem to matter that she could be a bitch, too. (Did you see Kerrigan waiting for the awards ceremony to begin at the Olympics? CBS cameras caught her rolling her eyes in disgust and saying, "Oh come on, give me a break. So she's going to get out here and cry again," referring to sixteen-year-old gold medalist Oksana Baiul. Someone had told Kerrigan the holdup was so Baiul could apply fresh makeup after sobbing over her victory, when in fact the delay was caused by someone misplacing a tape of the Ukrainian national anthem.)

Nancy got every benefit of the doubt. Tonya got squat.

But Harding wasn't going to leave skating without a fight. Perhaps in some recess of her mind she figured the skating world didn't fight fair, so why should she? Perhaps the botched attack was a last-gasp stab at defeating Kerrigan and winning the prize she had eyed all her life, an Olympic medal. But the attack only served to make Kerrigan a bigger and even saintlier star. It backfired, like so much in Harding's career. She was always working at cross-purposes. She wanted to win more than anything, yet refused to play the games necessary to do it. She hired lawyers, filed lawsuits, put up with the media invading her life so she could compete at Lillehammer — then arrived there completely unprepared, from not training enough to not bringing the right skate laces.

Some say figure skating will never be the same. Yes, it will. As breathtakingly beautiful as the sport can be, beneath its sequins and lip liner, beneath its kittenish exterior, beats the heart of a tiger looking for its next meal. It was like this before the Kerrigan attack, it will continue after. The attack was an aberration, certainly. But when one stirs together politics, pressure, jealousy, money and ambition, as elite women's figure skating does to a degree unmatched by any other sport, one is likely to see an explosion now and then.

Bill Bragg wants his daughter to skate so she'll learn valuable life lessons such as discipline, manners, time management and perseverance. Skating can do that. It's a wonderful teacher for children. But a parent would do well not to forget the life lesson of these last few months: From afar, an Olympic rink is shimmery and smooth, a blank sheet of great possibilities. Close up it can be awfully cold.

IAN THOMSEN

This Could Be the Start
of a Really Big Career

FROM THE INTERNATIONAL HERALD TRIBUNE

AND THE INTERNATIONAL Newsmakers Lifetime Achievement
Award goes to . . . Mrs. Tonya Harding-Gillooly-Von Bulow.
(Applause, much applause.)
Unfortunately, Tonya is unable to join us tonight.
(Laughter.)
But let us take this evening to review her sensational, spectacu-
lar career.
Tonya came from a troubled home in Oregon, and as a skater she
really wasn't the best. But in 1994 she rocketed to fame, becoming
an international celebrity at the age of 23 when her husband
pleaded guilty to arranging a bizarre attack on a rival American
skater.
(Nervous laughter.)
And when Tonya agreed to a plea bargain shortly after the 1994
Olympics — proving only that she knew of the conspiracy *after* the
attack — it looked like an anticlimactic conclusion to the most
sensational episode in American sport.
(Chuckles.)
Well, we all know now that that was only the beginning. Much
bigger things were in store for Tonya. Unable to travel beyond
Oregon, Washington and California because of her probation, she
spent those three years practicing the Asian arts of self-defense,
most notably karate. Inspired by a $2 million offer to become a

professional wrestler in Japan, she chose to remain in America. In 1997, she became the instant star of the new Ladies Professional Kick-Boxing Association.

(Highlights of Tonya kick-boxing appear on screen.)

Were the matches fixed or were they real? The debate raged as Tonya's opponents were carried out of the ring one after the other. Slow-motion replays showed dozens of her competitors suffering career-ending knee injuries, the devastating and practically unavoidable consequence of the "Triple Axel" — the name Tonya gave to her signature spinning air-kick.

Within months, stadium crowds of 100,000 and pay-per-view audiences in the tens of millions were following Tonya and her ex-husband/manager, Jeff Gillooly — she in her rhinestoned, muscle-bound, ugly figure-skating-style outfits, her lavender makeup visible from the farthest seat in the house, her hands in boxing gloves, a cigarette stuffed in her mouth in between rounds, and her ex-husband constantly shouting instructions up to her. With a glare she would spit the butt at him, the crowd roaring as she stomped toward her next victim, her French-braided head weaving back and forth like a cobra's.

(Lights dim for video.)

Question: If we could finally set the record straight, Jeff, did or did not Tonya help plan the attack on Nancy Kerrigan six years ago?

Gillooly: It was all her idea. I still can't believe I was the one who went to jail.

Question: Was it your idea, Tonya?

Harding: I think it's time the truth came out. I am ready to confess today that the idea was all mine. . . . NOT! Hah Hah! Hah Hah HACK Hah HACK HACK . . .

(Video freezes with Tonya in mid-hack.)

(Applause as the lights come back up.)

A generation of pre-teenagers who knew nothing about the 1994 Olympics were flocking around Tonya. Every has-been celebrity who sought to regain his or her fifteen minutes of lost fame could dare enter the ring for "an exhibition" against her, often with painful results . . .

(A montage of Tonya photographs: Leaning to hug Madonna on her stretcher . . . Kneeling to sign Shaquille O'Neal's cast . . . Standing by as Buddy Ebsen receives last rites . . . and relief as he regains consciousness . . .)

Then — disaster. During a rare tag-team match, Tonya rushes out to defend Gillooly from a double-attack by Roseanne and Tom Arnold, who are grappling to regain their place as America's most notorious couple. But for once Tonya's "Triple Axel" is misdirected — or is it? — as the kick takes out Gillooly's knee. The Arnolds seize the moment, casting the distraught would-be pixie and her ex-hit-man-husband from the ring in a heap. Tonya will never kick-box again.

Instead, she uses their millions to buy the Ice Capades, starring Katarina Witt. The show takes a new direction as Harding orders Witt to sit on a trap door over a pool of water and a sign that reads: DUNK THE ICE QUEEN. The interactive gimmick, initially successful, fades rapidly.

The remaining years are a whirlwind: The final break-up of their on-again, off-again marriage . . . Tonya loses the last of her savings, and her right pinkie, as the star of a sea-life extravaganza in which sharks are trained like dolphins . . . She applies to work with the Mother Teresa Foundation in India but is turned down after lying on her application.

Then, while starring in a questionable film biography of Sonja Henie on location, Tonya meets and falls head-over-heels in love with . . . Claus Von Bulow!

(Laughter and applause.)

Tonya really wanted to be here tonight. She sued the Swedish government to let her attend this ceremony, but they aren't going to let her leave until they find out why Claus fell into that coma last week. On a personal note, I have just this to say: Good luck finding out!

(Applause.)

Good night, and thanks for joining us. I've been your host, Nancy Kerrigan.

(She walks off stage holding Tonya's award. Standing ovation.)

Biographical Notes

Los Angeles native J. A. ADANDE is a graduate of Northwestern University. Before joining the *Washington Post* in 1994, he spent two years with the *Chicago Sun-Times*. He lives in Arlington, Virginia.

Following stints with the now defunct *Brooklyn Eagle* and *New York Journal American*, DAVE ANDERSON joined the *New York Times* as a sports reporter in 1966. In 1971 he became a sports columnist. Mr. Anderson is the author of nineteen books, most recently *Pennant Races: Baseball at Its Best*. In 1994 he won the Red Smith Award from the Associated Press Sports Editors for distinguished sports column writing.

PETER ANDREWS is a contributing editor for *Golf Digest*.

FURMAN BISHER has been sports editor of the *Atlanta Journal* since 1957. Over the course of his illustrious career, Bisher has won numerous awards, including the Red Smith Award, and he is a member of the University of North Carolina Hall of Fame, the National Sportscasters and Sportswriters Hall of Fame, the International Golf Writers Hall of Fame, the Georgia Hall of Fame, and the World Writers Cup International Hall of Fame. The author of more than one thousand magazine articles, Bisher has also written seven books, including *The Furman Bisher Collection*, published in 1989.

Baltimore native TOM CALLAHAN spent ten years as a senior writer for *Time* magazine before becoming a columnist for *U.S. News and World Report*. A contributing editor for *Golf Digest*, Callahan is the coauthor, with Dave Kindred, of the golf travelogue *Around the World in Eighteen Holes*.

GARY CARTWRIGHT, a senior editor for *Texas Monthly*, was a finalist for the National Magazine Award in 1986 in the category of reporting excellence. A frequent contributor to many national publications, Cartwright is also the author of several books, among them *Blood Will Tell*, and the coauthor of several movie scripts, including *J. W. Coop, A Pair of Aces*, and *Pancho, Billy, and Esmerelda*. His profile of Harvey Penick appeared in *The Best American Sports Writing 1994*.

A native of Los Angeles, novelist JAMES ELLROY is considered America's premier practitioner of crime fiction. He is the author of *Because the Night, The Black Dahlia, White Jazz*, and, most recently, *American Tabloid*.

ROBIN FINN wrote for the *Minneapolis Star* and the *Hartford Courant* before joining the *New York Times* as a sports reporter in 1985, where she now covers tennis and hockey. Her work has appeared in a number of national publications, including *Sport, Cosmopolitan, Crawdaddy*, and *The Hamptons*.

A native of Wichita Falls, SKIP HOLLANDSWORTH has worked as a reporter and columnist for the *Dallas Times Herald* and the *Dallas Morning News*. He also worked as a reporter and producer for *USA Today, Today*, and ESPN. Hollandsworth is a senior editor for *Texas Monthly*.

SALLY JENKINS is a senior writer at *Sports Illustrated*, for which she covers tennis and football. She was nominated for a Pulitzer Prize in 1985 for the stories she wrote concerning the death of basketball player Len Bias.

ROBERT F. JONES is the author of ten books, among them the novel *Blood Tide*, which was named a Notable Book of the Year by the *New York Times* in 1990. His articles, essays, and short stories have appeared in fourteen anthologies and numerous magazines. Jones is currently a contributing editor at *Sports Afield* and a columnist for *Shooting Sportsman* magazine. He lives in Vermont with his wife, two bird dogs, three cats, and countless flyrods.

PAT JORDAN is best known as the author of the classic baseball memoir *A False Spring*, detailing his career as a minor league pitcher. He is also a novelist and frequent contributor to a number of national publications. His profile of Whitey Herzog, "The Wit and Wisdom of the White Rat," appeared in *The Best American Sports Writing 1993*.

TOM JUNOD won a National Magazine Award for feature writing in 1994 for his work that appeared in *GQ*, where he serves as a contributing editor. He lives in Georgia.

DAVE KINDRED, the author of six books, wrote for the *Washington Post*, the *Atlanta Journal*, and the *National Sports Daily* before joining *The Sporting News* in 1991 as a weekly columnist. He is a past winner of the Red Smith Award for lifetime achievement in sports journalism.

TONY KORNHEISER is a columnist for the *Washington Post*. He is a frequent contributor to a number of publications, among them *Sports Illustrated, The Sporting News,* and *Ladies Home Journal.*

MARK KRAM is a contributing editor to *Esquire* and a screenwriter. His story about the injuries suffered by professional football players, "No Pain, No Game," appeared in *The Best American Sports Writing 1993.* A story by his son, Mark Kram Jr., appeared in last year's edition.

Columnist JIM MURRAY of the *Los Angeles Times* has won virtually every award available to sports writers, including the 1990 Pulitzer Prize for Commentary. Murray spent his formative years as a reporter for the *New Haven Register* and the *Los Angeles Examiner* before joining *Time* in 1948. In 1954, Murray helped launch *Sports Illustrated.* He joined the *Times* in 1961. Murray is a member of both the Baseball Hall of Fame and the National Sportscasters and Sportswriters Hall of Fame.

RICK REILLY's story "What Is the Citadel?," about the athletic program at the Citadel, appeared in *The Best American Sports Writing 1993.* Reilly has been with *Sports Illustrated* since 1985, where he is a senior writer.

STEVE RUSHIN's overview "How We Got Here" appeared in the fortieth anniversary issue of *Sports Illustrated,* where Rushin is a senior writer.

JOAN RYAN is perhaps the best known female sports journalist in America. She joined the *San Francisco Chronicle* last year following a long tenure as columnist at the *San Francisco Examiner.*

JAY SEARCY has spent forty years in sports journalism, most recently with the *New York Times* and the *Philadelphia Inquirer,* for which he served as executive sports editor before returning to writing in 1986. Searcy was twice named Tennessee Sportswriter of the Year, and was honored by the Associated Press Sports Editors for feature writing in 1987 and 1988.

BLACKIE SHERROD is a native of Texas. After playing wingback at Howard Payne College, he served in World War II as a torpedo plane gunner. Sherrod, an award-winning columnist, joined the *Dallas Morning News* in 1984 following stints with the *Fort Worth Press* and the *Dallas Times Her-ald.* A past winner of the Red Smith Award, Sherrod is the author of *The Blackie Sherrod Collection.*

GARY SMITH is a senior writer for *Sports Illustrated.* This is his third appearance in *The Best American Sports Writing.* His story about high school basketball on a Crow reservation won the 1992 National Magazine Award for feature writing.

JERRY TARDE is the editor of *Golf Digest* and author of *Golf for a Lifetime*.

IAN THOMSEN was a sports writer for the *Boston Globe* and the *National Sports Daily* before joining the *International Herald Tribune* in 1992. After spending three years based in Paris, he has moved to London, where he lives with his wife Maureen and daughter Jacqueline.

GEORGE VECSEY joined the *New York Times* in 1969. Over the course of his career with the *Times* he has served as a national correspondent, Long Island correspondent, and religion reporter. In 1982 he was named a columnist, joining Dave Anderson in writing "Sports of the Times." Mr. Vecsey lives in Port Washington, New York.

BOB VERDI is a columnist for the *Chicago Tribune*. In 1980 he was named Sportswriter of the Year by the National Sportswriters and Sportscasters Association, and in 1992 Verdi was recognized as the Illinois Sportswriter of the Year for the fourteenth time. Originally from Port Washington, New York, Verdi lives in Northbrook, Illinois.

MICHAEL WILBON finished second in the column writing division of the 1994 Associated Press Sports Editors competition. A columnist for the *Washington Post*, Wilbon has contributed articles to *Sports Illustrated* and *TV Guide*.

Notable Sports Writing of 1994

SELECTED BY GLENN STOUT

Revolution. *LA Weekly,* April 1–7,
1994

LISA DePAULO
Biting Back. *Philadelphia,* July 1994
BONNIE DiSIMONE
Years of Tears, Year of Hope. *The
Cleveland Plain Dealer,* March 20,
1994
MIKE DOWNEY
Zaniness in Zaire. *The Los Angeles
Times,* October 30, 1994
TODD DREW
Siscone and Barney Take One Last
Shot. *Speedway Scene,* October 21,
1994
CHRIS DUFRESNE
No Tear for Fears. *The Los Angeles
Times,* September 19, 1994

TOM FARREY
Desperate for the Winning Edge.
The Seattle Times, February 6, 1994
TOM FAULKNER
Balls Strikes and Class
Consciousness. *The Detroit Free
Press Magazine,* August 28, 1994
JOHN FEINSTEIN
Peace of Mind. *Golf,* July 1994
JEFFREY FELSHMAN
Blind Alley. *Chicago Reader,* July 15,
1994
PAT FORDE
The Dream Team. *The Courier
Journal Scene,* September 10, 1994
DAVID FOSTER
I'm Sorry. *Gray's Sporting Journal,*
March 1994
MIKE FREEMAN
Corraling the Cowboys. *The New
York Times Magazine,* August 7,
1994

ANN GERHART
Making a Play for Jeffrey. *Inquirer,*
August 28, 1994

MICHAEL GLAB
Fight Like a Man. *Chicago Reader,*
September 9, 1994
PATRICK GOLDSTEIN
Father Figure. *The Los Angeles Times
Magazine,* March 13, 1994
MICHAEL J. GOODMAN
Pumped Up. *The Los Angeles Times
Magazine,* April 3, 1994
BUD GREENSPAN
Milestone Mile. *The Los Angeles
Times,* May 6, 1994
DAVID GUTERSON
Moneyball! *Harper's,* September
1994

RAN HENRY
Barbarians at the Gate. *Tropic,* May
1, 1994
JOHNNETTE HOWARD
For Navratilova, It's Time to Just
"Be." *The Washington Post,*
November 15, 1994
DESSON HOWE
For Kicks. *The Washington Post
Magazine,* June 5, 1994

PAT JORDAN
Thin Mountain Air. *Philadelphia,*
April 1994

TOM KERTES
Frosh Prince. *The Village Voice,*
November 29, 1994
MICHAEL KIEFER
The Flying Leininger Brothers. *New
Times,* August 4–10, 1994
CURRY KIRKPATRICK
Sports, Most Foul. *Newsweek,*
January 17, 1994
MARK KRAM JR.
The Graduate. *Philadelphia,* June
1994

BILL LITTLEFIELD
So Short, So Good. *Yankee,* May
1994